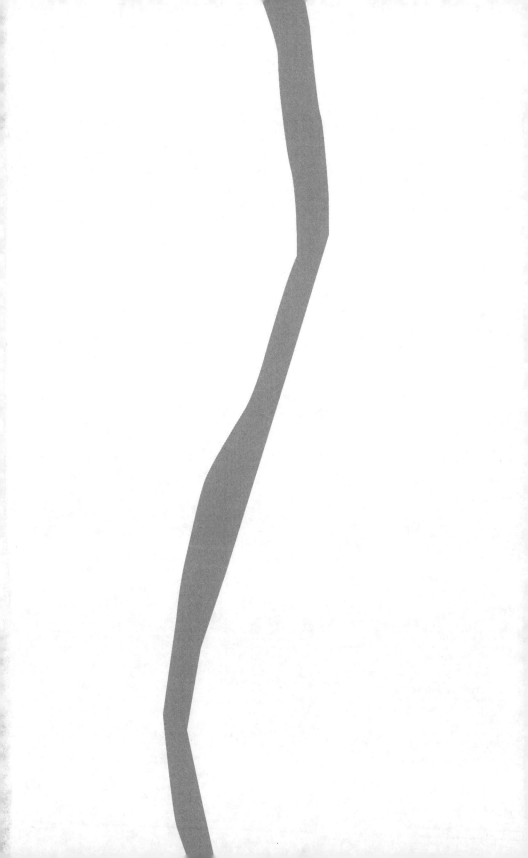

RUN TOWARDS THE DANGER

CONFRONTATIONS WITH A BODY OF MEMORY

SARAH POLLEY

With illustrations by Lauren Tamaki

PENGUIN PRESS

NEW YORK

2022

PENGUIN PRESS
An imprint of Penguin Random House LLC
penguinrandomhouse.com

Interior illustrations © 2021 Lauren Tamaki

ISBN 9780593300350 (hardcover)
ISBN 9780593300367 (ebook)

Printed in the United States of America
1st Printing

Set in Fournier MT Pro
Designed by Kelly Hill

Mrs. Beverley Panikkar let me write stories all day every day in Grade 2 and told me I would be a writer one day. I told her years later that if I ever wrote a book, I would dedicate it to the space, presence, and attunement she gave to the children she taught. So here you go, Bev. And thank you.

Made possible by Eve, Aila, and Amy,
who have rewritten my life.
I love witnessing your stories unfold,
and you with them.

Contents

Preface   *1*

Alice, Collapsing   5

The Woman Who Stayed Silent   69

High Risk   103

Mad Genius   143

Dissolving the Boundaries   175

Run Towards the Danger   209

Endnotes   *249*

Acknowledgments   *251*

Preface

"Living backwards!" Alice repeated in great astonishment. "I never heard of such a thing!"

"—but there's one great advantage in it, that one's memory works both ways."

"I'm sure mine only works one way," Alice remarked. "I can't remember things before they happen."

"It's a poor sort of memory that only works backwards," the Queen remarked.

—Lewis Carroll, *Through the Looking-Glass*

The working title of this book was "Living Backwards," inspired by the Queen's suggestion to Alice that memory can work more than one way. "Living Backwards," though, sounds like a memoir that covers the scope of a lifetime. If this were a memoir or an autobiography, it would be woefully incomplete. I am both far luckier than these essays would imply if they were read as a map of my life, and I have experienced more trauma than I have given chapters to.

I originally wrote these essays as stand-alone pieces. I wrote some of them over many years, in some cases decades, abandoning them for long stretches, unsure if I had the courage to finish them or if they had a place in the world. As the essays began to shape themselves into a book, I realized that the connective tissue between them was a dialogue that was occurring between two very different time frames in my life. The past was affecting how I moved through the world, while present life was affecting how the past moved through me.

I've been acutely aware that my childhood experiences inform my current life. I have, until recently, been less conscious of the power of my adult life to inform my relationship to my memories. When I was lucky enough to have experiences in adulthood that echoed pivotal, difficult memories, and to have those experiences go another, better way than they had in the past, my relationship to those memories shifted. The meaning of long-ago experiences transformed in the context of the ever-changing present.

The past and present, I have come to realize, are in constant dialogue, acting upon one another in a kind of reciprocal pressure dance.

When I first met concussion specialist Dr. Michael Collins, after three and a half years of suffering from post-concussive syndrome, he said, "If you remember only one thing from this meeting, remember this: run towards the danger." In order for my brain to recover from a traumatic injury, I had to retrain it to strength by charging towards the very activities that triggered my symptoms. This was a paradigm shift for me—to greet and welcome the things I had previously avoided.

As I recovered from my concussion, "run towards the danger" became a kind of incantation for me in relation to the rest of my life. I began to hear it as a challenge to take on the project of addressing and questioning my own narratives.

What follows are some of the most dangerous stories of my life: the ones I have avoided, the ones I haven't told, the ones that have kept me awake on countless nights. These are stories that have haunted and directed me, unwittingly, down circuitous paths. As these stories found echoes in my adult life, and then went another, better way than they did in childhood, they became lighter and easier to carry.

These stories don't add up to a portrait of a life, or even a snapshot of one. They are about the transformative power of an ever-evolving relationship to memory. Telling them is a form of running towards the danger.

Alice,
Collapsing

"I could tell you my adventures—beginning from this morning," said Alice a little timidly: "but it's no use going back to yesterday, because I was a different person then."

—Lewis Carroll, *Alice's Adventures in Wonderland*

At least twice a week, I used to find myself in a periwinkle-blue poufy dress with a white pinafore. My stockings were striped and my hair was held firmly by a headband that dug into my head behind my ears. My breasts, still tender and growing, were painfully flattened by a tensor bandage. It was a dream that I frequently found myself in, where nothing anyone around me said made any sense and it was all hostile: hostile towards my common sense, hostile towards my youth, hostile towards my growing up. I knew I didn't want to be a child; I wanted to be a queen but I didn't want to be left alone, or tested, or made fun of or to do all the things that seemed to be necessary to become a queen. I would follow corkscrew paths. I had to run in order to stay in the same place. People would scream in pain before they were hurt. There was a mint in my mouth for good luck. I wanted to kill myself.

Sometimes when I woke from this dream, I remembered that I was, in fact, wearing a rose-coloured dress and not a blue one. Sometimes I corrected my subconscious. Most of the time, though, I woke up incapable of differentiating the portrait of myself from the iconic John Tenniel illustrations, coloured in modern reprints. I wonder if Alice Liddell had had the same problem.

The real Alice was a sullen-looking child with dark hair and eyes. In one of the photographs that Charles Dodgson (Lewis Carroll) took of her, "The Beggar Maid," she looks alarmingly sexual, taunting him, challenging him to want more. At least that's how I viewed the photograph when I was a young teenager. As I look at the same photograph now, as a grown woman, I wonder what instructions the adult taking the photograph gave to her to produce such an alarming effect. In the books and movies that were consumed by millions, though, Alice is golden and fair, WASPy beyond measure, and exudes innocence. The books, *Alice's Adventures in Wonderland* and *Through the Looking-Glass*, have passed through children's hands for over a century now, cloaked in this deceptive costume.

Ever since I can remember, these books inspired a terror and an exasperation in me. Every one of Alice's attempts to make sense of her new, irrational world, to find anything approximating normalcy, or to simply get home is thwarted by mean-spirited creatures with their own irrational systems of logic. Despite my father's love of these books, I never, as a young child, wanted to hear them read at bedtime. They left me exhausted, haunted by a kind of relentless uncertainty. I feared that if I took any time to live inside these stories, the walls and ceiling of my childhood bedroom might soon collapse into dust and be replaced by kooky angles of drywall.

As an adult, I experience this same aversion to movies that remind me of the *Alice* books or that mirror this same quality of someone constantly trying to get somewhere and failing. Movies like *After Hours* make we want to scream. They make me feel nauseous and aggravated and goosepimply.

I hate stories in which people can't get to where they're going.

As there seemed to be no chance of getting her hands up to her head, she tried to get her head down to them, and was delighted to find that her neck would bend about easily in any direction, like a serpent. She had just succeeded in curving it down into a graceful zigzag . . .

"But I'm not a serpent, I tell you!" said Alice. "I'm a—I'm a—"

"Well! What are you?" said the Pigeon. "I can see you're trying to invent something!"

"I—I'm a little girl," said Alice, rather doubtfully, as she remembered the number of changes she had gone through that day.

—Alice's Adventures in Wonderland

When I was fifteen years old I got caught through the looking glass in a pink dress, in a crisp white pinafore, with my breasts bound, playing younger than I was. My spine had by then bent—perhaps, I thought then, under the weight of grief—to a forty-five-degree angle, so along with the tensor bandages pulled tightly across my chest, the pink dress itself was lined with various strategically placed pads to make my shoulders, my back, and my waist appear symmetrical. Even then, it took effort to appear straight. On two-show days I would begin to sag sideways, the tips of my left hand's fingers almost touching the side of my left knee. One of my left ribs, just under my breasts, protruded so much that it created a noticeable lump right in the middle of my torso, causing the right rib to slough out of view.

I knew I had to wear a hard plastic brace sixteen hours a day to make my body grow straighter, but I didn't, so every few months I, and others, noticed that I twisted and bent a little more. By this point I knew I was close to needing major surgery to correct the curve, but that was to be my choice too, having no parent to oversee such choices. The surgery terrified me, not only the idea of being cut into and operated on for ten hours, having my spine stretched out, fused, and a pound of metal attached to it, but also I couldn't think who would take care of me while I recovered. I had stopped going to regular follow-ups at the hospital a long time before, had stopped wearing the brace around my body sixteen hours a day as prescribed, had stopped thinking about what the consequences of my negligence could be. I knew that I was free to keep twisting and curving and sloping and that nothing, ever, would stop me. There was no adult who could force me straight.

But I wondered, now, at fifteen years old, if the thing I had feared the most, the prospect of this major spinal surgery, could liberate me from something I found myself fearing even more: walking even one more time onto a stage at the Stratford Festival.

I had been diagnosed with scoliosis four years earlier during a routine insurance medical for the television series *Road to Avonlea*. The doctor asked me to touch my toes, and then spent a while tracing the protrusion of my spine with his fingers. When I stood up straight again and looked at him, his brow was furrowed.

It somehow made sense to me to be told that I wasn't straight, that my spine was curving nonsensically to the right at the top and to the left at the bottom. My world had started curving out of shape the previous year, and my own body curving alongside it gave things a logical symmetry. It also made sense of a few things that had been mysterious to me about my ever-changing body, chiefly (and most important to my eleven-year-old self) the noticeably lopsided breasts that had begun to emerge, the left one growing large and ripe while the other one remained almost nonexistent.

I was alone in the examining room with the doctor when he made the discovery, and when he said the word *scoliosis*, it sounded like death. My mother had died just months before, and my experience of diseases was that they didn't hold back. They took you and maimed you and ended you. So when I heard the diagnosis of something with a -*sis* on the end of it, I assumed that my days were numbered. He referred me to the orthopaedics department at Toronto's Hospital for Sick Children, and that is where I found myself a month later, in a waiting room with similarly crooked kids, all of us waiting to hear how badly we'd been bent out of shape.

After a trip to the X-ray machine it was determined that I had a thirty-eight-degree curvature in my thoracic spine. I stared, transfixed, at the X-ray. It was strange to see that my own spine, lit from behind by the light board, had been hiding secrets from me. For years it had been surreptitiously bending itself into the ugly beginnings of a coil. It seemed impossible that I could be so deformed. Impossibly scary, and impossibly lucky.

The feeling of being lucky was one I kept to myself. There had been a part of me that, while my mother was dying, had relished having a parent with cancer. *Cancer* was a powerful word, one you could throw around with immediate results. It seemed to inspire a focus from people. They looked at you with what was supposed to be sympathy but felt, in fact, like a kind of exaltation. When my mother had cancer, I felt as though I was suddenly transformed into a sallow child of tragedy, imbued with a kind of magic that only children close to grim events can be. I was comfortable in this role, and delighted to help move the play forward, saying the word *cancer* in a hushed tone with an accomplished look of dread, reporting on my mother's latest surgery or round of chemotherapy with my eyes downcast and bashful in the face of the enormous attention it garnered. It helped that I never once really believed my mother was going to die. It allowed me the space to focus on other people's reactions and to delight in the special place I had earned in their hearts. I knew I was exaggerating, making it up. Deep inside, I believed that my mother had something very innocuous dressed up with a scary word, and I was just using the drama of this disease to get attention. I believed this until her actual death, which, for a long time, some part of me felt I was responsible for. By playing the part of the child with the dying mother so convincingly, I believed I had summoned a bad ending.

But I had missed the word *cancer* these last months. And now part of me was glad to have one to take its place.

I found out early on in my appointment with the orthopaedic surgeon at the Hospital for Sick Children that scoliosis wouldn't kill me. This was good news and bad. Good, because I'm pretty sure I didn't want to die at that point in time. Bad, because it limited my ability to create that same kind of wonder in adults that a dying mother had. "How did I get it?" I asked the doctor. She told me it was genetic. Since no one else in my family had scoliosis, I decided that it must be grief, the sadness I couldn't yet feel about my mother's death, bearing down on me until my spine bent, forcing me to feel it any way it could.

There were a couple of ways to treat scoliosis, according to my doctor. The first option, for the less severe cases, was to wear a tight plastic brace, which wrapped around the torso, for sixteen hours a day in the hopes that it would alter the course of the curving spine as the pubescent body continued to grow. The more severe cases had to be operated on. The spine would be stretched out, fused with graft from the hip bone, and two steel rods would be placed on either side of the spine to keep it in place as the graft took hold and hardened. The rods would be attached with many hooks and nuts and bolts, adding up to about a pound of metal in the back.

I was on the cusp of these grim options. I was fitted within the month for a total-contact thoraco-lumbar-sacral orthosis (TLSO) brace. This was a relief in itself, as the other brace option, which was horrifically detailed in *Deenie*, a Judy Blume book I had read, was the Milwaukee brace, which included a Frankenstein-esque ring of metal around the neck. The one I was being fitted for, the TLSO brace, came up to just below my chest in the front, though in the back it came up to just below the neck. It was hard plastic, with two thick Velcro straps that ran across the front, attached to the brace by eight little metal discs, giving it a robotic look. Most humiliating, the brace had been made from a cast of my body, so there was the actual shape of my body right there in front of me and anyone who saw the brace, hips just forming, rib cage uneven, a body in progress. Firm pads were strategically placed on the right side, where my upper and middle back fit into the brace, to help push my spine as it grew into something approximating straightness. There was also a hard pad in between these two, on the left side, to try to push the bottom part of the S into straightness. When they first strapped me into it in the hospital, I felt like I couldn't breathe. I was told I would get used to it, though the hard pads digging into my spine would likely give me welts for the first while. I was shown how to put it on, though not given a practice run putting it on by myself there at the hospital.

It turned out that getting it on at home alone was almost impossible. Pulling clothes up over it required some doing. Living in a body that changed suddenly and unpredictably with puberty required some doing, even without being strapped into a hard plastic brace.

It was recommended that I sleep all night in the brace, to cover at least half of the sixteen hours I was required to wear it, especially since I had to work on the television show *Road to Avonlea* during the days, and it would be hard to be as physical as I needed to be in certain scenes while wearing it. The first night, I struggled to pull the straps to the markings they had made with a pen at the hospital to show me when it was pulled tight enough. After a long struggle, I cried out that I couldn't do it. My dad ended up pulling me into the brace. I hated having him close me into that contraption. I was red with rage. He didn't deserve my anger, but he was the only parent in sight and no eleven-year-old girl wants her dad manipulating her body. After that first night, I pulled the straps away from my body with every bit of strength and frustration I had, hurting my arms and hands and crying with the effort, but managing, crucially, to avoid needing my dad's assistance.

This hard, tight contraption was constricting and sweaty and it was difficult to sleep. After two days I had big red welts in all the places where the pads touched my skin. The thin undershirts I was given to wear underneath the brace were drenched with sweat when I took it off in the afternoon. After my mother died, my dad and I didn't do laundry, ever, so they soon smelled terrible, and my eleven-year-old brain didn't compute that the solution to this problem might be to just wash them.

I had to buy new clothes to accommodate the extra thickness the brace added to my body, so my on-set tutor and guardian, Laurie, who worked on the TV show I was on, took me out one weekend to a department store, where I sobbed in a change room as I realized I couldn't bend over in the brace to pull up my pants. I became terrified of gym class at school, and beforehand I would steal into a bathroom stall to take off the brace out of view, and return after class to put it back on. But pubescent children are aggressively observant, and by the end of my first day at school in the brace, a friend remarked loudly, in front of a group of kids, that I had "no butt." And then she wanted answers from me. "Are you aware that you don't have any butt?" The brace went straight down over my back and flattened me. I was dumbstruck with shame.

They had to remake all my costumes for *Road to Avonlea*, so I spent a lot of time standing in front of three or four people, in my underwear in the brace, while women and men took measurements and held bolts of fabric up against my torso. I felt more exposed than if I had been naked.

After about two years, I realized that no one would notice whether I continued to wear the brace or not. A young teenager often requires enforcement from an adult to do uncomfortable or painful things for their own good. My dad was not an enforcer, and it dawned on me that he probably wouldn't notice or care if I took a break. I started by skipping the occasional day, and then eventually stopped wearing it altogether. My spine, released from the prodding of the brace's pads, began growing amok, while I tried to compensate for my breasts, which were growing wildly uneven, by wearing push-up bras that would create a kind of shelf of one continuous breast rather than two uneven ones.

By the time I was fourteen years old, my right shoulder blade jutted out dramatically farther than the left one, and I slumped over to the left, so far that my left fingertips touched the side of my knee if I relaxed my body. I almost never did. I walked around forcing myself straight, forcing my right shoulder back and my torso upright, no matter how much it hurt. I would comment on how well the brace seemed to be working, loudly, and without provocation, at work and when relatives would visit. I didn't want to risk anyone asking me about whether or not I was wearing that torturous contraption. I went to a follow-up appointment at the Hospital for Sick Children, where a jocular orthopaedic surgeon said things like "You're a good kid, Charlie Brown" and "Well, you're getting close to the point where we may have to consider surgery soon, but you've escaped the knife this time!"

I decided, since my mind was made up to rid myself of this godawful brace, that it would be prudent to stop going to my checkups, lest someone get it into their head to cut my back open and fix it. Lest I didn't "escape the knife" the next time.

By fourteen, I had moved out of the family home in Aurora where I had lived alone with my father, and no one would ever know again whether I was missing my appointments or not.

My father, after my mother died, had fallen apart. It's possible that he was always apart, and my mother had just, for many years and with great effort, held him together. Or perhaps he fell apart in a manner that many men of his generation would have after the woman who had done every practical thing in their lives for them for years died. His falling apart didn't seem to cause him concern. Or perhaps it did and he just couldn't fathom what to do about it. And so he did nothing. My siblings, who were all much older than I, had moved out of the house a long time before, leaving the house empty when I was at work or school. My dad sat in front of the TV all day, every day. At night he would play endless games of solitaire. I fell asleep, many nights, to the rhythmic *flick, flick, flick* of his cards on the coffee table, hearing them wind down into shorter numbers of flicks as he got closer to the ends of the lines of cards as he finished setting up the game. The cards became grimy, with little patches of black dirt on them. They had a specific sharp smell of filth that I can still conjure to this day. After a couple of years, the cards were so faded from constant use that it was impossible to see what the images on many of them had been. Was this a new challenge he had created for himself, to have a hand in imagining what the cards might be as they grew impossible to decipher? My guess is that he would say it was just laziness, it was too much effort to buy a new pack. My dad spoke often of his idleness with resignation and a dash of glee, which made it seem as though a relaxed charm was responsible for all the things he hadn't done and wasn't doing.

Shockingly, after my mother died, he slowly learned how to cook, which was quite extraordinary for a man over fifty who had never even made himself a sandwich. He didn't, however, learn how to clean. I don't ever remember him doing laundry. Not once. When the sheets became unbearable on my bed, I simply took them off and slept on the bare mattress or moved to another empty bedroom in the house. This went on for years.

One year, we went to my Auntie Ann's house for Christmas. I was struck by how clean and comfortable things were in her house, in such marked contrast to ours. I was used, by now, to a thick layer of dust covering every surface. On the car ride home, I made a meticulous list of every surface in the house that I would clean, in order, when we got home.

The next day, I fished around in the back of the cupboard under the sink for cleaning supplies and found some rusty cans of Pledge and a bottle of Vim that hadn't been touched in a long time. I worked my way through my list of surfaces to polish as though it was more reliable than my eyes. I cleaned every surface in the house, cloths turning black from a single wipe over a side table or mantelpiece. My dad looked at me, eyes wide, shaking his head. "You've gone mad," he said, somewhat admiringly.

But the house soon went back to its business of collecting dust, and I lost enthusiasm for doing another three-day stint of cleaning. Eventually there were messes that couldn't be cleaned up anyway. The cigarette burns in the arms of the recliner my dad would fall asleep in while watching soccer, the TV blaring so loud it could be heard from the end of the driveway. Corners chewed off the furniture by my untrained bichon frise puppy, Mookie, as my dad cursed and swore.

When I was thirteen, my father and I went on a trip to Europe. We went to France, Greece, and England. I had conceived this trip and offered to pay for it out of my acting earnings, and my dad had said yes, making it contingent on my giving permanent custody of Mookie to Auntie Ann and my cousin Sarah in Stratford. As I lived an hour and a half away from the school I attended for a small portion of the year, I was often isolated from all friends except my dog, who no one had bothered to train, who still pissed and shat on the floor every day, and who I loved desperately as he slept with his little chin perched on my neck at night. I can't figure out exactly why I agreed to give up Mookie, except that I think I knew that he was being terribly neglected; when I was at work for twelve to fifteen hours a day, my dad would often not let him out or even put out food for him. The dog was my responsibility. Those were the terms of the contract my parents had made with me when they agreed to get me a puppy as my mother was dying. My father was not flexible on the terms, whatever my work or school obligations.

The trip to Europe was an agony. It turned out that while I wanted to see all these places (the Eiffel Tower! the Tower of London!), I did not want to see them with my father, who made increasingly strange jokes about us being a couple. He would say, loudly, after requesting a room with only one bed as he checked us into a hotel in Paris, "Ha! It's as though we are Humbert Humbert and Lolita!" I flooded with rage and humiliation and tried not to look at him for days. It didn't stop him from repeating the joke many times. These types of jokes were in keeping with his lack of regard for sacred cows in conversation and in humour, but I just wanted to go home where I could get away from him.

My one fond memory of our trip was a day we spent visiting the British Museum in childlike wonder together. He bought me two prints of maps of the world from the gift shop. They were drawn hundreds of years ago. The continents drawn on these rudimentary maps were too close together, or too far apart. Young, sloppy-looking sketches of a world that hadn't yet been accurately discovered.

The following summer my dad played golf all day, every day, leaving me alone, dogless, in the hollow, filthy house. I would smoke cigarettes, read books, and do stretches in my room. I remember pulling my leg up and towards myself while I lay on my back and thinking, in a logic that seemed obvious to my thirteen-year-old self: "Okay. I'm basically grown now. I smoke, I have my period. Now all I have to do to be an adult is have sex. And get out of here."

By fourteen I had moved in with my brother's ex-girlfriend Laura, a twenty-four-year-old assertive, emotionally generous woman who had a two-bedroom apartment in north Toronto. On a visit to see her in the city one day, I asked if I could move in and offered to split the rent, and as she had always felt protective and fond of me, she agreed. I told my dad about my plan, and it made rational sense to him that I wanted to move out. He prided himself on "not being a father but a friend." He didn't believe in any separation between children and adults and the conversations they should or should not have. Nothing was sacred, all were equal. We had, for years now (on the nights when I didn't have to work the next day, leaving him to play solitaire by himself), stayed up late at night together, smoking cigarettes, talking about books. By the time I was thirteen I had read all of D.H. Lawrence's books, and then on to the Bloomsbury group's work, with my father as my guide and nightly book club. Whenever I suggested a new book, he insisted that we do a lot of reading leading up to it, to give it context. (It took us about six months of background reading to get to James Joyce's *Ulysses*.) One night, he told me that when he was my age, he had had a nervous breakdown. He had wanted to learn everything all at once, and his hunger for learning was so voracious that it began to consume him. He became manic, unable to rest, and after weeks of sleepless nights, reading, working on math problems he had created for himself, and unable to satiate himself with knowledge, he fell apart completely. He was a working-class kid, but the headmaster had taken a liking to him, and the school he went to raised funds for him to go on a vacation to recover his sanity. Spurning sleep to stay up with him, reading and talking, I understood his story, his hunger, on a visceral level. (This story, by the way, was disputed by some members of my dad's family, who have no memory of it whatsoever.)

When it came to learning—or indeed any activity of any sort—my father believed that everything must be for the sake of itself rather than some greater ambition. The story my father told most often about himself as a youth was one in which, at the last moment, he ran in a race he had not trained for. He had been asked to replace a sick runner to represent his school. Not caring about running particularly, and knowing he had no chance of winning, he made a game for himself: he would treat the passing of each runner in front of him as a major victory. And so he ran the race this way, trying to pass each runner as though it were the end goal, celebrating each small triumph, until the end, when he suddenly realized there was only one more runner in front of him. He gunned towards the finish line, bewildered by the unexpected ending of having won the entire race.

It was a self-aggrandizing story, but he told it with such intense drama that, listening to it, you rooted for him to pass each person he was racing against and celebrated with him each time he did. This was emblematic of his relationship to success. He believed it was acceptable only if it had been realized effortlessly, without ambition, almost by accident, and born out of a love of the moment, a commitment to overcoming the present, immediate challenge, instead of a long-term strategy. I loved his stories, and their out-of-step-with-society perspective, even if I had heard most of them a thousand times.

So it wasn't an unhappy relationship with my dad, just a very complicated one, just a very adult one, in a house that was falling apart with mice and moths infesting many rooms, and far too many conversations about the tragic pathos of pedophiles.

Shortly after I moved out of my dad's house, I fell in love with a boy at my high school. He was four years older than me, moody, cynical, and funny; he wore a black overcoat every day and called himself Eddie Mars. It took me months to discover that this wasn't his real name but one pilfered from the classic film *The Big Sleep*. His real name was Corey Mintz. I loved him and I was loved by him. Even now, at forty-one, I can look back on this relationship and say that what was between Corey and me really was love. He had a terrible relationship with his father and stepmother, who he lived with. My mother was dead, and my father prided himself on not being a father. We were parentless, and so we became each other's parents.

At the time I met Corey I had already been cast in *Alice Through the Looking-Glass* at the Stratford Festival the following summer. I was scared of being onstage generally, but performing at Stratford for the first time and getting an immersion in theatre education sounded like a more intellectual pursuit than the TV show I had been contractually bound to for years, and my Auntie Ann, cousin Sarah, and her daughter Rebekkah, all of whom I adored, lived there. But I don't think I said yes to the opportunity for any of those reasons. Even though I had little interest in acting at that point, I think I said yes because my dad, when he heard that I might play Alice, had a kind of histrionic reaction of uncontainable joy. It wasn't just that he found my character on *Road to Avonlea* boring (something he told me even when I was twelve and locked into my contract for a few more years). He was obsessed with the *Alice* books, and even more so with Charles Dodgson (Lewis Carroll) and his love for Alice Liddell. I had watched *Dreamchild*, a film about their relationship, with him several times as he gasped and wept beside me. He found the unrequited love of a grown man for a child exquisitely moving, and he cried every time he saw Ian Holm attempt to profess his love for Alice and fail.

At one point in the film, Alice's mother has a conversation with Alice about her daughter's strange interactions with Dodgson.

"Mr. Dodgson seems to confess a remarkable number of things to you," Alice's mother says.

"He says that every man should have someone he can trust his secrets with," Alice replies.

"But why on earth should he say that to *you?*" her mother asks, concerned.

"Because he loves me, of course," says little Alice.

In the film, Dodgson constantly feels rejection and humiliation when he is with Alice. Dodgson has a stutter, which the Liddell girls mock behind his back and struggle not to laugh at in front of him. Each time he is about to lay himself bare and profess his love to Alice, she turns away, or manages to dodge the conversation. In one particularly haunting moment, Dodgson is staring lovingly at Alice while rowing her down a river on a perfect summer day, and she intentionally splashes him in the face. He is hurt and humiliated. When Alice's mother reprimands her for her cruelty, he does his best to cover for her, to say that it is of no concern. His attempt to smooth over the situation and to leave Alice free of consequences for her actions only makes the moment sadder. The film overall, as I saw it then, took the sympathetic side of a grown man who is in love with a little girl. In fact, the experience of watching this film so ingrained in me the perspective of the older man in this dynamic that my first (autobiographical) film script, many years later, took the side of a man who had stalked me as a child, and painted me as a hideous brat. (I never made that film.)

I was raised with the relationship between Dodgson and Liddell as an iconic one: the pathos of the older man, the coldness of the child who rejects him, mocks him. I never questioned it as being odd that my father shared this world, this perspective with me, so constantly. Though I hated the *Alice* books themselves and the feeling of being trapped in a prison of the frustration they left me with, I was able to feel intense sympathy for Dodgson as I watched the movie alongside my father. I was able to hate Alice, the child who broke his heart. It was this Alice—precocious, self-aware, sexual, and powerful—that stayed with me. It was this Alice that I thought I was going to Stratford to play.

"What size do you want to be?" . . .

"Oh, I'm not particular as to size," Alice hastily replied; *"only one doesn't like changing so often, you know."*

—*Alice's Adventures in Wonderland*

In my real life at fifteen years of age, I felt myself to be a woman, fully grown, with full breasts, living by now with Corey in an apartment far away from any parent. In Stratford I was suddenly a child again, mothered by my aunt and cousin as though I were very little, my body literally bound into smallness onstage as Alice. In any given hour I was growing and shrinking, growing and shrinking, like Alice drinking the various potions in Wonderland. I had gone through the looking glass of my own life. In Toronto I was completely independent—monitored by and connected to only my nineteen-year-old high school dropout boyfriend. In Stratford in that summer of 1994, I had the two most maternal women in the world tending to my every need, feeding me delicious food, reading classic books with me on huge plush couches in a house full of flowers and intricate wallpaper. I contributed exactly nothing to the household. I'm not sure if I ever even brought a dish to the sink after eating from it, so relieved was I to sink into the indulgence I was experiencing after years of being prematurely independent. If I had a small cold, my aunt would call the theatre to say I couldn't possibly come in for rehearsal because I was sick. I had never before, even with high fevers, vomiting, and strep throat, missed a day of work on a film set. I went from being motherless in Toronto to being mothered beyond reason in Stratford.

My Auntie Ann and my cousin Sarah made three beautiful meals a day. There were dozens of soft, gorgeous places to sit. Everything seemed baked in flowers. Blossoms and vines crawled up the walls in traditional wallpapers. Even the armchairs had extensions to be sprawled out on.

While Rebekkah, Sarah's ten-year-old daughter, either read with us or watched endless episodes of *Star Trek*, we would spend hours drinking tea and reading together in the afternoons, either on the feather cushions of the living room couches or, on hot days, while sipping lemonade on the shaded porch, verdant with hanging plants. At night I'd put on little performances, imitating my brothers and sisters, and pulling Rebekkah into the act. Auntie Ann and Sarah laughed harder than they likely meant to at my jokes. They were the two most well-read, astute women I have ever met. Sarah, who was quiet, thoughtful, and wise, had studied English literature and had edited a poetry magazine by the time she was seventeen. A single mother in her twenties, she had dedicated her life to her child and to making the world feel safe and possible for her, while running a small store filled with beautiful things, some of them made by her mother.

My Auntie Ann was an extraordinary artist who was now dedicating herself to making exquisite things in a way she hadn't had time to while raising her five children. She had gone to art school in England when she was young and around that time met a Canadian scientist and fallen deeply in love. She recounted to me how he had told her early on, in plain terms, that he wanted to marry a woman who would stay home and take care of children while he worked. She loved him, and agreed. Though she'd had what sounded like a happy marriage before her husband's death from cancer, and five children she adored, as she told me this story she stared off into space for a moment and said, "I sometimes wonder why I agreed to give it all up so easily." But her art never stopped. She made exquisite dolls based on characters from Shakespeare and Molière; convex mirrors with sculpted and painted frames that reflected back to you the off-kilter nature of the world, and of yourself.

Sarah was reading all of Fay Weldon's books that summer, and would get our attention every now and then to read out an especially funny line. I read George Eliot, starting with an old, musty copy of *Silas Marner* that I loved the smell and weathered texture of and continuing with the books my aunt brought home from the library every week. Once I looked up from my book and said, to no one in particular, that I had felt depressed for a lot of my life. Auntie Ann didn't look up as she said, "Well, that's not so bad. It's a sign of intelligence. It's the village idiot who walks around all day with a big smile on his face." She managed to combine the warm, nurturing haze she created with an acerbic wit worthy of Dorothy Parker and an intolerance of the flaws in many of the people she encountered. If you were inside her bubble you were doted upon and loved beyond reason. If you weren't, you might be torn to shreds, which, for better or for worse, made the love I experienced in that house feel even more authentic and rare. I loved being in her small collection of cherished things.

(Later in life, when Auntie Ann lived alone and was beginning to feel isolated, she surprised everyone by joining a seniors' group, thinking she should make more of an effort to have more friends. To her horror, some of the people in the group started calling her, actually wanting to become her friend. She recounted this as a chilling horror story, replete with details of how stupid they all were, inviting her to barbecues, which she called "carcinogenic nonsense." She laughed so hard she cried at her naïveté in thinking she might like these people, as well as at her own intolerance of them. At another point, she joined a group called the Culture Vultures, which travelled around by bus to interesting places. She lobbied them to change their name, as the people in the group weren't, in her opinion, cultured or even very interesting.)

I have never, before or since, felt so taken care of, so bathed in feminine love as I did that summer. Sometimes as we read together, my beloved dog Mookie, who I had given up years before, would come and put his head on my lap, a recognition in his calm. I would try not to feel his weight, try not to feel the love and sadness that his presence evoked in me. I think I took him for a walk once in five months. I simply couldn't find it within me to love a creature I had abandoned.

"Who are you?" said the Caterpillar.

This was not an encouraging opening for a conversation. Alice replied, rather shyly, "I—I hardly know, sir, just at present—at least I know who I was when I got up this morning, but I think I must have been changed several times since then."

"What do you mean by that?" said the Caterpillar sternly. "Explain yourself!"

"I can't explain myself, I'm afraid, sir," said Alice, "because I'm not myself, you see."

"I don't see," said the Caterpillar.

"I'm afraid I can't put it more clearly," Alice replied very politely, "for I can't understand it myself to begin with; and being so many different sizes in a day is very confusing."

—Alice's Adventures in Wonderland

The first read-through of *Alice Through the Looking-Glass* in the rehearsal hall began with James Reaney (who had written the adaptation for the stage) speaking to the cast about Lewis Carroll and his relationship with Alice Liddell. I can't remember exactly what he said, but he addressed the underbelly of the book, the longing in it and the subtext—which can hardly even be called subtext when it's so obvious—that Dodgson was most likely a pedophile, in love with the real Alice for whom he wrote the books. *Through the Looking-Glass*, written years after *Wonderland*, was written in sadness and nostalgia. Dodgson had become estranged from Alice Liddell and her family after an incident on one of the river outings they took together. Dodgson's journal is missing three crucial entries from these days, torn out after his death by a protective family member. It is not clear what happened that day, but it has long been speculated that Charles Dodgson crossed a line with Alice Liddell that propelled her mother to finally break contact between him and her family.

James Reaney's thoughtful analysis of the undercurrents of the *Alice* stories was fascinating to me, and I felt as though he was talking about the story I had always known. Marti Maraden, the empathetic, joyful director, got up after James had left to say that while everything James had shared was very interesting, and likely even true, Dodgson had also written this tale "to delight children." That was the spirit in which we as a company would be moving forward as we presented this play. We would mount this production, she said again, "to delight children." She said that several times, to make sure it sunk in, and I think, perhaps, to inoculate us against the perverse paths we might be tempted down. We were there to delight children. Something clanged in me, dissonant, an echoing gong of an inner knowing; something felt off, something felt strange. I pushed it away. I was here, as it turned out, "to delight children." Not to conjure the Alice of long ago whom Dodgson fell in love with, not to call forth the spirit of the twisted sexuality in the relationship between the writer and his young muse. "Delight children" was my marching order. (I mustn't tell my father.)

I was nervous as I read my part in front of the cast during that first reading of the play. I hadn't yet begun my voice lessons, so my voice was small and scared, a voice meant for film and television, not the stage. Afterwards, the lovely Bill Needles (who would play the White King) and Mervyn Blake (the Red King), in their seventies and eighties respectively, came up to tell me that they loved my reading. I don't think it was true, but they were exceedingly kind to me throughout my time at Stratford.

Douglas Rain, a legendary classical actor who had also been the voice of HAL in the movie *2001: A Space Odyssey*, and who had been a terrifying icon at the festival for years, nodded curtly and gruffly said, "Hello. I couldn't hear you." I smiled at him. I liked him right away. There are certain people from whom you can immediately intuit that their fiercest expression of warmth is brutalizing honesty. He looked at me grinning back at him, and I think he saw that flash of recognition. I saw him try to suppress a smile as he walked away. But I was scared. I was scared of my voice and how small it was. I was scared that no matter how hard I worked in the little time I had, it wouldn't get bigger. I was right to be scared.

I was put through a veritable theatre bootcamp every day. On top of rehearsals, I had daily intensive voice sessions with an incredible voice coach named Janine Pearson and movement lessons with a brilliant Alexander Technique coach named Kelly McEvenue. The idea was to cram four years of theatre school into six weeks, so that I, who had never been in a play before, could take on the task of being the lead in a play at North America's largest classical repertory company, in front of twelve hundred people, sometimes twice a day, playing a part that had more onstage time than Hamlet. (During a dress rehearsal one day, Douglas Rain commented: "My god, you *never* leave the stage! Even Hamlet gets to leave the stage every now and then.")

In the evenings I would try to memorize my lines, something that had terrified me even when I was working in television, where there was at least a possibility of doing a scene over again if you forgot a line. Now, after rehearsals, and when I was done with my schoolwork for the day, I needed to learn a two-hour play. Perfectly. After each line-learning session alone in my bedroom, I felt dizzy with fear.

In the rehearsal hall, though, I was never alone. From Janine I learned how to stretch, how to breathe deep down into my diaphragm, to use it to make a sound that would reach from my deepest self to the back of the enormous theatre and pitch up towards the large balcony. I was to be aware of the back of this balcony with every word. I was to pay as much attention to the final consonant of a word as I did to the beginning. In everyday speech, Janine explained to me, people often trailed off towards the end of a word, swallowing its final sound. Onstage I was to treat this last consonant as if it had another, final sound to reach for, or as though the word might continue on after it would normally end. I worked hard on this particular point, as my tendency in rehearsal was to let those last sounds float off as I did in regular speech. Janine was rigorous, demanding, and exceedingly warm and kind. By the end of our sessions I had discovered a voice more powerful than I could have ever imagined having. I didn't lose my consonants anymore to a lack of effort at the ends of words. I didn't give up on words before they were completely said.

But the time I had simply wasn't enough to make up for a lack of theatre school, and by the time the dress rehearsals rolled around, Marti and the stage manager had reluctantly decided to mic me. I felt this as an acute failure of my work ethic, and I felt as though I had been given up on. And in that first moment of a mic being hidden in my hair, I gave up a little on myself.

In my movement classes, Kelly taught me how to walk, how to stand, how to make my body alive and present at all times. When my back was to the audience, I was to imagine that I was at a party and a boy I really liked was behind me. Though I was facing away from this imagined boy, my body's energy and its language was all directed to and for him. It was a helpful image and one that my teenage self immediately connected with. But no matter how hard I worked at it, I couldn't straighten my twisted, hunched body. Kelly would massage the muscles that had become increasingly squeezed and trapped in the small space between my upper spine (which had migrated even farther to the right) and my right shoulder blade. She taught me how to hoist myself straight more efficiently, and with less pain, to create the impression of balance. But I was crooked, there was no doubt. The costume department sewed pads into all the places my body was asymmetrical. They filled in the area between my shoulder and chest where there was a gap due to the increasing hunch on one side. They created a shoulder blade pad for my left shoulder to compensate for the one on the right that protruded. Another large pad ran alongside my left rib cage to even it out with the right one. And then, of course, there was the tight tensor bandage that bound my breasts to make me look like a prepubescent girl.

It felt strange that these breasts, which had become such currency in my life now that I was a sexual person, were being obliterated every time I put on my Alice costume. After straining to grow up and past my childhood for so long, I was now actively disappearing the maturity I had gained through much struggle. This felt strangely in continuity with my childlike life at my aunt and cousin's house. Instead of being a woman, living on my own, which is how I had been living far too early, I was no longer an adult but completely taken care of, with no expectations around the house or responsibilities, being forced back into the body of a child.

By this point, it may be obvious that a nervous breakdown of epic proportions was in the offing. This dichotomy between my womanly body, which was in a kind of collapse, and the oddness of experiencing a sort of reversal of puberty and hard-won independence, twisted with the knots of a story written by a likely pedophile that contained echoes of my relationship with my father, was a powder keg for my subconscious.

It wasn't at all clear to me, though. In fact, I loved the rehearsals. I loved watching the play slowly take shape, the opportunity for play, for experimentation, and the room to try something and have it not work without its inducing panic, which was almost always the case on the TV shows and films I had worked on, which were constantly behind schedule, over budget, and under the gun. The work of theatre seemed like intellectual, creative work, whereas almost everything else I had performed in seemed industrial or about producing a product as quickly as possible. It had often been about finding the *fastest* way to a result instead of the *best* way. And, most surprisingly, theatre was *fun*. I wasn't used to work being fun. But theatre people, it turned out, had reinvented fun.

The people I was working with were a wildly smart, vibrant cast of characters with far more integrity and intellect than their TV and film cousins. They were there because they loved Shakespeare and great text. They were there after studying great works of literature for years. I encountered none of the egos I was used to in film and television, where one narcissistic personality or unstable thespian could hold up a day and harpoon a schedule. There were crazy, larger-than-life characters, to be sure, but they were people who did the damn work, expressed themselves fully, and took up space in a way that I found mesmerizing as opposed to alienating. I shared a dressing room with Michelle Fisk, who played the Red Queen. She was electric; she owned the stage with her huge voice and commanding presence; she was achingly maternal, kind, and forcefully on my side from the first day.

Every now and then, I would try to sneak into the rehearsals a little bit of who I felt the real Alice Liddell to be. I tried to be snappish and judgmental with Douglas Rain's Humpty Dumpty, allowing a kind of provoking flirtatiousness to seep into my performance. I saw Douglas clock this, and saw a small, perplexed smile grow in his eyes as he peered at me sidelong from his giant egg costume. I was quickly directed into a much more innocent exchange, letting him play the salty while I played the sweet.

The White Knight, who Alice meets towards the end of the book, is clearly based on Dodgson himself, a bumbling, incompetent eccentric who so wants Alice to be okay and ultimately helps her to find the final square of the chess game, where she will turn from a pawn into a Queen, thus abandoning him. In these scenes, with Tom Wood playing the White Knight, I played a peculiar concoction of love and scorn. These dynamics were familiar to me. I had spent a life on film sets, my puberty unfolding in front of dozens of men with no sense (or care) of what was appropriate to say or not say in front of children or of the boundaries between adulthood and childhood. The size of my breasts had been commented on, often, through the years. I had experienced unhidden yearning from people three times my age. I had heard explicit conversations about sex or had had them directed straight at me. I dealt with all this by wielding the only power I had, which at the time felt very real and potent: I could mock these men to their faces, I could say whatever I wanted, I could be as mean and bad and hurtful as I pleased. Because we both knew that, as a child who had felt their desire, I had something on them.

After sneaking these strange, unearthed elements into the scenes with Humpty Dumpty and the White Knight, I was told to be nicer. When I responded, nervously and gently, that I didn't think the real Alice had been particularly "nice," I was told, once again, that this was a play "to delight children," and that while there may have been some troubling undertones in the relationship between Dodgson and Liddell in real life, this play was to be presented as something to bring magic to the audience, not uncomfortable questions of sexuality and pedophilia. I again felt that clang of dissonance between what I was being asked to play and what I understood the play to be, but I quickly pushed it aside, involved myself in the easy, joyful company of the cast, and closed my eyes when it felt, at my next costume fitting, as though my breasts were being bound just a little bit tighter.

In the evenings, I'd do schoolwork to keep up with my classes and study my lines again. Every time I sat down to run my lines on my own, I had a kind of sinking feeling. Away from the loud camaraderie of the big, colourful cast and my supportive coaches, I would realize that *I alone* was Alice. I had to carry this play. I had to remember *all of these lines at the same time.* There would be no second takes once we went into the run of the play. But before I could panic for long, morning would come and the games would begin again, along with the intensive training from Janine and Kelly and the support, care, and nurturing of Marti.

As evening came again, I would remember that I still hadn't taken on the true challenge of being in front of an audience. I tried not to think about how different it would feel when the seats in the theatre were no longer empty.

On the day of the first preview, I had a little round mint in my mouth that I had taken out of a bowl in the green room. I chewed through the remainder of it anxiously as I waited behind the curtain for the house lights to go down. Tom Wood came up to me and whispered, "Break a leg." I turned to him and said, "I just hope I don't suck." He laughed. I went onstage in the dark. I took my place in an armchair, a fake little kitten in my hands, in front of the mantelpiece that held the huge, ominous looking glass that I was to go through for the next two hours. The preview went mercifully well. I was full of adrenalin and it felt like flying, to be at the centre of something so momentous.

The success of the first show left me with some rather rigid superstitions. I made sure to always have one of those same mints in my mouth and to be almost finished chewing it by the time the lights went down. I asked Tom to come up to me before every show and say "Break a leg" just as the lights finished dimming. I would say, in the exact same tone of voice I had before the first preview, "I just hope I don't suck." I would ask him to laugh in exactly the same way. He sweetly obliged. And then I would, night after night, slip into the armchair in front of the mantelpiece under the cover of the darkness, able, for those few seconds before the stage lights came up on me, to see the anticipation and excitement in the audience's eyes, many of whom were children, there to be delighted.

When previews began, a sign-in sheet was posted near the door of the backstage area. There was a list of the cast, and beside each name there was a blank space for us to initial when we arrived at the theatre, so that the stage manager would know we were there before the performance started. I began to notice that the box next to Douglas Rain's name was always empty. I asked Michelle about it, and she said something to the effect of "That's his thing. He just doesn't sign in." I knocked on Douglas's door. By now, Douglas and I had a rapport that had turned into something of a sideshow, I as the provoking, irritating teenager, he as the cranky old man who suffered no fools and wasn't used to being trifled with. "Douglas," I said, "why don't you sign in? *Do you think you're so good but you're not?*"

"That's not even a real question." He continued putting on his Humpty Dumpty makeup and asked me to leave.

"Why don't you sign in? What's your problem?"

"I'm a professional," he hissed. "Of course I am here when I am supposed to be here. I don't need to *sign in* to do my job."

I rolled my eyes. From that day onward I signed in for Douglas with cheery, jocular messages to the rest of the cast. One day I wrote, "OH MY GOD! I just LOVE you all SO MUCH! HAPPY HAPPY JOY JOY!" Some days I would write things to the effect of "Do you, like, LOVE your job? I do!!! Have an amazing show, everyone! I appreciate you so much!" I would punctuate the comments with drawings of rainbows and happy faces and smiling suns.

More than one cast member advised me that this was not a good idea and that I did not want to provoke Douglas's fury. Indeed, I had seen his genuine rages before. Mervyn Blake, who was playing the part of the Red King, was well into his eighties and had been part of the Stratford Festival when it was still operating out of a tent in the 1950s. He was frail by now, walking with difficulty with a cane. He had been in an army regiment that had liberated Bergen-Belsen and had sustained considerable trauma that sometimes came up in his sleep. (Someone who had roomed with him on tour told me he would often wake up screaming.) He was warm, always smiling, and universally loved. He was also the first Stratford actor to appear in every one of Shakespeare's plays. One day, in dress rehearsals for the Humpty Dumpty scene, as Douglas was perched with his ridiculous egg head and tiny prop legs on a fence, Mervyn took a moment to watch the rehearsal, delighted, from the wings. When he let out an appreciative laugh, Douglas *exploded*. He screamed that it was unprofessional, distracting, and amateurish for Mervyn to be standing there watching while we were rehearsing. At some point he stopped addressing the shocked old man directly and started screaming at Marti, "*HE SHOULD KNOW BETTER BY NOW!*" It was terrifying, and I felt my heart crumble for Mervyn, who stood stunned and alone in the wings. The warnings to be careful of Douglas were not unmerited. I just couldn't help myself.

One day I arrived to see Douglas staring at the sign-in sheet, reading all of my entries in his column and smiling to himself. By the time he got to the end of the preceding week's sign-ins he was shaking with laughter. He turned around and saw me, and his face turned to steel. But I felt, in that moment, that in a far-removed and utterly unselfish way, he appreciated me. My body went weightless with the sensation of victory.

Opening night arrived. My dad, my siblings, my mother's sister and her husband, and many of my cousins had come into town for the big opening. I stood backstage. I sucked on my mint. I told Tom I "hope I don't suck" after he said "Break a leg." He laughed. I made my way in the dark to the armchair. I felt as though I might throw up. My voice, when I started to speak, was shaking. It wasn't just shaking inside me; it was shaking on the outside too. I couldn't control it. I was terrified. A wall of fog rose up as I went through the looking glass, and then the set piece of the mantel and giant mirror were wheeled away by the company members. I had a conversation with a gnat. And then I heard my father, somewhere towards the back left-hand side of the theatre, cough. Something about that cough made everything settle. I was onstage. I was the lead. I was Alice. I was acting with the voice of the great Douglas Rain, who was voicing said gnat. I was going to be just fine. I felt a sudden joy at being there, the thrill of making people laugh or gasp in real time. The thrill of delighting children. I never wanted to be anywhere else.

Towards the end of the play, Alice meets the White Knight. His first words to her, after doing battle with the Red Knight over who will lay claim to her, are, "It was a glorious victory, wasn't it?"

Alice replies, "I don't know. I don't want to be anybody's prisoner. I want to be a Queen."

The White Knight says, "So you will, when you've crossed the next brook. I'll see you safe to the end of the wood—and then I must go back, you know. That's the end of my move."

The White Knight is bumbling, nervous, unable to really manage in any reasonable way in the world. He shows Alice a little box he keeps "clothes and sandwiches in," which he carries upside down "so that the rain can't get in." He hasn't realized that he has left the box open, which means he is losing everything he has as it falls out. He tells Alice about absurd, nonsensical inventions that have no practical purpose, like anklets around his horse's feet to "guard against the bites of sharks." The character was played by Tom Wood, my pre-show bringer of good luck. He was almost painfully gentle and sweet to me. When I met him, out on that stage in that scene, it signalled the play was almost at its end. He sauntered up to me, with an actor playing his horse close behind him.

In Lewis Carroll's original scene from the book, which was nearly identical to the scene we played, he writes:

Of all the strange things that Alice saw in her journey Through The Looking-Glass, this was the one that she always remembered most clearly. Years afterwards she could bring the whole scene back again, as if it had been only yesterday—the mild blue eyes and kindly smile of the Knight— the setting sun gleaming through his hair, and shining on his armour in a blaze of light that quite dazzled her—the horse quietly moving about, with the reins hanging loose on his neck, cropping the grass at her feet—and the black shadows of the forest behind—all this she took in like a picture . . .

I heard my dad cough again, deep in the middle rows somewhere. I looked out into the black chasm of the hidden audience. I looked back at Tom, singing.

As the Knight sang the last words of the ballad, he gathered up the reins, and turned his horse's head along the road by which they had come. "You've only a few yards to go," he said, "down the hill and over that little brook, and then you'll be a Queen— But you'll stay and see me off first?" he added as Alice turned with an eager look in the direction to which he pointed. "I shan't be long. You'll wait and wave your handkerchief when I get to that turn in the road! I think it'll encourage me, you see."

"Of course I'll wait," said Alice: "and thank you very much for coming so far—and for the song—I liked it very much."

"I hope so," the Knight said doubtfully: "but you didn't cry so much as I thought you would."

I felt myself on the verge of a sob. Some deep sadness at having to say goodbye to the kind, messy, vulnerable, incompetent, loving White Knight gushed up. In rehearsals, James Reaney had told us that the White Knight was Charles Dodgson saying goodbye to the Alice he had known and loved, as she had fled into adulthood. And this moment he had written was Alice giving him the send-off, a goodbye full of grati-tude, which she likely had never given him in life. A small, guttural moan escaped from me, which I quickly suppressed. I saw an assistant stage manager turn quickly from the wings to see what had happened. I took a deep breath and continued.

"I hope it encouraged him," she said, as she turned to run down the hill: "and now for the last brook, and to be a Queen! How grand it sounds!"

After the show I rode back to my aunt's house with my father and siblings. My father talked about how mesmerizing the play was, how brilliant I was. My sister Jo said, "I disagree. It sort of played like an innocent, sweet tale. But I don't think that's what it is. The books are more complex than that. And Alice seemed so *sweet*. I don't think that's who Alice is. Alice is smart and provoking and bratty. That's how I always thought it should be played." I felt sick. I felt I might vomit. I opened the window. She was right, of course.

I had sixty-five shows to go. And now I feared that for the many months of shows to go, I would not be able to hide the lie of my performance from myself.

I managed to push this criticism out of my conscious mind, but the dissonance I had felt throughout rehearsals had now been clearly articulated. It was a discomfort I could no longer rid myself of by avoiding thinking about it. A seed had been planted that would grow.

Despite this clash between belief and performance that I now felt while performing the play, my life for those first twenty shows feels like a dream to me now, a picture of overindulged childhood and creative excitement. By day, there were the long hours of delicious food and reading great books with two vibrant, maternal women. By night, I was performing with some of the greatest actors I have ever known, ending with a standing ovation after every performance. It was thrilling. Until it wasn't.

Around the twentieth show, I began to tune out. I still loved the time with my aunt and my cousin, but it was at strange odds with the life I was building outside of this pause in time. I was in love with, and separated from, Corey. He was allowed to visit, but not to share a bedroom. Corey was not within my aunt's small collection of treasures. (To be fair, he was hard-edged and cynical and lacked any diplomacy.) I could feel that she disliked both his presence in her house and what he symbolized: that I would be moving out one day. My aunt said, somewhat wryly as she set up the guest bedroom for Corey, that she didn't want any "copulation" in the house because her granddaughter looked up to me. I was being loved and pampered and nurtured like a child, but I also had some of the limitations of a child, and though these limitations now seem reasonable to me, being a child wasn't something I was used to, either then or during most of my childhood. A part of me was home-sick for myself—the self that felt much older than fifteen, the self that lived free from rules and restrictions and the other taxes of being taken care of, the self that I felt I had earned, fair and square, through years of adult responsibilities.

And the show itself was now boring to me. I was on a kind of automatic pilot, for the most part thinking of other things while saying the lines I had said so many dozens of times before. I felt no fear, but neither did I feel much joy or engagement. My main joy in the production now came from the practical jokes the cast played on each other, the sudden glimpse of someone naked in the wings as I delivered lines and had to keep my face straight. The play now performed itself, without much effort. I wasn't really there, consciously, for much of it.

I've always wondered what my performance looked and felt like to an audience during those second twenty shows. Did I seem disassociated? Or was my performance of Alice, as it had been guided, so separated from anything real in me anyway that there wasn't much of a difference from the shows when I had been more consciously present? What I do know is this: not being conscious of myself in those twenty or so "auto-matic pilot" shows had consequences.

On my days off, I took the train to Toronto to see Corey. We had a place together in the Gay Village, a sixth-floor boxy apartment with little light in a 1960s high-rise. It had no furniture. We would sleep on the floor together, our possessions limited to two little candle holders with cut-outs in them that cast stars on the ceiling as we lay together in sleeping bags. We also had a goblet with grasshoppers carved into it, given to me by the legendary actor Bill Needles, who had told me he thought Corey was "adorable." He told me that he had had this grasshopper glass in every house he had lived in as an adult and it had brought him good luck. "It's time to pass it along to someone who needs it," he had said.

One day, when I returned to Stratford from a night in Toronto, the stage manager asked to speak with me before the show. As I went to my dressing room, I noticed several of the cast looking at me sympathetically. I started to have the sense that I was about to be told something unpleasant, something that everyone else already knew.

Marylu, the stage manager, asked me if I knew that for the past few shows I had been adding a vowel to the end of nearly every word. I said no, but that Janine had told me to imagine there was a vowel at the end of every word. Marylu emphasized that I wasn't just imagining these vowels anymore. I was actually *saying* them. I was shocked. As I felt my body burn into what felt like a dangerous heat, I thanked her for informing me (though I secretly wanted to kill her for doing so) and said that I would stop doing it.

The next show, I was not on automatic pilot anymore. I heard every word everyone said. I heard every word *I* said. And every word that should have ended in a consonant had a vowel tacked right onto the end of it, like a wagging, gleeful tail. I could hear myself now, clearly, but I couldn't change what I heard.

(My one-and-a-half-year-old, who at this moment is learning to speak, does the exact same thing. She says "hot-a" instead of "hot." She says "mad-a!" instead of "mad." Everyone finds it hilarious. Sometimes I do too. Often, though, I find it makes my heart skip a beat. Because the night I first heard myself speaking this way was the beginning of the end of my surviving my previous life.)

I went back to Janine. I worked with her for hours the next day. Now we had to undo much of the work we had done together. I needed to be willing to let the ends of words go again instead of hitting them with the imaginings of a continuation. I just had to let them bleed out into silence. This act felt irresponsible, like a kind of abandonment of the words—an abandonment of Lewis Carroll's words. It was painful and felt like an arduous process, but after two shows, the phantom vowels had disappeared.

Douglas Rain appeared at my dressing room doorway after I had done my first show with vowel-free word endings. He looked at me with an intensity, almost a ferocity, in his eyes. He said, "I have never seen *anyone* fix such a *major* problem so *quickly*."

As I left the theatre that night, I received squeezes on my shoulders and hugs and congratulations. Until then, I had not realized what a big problem, and what a widely *recognized* problem, it had been. What had the *audiences* thought? It must have been crazy to watch a two-hour play with someone speaking with such a noticeable tic.

One thing felt certain to me. If I went back on automatic pilot, or let my guard down ever again, I would fail. I would fail spectacularly. I now had proof. Horrible, humiliating proof.

THE UNRAVELLING

"Take care of yourself!" screamed the White Queen, seizing Alice's hair with both her hands. "Something's going to happen!"

And then (as Alice afterwards described it) all sorts of things happened in a moment.

—Through the Looking-Glass

The tic in my speech had been resolved, but now a new problem had arisen. This one had teeth and scales, a kind of giant smelly, angry Jabberwock that was bearing down on me.

Now I was afraid of going onstage.

I was afraid in a way that drenched my whole body in sweat in an instant and made my heart smash so violently within my chest that I thought it might explode clear through my skin. I was afraid to go onstage, but I was also afraid of my voice. I was afraid of how my mouth shaped words. And I was afraid that the automatic pilot I had been on for the previous twenty shows had been responsible for getting me through them. I had remembered all my lines on automatic pilot and there had been no problems. Now that the auto mode had been turned off, what if my conscious self couldn't remember them? And what if (and this thought made it hard to breathe) anyone found out that I was afraid to go onstage? What if this fear was known and spoken of by others? I cannot, sitting here, in my forty-one-year-old body and brain, remember what it felt like to be certain that expressing a fear would make it worse, that the humiliation of people knowing I had a fear could be worse than the agony of living with it alone and unexpressed. But at fifteen these things were patently obvious to me and as I was in conversation only with myself on this matter, there was no other way of thinking of this situation within the limited confines of my panicked brain.

Mornings were usually okay. I would wake up and begin the day of reading with my aunt and my cousin, and find myself pleasantly surprised by my general calm. Then, around two thirty, as the day veered closer to evening than morning, some kind of state-of-emergency switch turned on, and the tyranny of seven thirty (as the great Canadian actor Brent Carver called it) loomed over me. I couldn't do it. I knew I couldn't. I couldn't go out on that stage under any circumstances. But I had to. There was no way out. I would go to the theatre, my legs heavy, feeling like a condemned person walking to the guillotine. I would chide myself for this overly dramatic image, but I was fairly certain that if I had to go onstage that night, I would die. But, I thought, I would die more *painfully* if I told anyone how I felt and experienced the shame of their knowing I was afraid.

It never even *occurred* to me that I was likely surrounded by people who had experienced stage fright and had, over many years, learned techniques for managing it. In retrospect, I was in a town of people, a significant percentage of whom likely had a lot of expertise in this matter. It pains me now to think of how helpful Michelle Fisk, who played the Red Queen, would have been. She was always incredibly kind to me, and hid her maternal instincts towards me in small gestures of care so as not to make me feel diminished by them. Nonetheless, it never once crossed my mind to tell her, or anyone else, including Auntie Ann and Sarah, who loved me, would have done anything for me, and were resourceful.

I started to arrive at the theatre earlier and earlier. Initially, at the beginning of the run, I would arrive at the theatre early to go into the basement rehearsal space, a dark, carpeted room with no windows, to stretch and do vocal warm-ups. By week two of my stage fright, I was arriving hours early, locking the door and beginning what was now no longer a warm-up but about an hour and a half of sobbing on the floor in a fetal position.

As I waited in the wings for the lights to go down, my before-show rituals with the mint and Tom took on a frantic tone. If he wasn't there by my side to say "Break a leg" earlier than he should be, I would run to the end of the line of actors waiting to go onstage to find him and grab him, my nails digging into his arm, in thinly concealed panic. Now I had two mints, one in my mouth and one already ground down to the appropriate size, to ensure I got the exact sound of the *crunch* I was used to after I said "I just hope I don't suck." The rituals became more and more critical to my survival, to ensuring that something didn't go terribly wrong, to ensuring I didn't become engulfed forever by the world behind the looking glass.

Now every scene, every set piece, signified to me only how close or far the performance was to being over. The Gnat scene was bad. Almost nothing had happened yet; I was still close to the beginning. Ditto for the White Queen scene and the Tweedledum and Tweedledee scene. It was around the Humpty Dumpty scene that I started to relax a little. As I saw Douglas, perched in his ridiculous giant egg costume, tiny legs dangling off the wall, I knew I was heading into the home stretch. I also felt, every now and then, Douglas's eyes on me, seeming to notice something, projecting some kind of concern or warmth that I hadn't noticed before. I wondered if he could see my fear. I was terrified that he could, but I was able, for those brief moments with me as Alice and he as a grouchy giant egg, to also feel soothed by the possibility of his knowing me.

And then one day, the fear turned to madness, and I myself went through the looking glass. During one performance, as the fog rose in the giant mirror in the first scene of the show and I shimmied down onto the chair on the other side, something more disturbing than stage fright began to grow in me. I started to feel convinced by the nonsense of the world I had entered. When Alice had to run in order to stand still, I felt anxious and resentful of the arbitrary rule I was being forced to follow by the imperious Red Queen. When I asked what road to follow and had a character recite a poem to me instead of giving me a direction, I became genuinely incensed. Not incensed as Alice. Incensed as Sarah. I started to become more and more furious with each passing show. Conversations such as the one where the White Queen claims there is "jam tomorrow and jam yesterday—but never jam today" made me livid. I didn't like that the answers every character gave me in response to my queries were so infuriatingly twisted and circular.

ALICE: I'm sure I didn't mean—

RED QUEEN: That's just what I complain of! You should have meant! What do you suppose is the use of a child without any meaning? Even a joke should have some meaning—and a child's more important than a joke, I hope. You couldn't deny that, even if you tried with both hands.

ALICE: I don't deny things with my hands.

RED QUEEN: Nobody said you did. I said you couldn't if you tried.

WHITE QUEEN: She's in that state of mind that she wants to deny something—only she doesn't know what to deny!

I began to feel trapped behind the looking glass, as though the worst imaginings of my smaller self, the one who had resisted these stories at bedtime in the first place, had come true.

"So I wasn't dreaming, after all," she said to herself, "unless—unless we're all part of the same dream. Only I do hope it's my dream, and not the Red King's! I don't like belonging to another person's dream," she went on in a rather complaining tone: "I've a great mind to go and wake him, and see what happens!"

—Through the Looking-Glass

As the play progressed, I became more and more lost to the world I knew. It was as though the frustration I had felt when hearing these stories as a small child had suddenly taken a growing pill and had taken over my whole body.

Now, when I said goodbye to the White Knight in that penultimate scene, I could not stop the tears from flooding down my face as I said *"I hope it encouraged him."* I watched him, losing his things out of the hole in his sack, as he trotted on alone, unawares. I wished there was something I could do for him. I hated Alice Liddell for abandoning Charles Dodgson by fleeing her childhood into womanhood. I hated that my dad left chicken pot pies on the stovetop for a week, insisting they didn't need to be refrigerated, or that he made the red cabbage three weeks before Christmas dinner, and that the cards he played solitaire with no longer had images on them. I tried to block out the mornings I had woken up to find him, still sleepless, staring at reams of papers on the dining room table, full of tiny, neatly written mathematical equations, numbers doubling and quadrupling until he ran out of space in the millions. (I later discovered he was trying to ascertain how many humans had had to copulate in order to produce him, and how many of those couplings were likely rapes. "How much violence was I the product of?" he said, looking helpless and childlike.) I wonder, in retrospect, if these moments were signs of a typical eccentric Englishman who'd never had to do a single domestic duty until his wife died, or of mental illness, or early signs of the dementia that would be diagnosed many years later. I suppose I'll never know, and there is something I can't help but find funny about how closely these states might resemble each other.

When I had moved out of my father's house the year before I went to Stratford, he didn't argue with me. He didn't suggest that we move closer to my school and my friends so that I might be inclined to stay with him. He just let me leave. It wasn't a lack of love, I don't think, but a habit of being passive, of avoiding conflict, of letting go every day in a way that still provokes both admiration and fury in me. And once I left, we didn't speak unless I called him. He never said "I love you" when he said goodbye. So I started to say it to him. I said it insistently, consistently, until one day he had learned how to say it back to me. I already knew that he loved me, but it could be vague and hard to pin down. His love was all around the edges, but sometimes it was hard for both of us to see, I think.

On a visit home one weekend shortly after I had moved out, I found a half-written letter to his sister Janet in England. He wrote that a mammal's purpose in life was to bear and raise their young. Now that I was gone, his life had no purpose. He'd thought he would have a few more years left of purpose. But I had left so young. He wrote this in a detached, intellectual way that implied it was a subject of some interest but not heartbreak. I later found a reply from his sister in which she attempted to comfort him, saying, "I'm sure your Sarah will change her mind and come back to you soon." But I never did.

Around this time, my dad, when I would see him occasionally, would sing to himself, with a little side grin, "How ya gonna keep 'em down on the farm, after they've seen Paree?"

Standing on that stage, convinced I had gone through the looking glass, I knew I didn't want to be a Queen. I didn't want to wave good-bye to him. I was moving away from my childhood, but I was also strangely caught and bound to it for this one, endless moment, in which I had to perform and remember all the words. And not add vowels to the ends of the words.

I cried every time I said goodbye to the White Knight. I cry now as I imagine the farewell. It guts me to remember comforting this bumbling fool of a sweetheart as he must leave behind the child that loved him— and that he loved.

Somewhere around this time I was given a note by stage management saying that while I could play a note of sadness in saying goodbye to the White Knight, I needed to stop short of turning it into a tragedy. I tried to tone down the sadness. But I couldn't. I still can't.

Recently, when I described this moment in the play to my therapist and the scenes of Dodgson's rejection by Alice in *Dreamchild*, I tried hard to talk about my anger at being made to feel sad for the grown man instead of for the child, but all that came out of me was the sadness itself, a sadness so fierce I couldn't speak for my sobbing. My therapist said, quietly, "There is something tremendously sad about being a pedophile. To love a creature you can't have. To know that that love is bad. To know that you are bad for having these feelings, even if you don't act on them. It's tremendously sad."

When, at the end of the play, there is a large dinner party that descends into chaos and confusion (there is an argument with an angry pudding, candles shoot to the ceiling, Alice ends up sitting beside a leg of mutton instead of the White Queen) and Alice finally destroys the looking-glass world by ripping off the tablecloth in a fit of rage, the rage in me was real. "I CAN'T STAND THIS ANY LONGER!" Alice screams. I often had tears flying out of my face when I screamed this line. I often caught Douglas's eyes at the end of the table and saw in them a flash of recognition of the real snapping inside of me.

It wasn't just the play itself that started to drive me mad. So did the audience, the sea of faceless strangers who sat quietly together in the dark, unseen and safe with their rustling programs and snapping gum and glugs of water, while I inwardly collapsed every night in front of them. When the lights were down between set pieces, or between acts, I would study their impartial faces as they reached into their purses for lip gloss or studied their programs. What kind of monsters would purchase tickets and bring their children to come to see me fail? Couldn't they see I was a child? (Though certain of being an adult, I invoked the state of childhood as a weapon against anything that struck me as unjust.) What kind of perversity in people leads them to pay money to watch someone so young walk a tightrope they will surely fall off? I thought to myself. I resented them all.

One day, around this time, Douglas Rain appeared again at my dressing room door. I heard Michelle, beside me, give a little start. He had a tomato in his hand. He held it out towards me. He said, "Here. I grew it in my garden."

I laughed. "A tomato?"

"I have more," he said. "You could cook something with them."

I laughed again and went into the jocular, needling mode I always had in interaction with him. "Cooking is boring," I said.

"Do you know what cooking *is?*" he hissed, enunciating every sound. "It is taking something ordinary, like this tomato, and by adding— *what?*—it becomes something *extraordinary.*"

I stared at him, uncomprehending.

"I said by *adding what* does it become extraordinary?"

"Heat," I said.

"Correct," he said.

He put the tomato on the counter and looked at me for a moment longer than usual, as though trying to assess what was going on behind my eyes. I looked away. If anyone was going to discover the secret of my terror, it was him.

When I got to the end of each of these jagged shows, I felt a kind of elation and adrenalin I have not felt before or since. I would wait behind the theatre, beside the loading dock where set pieces were wheeled in and out, for my aunt or cousin to pick me up. I would get into the car, covered in sweat and relief, and my breathing would be calm until around two thirty the next afternoon, when it would all begin again.

But the panic of two thirty started to become one thirty, which started to become twelve thirty. The starting gun for my terror seemed to go off earlier with each passing day. I kept telling myself, "Only twenty-five more shows to go," "Only twenty-four more shows to go," counting down the days until my release from the prison of my fear. And then came the news, greeted with elation by a cast of actors who made the majority of their income only in the summers, that the play had been picked up for a winter run at the Winter Garden Theatre in Toronto. When I heard the news, I felt nauseous. I forced a shaky smile onto my face. In our dressing room, Michelle expressed her relief at knowing income was coming in over the winter. She had two small children, Katie and Max. She said, "I can finally get Katie a carpet for her room. Her floor is so cold, and she keeps asking for a carpet. I can finally get one for her." She had tears in her eyes. So did I. It was such a simple thing for a child to want, this carpet.

My counting down of the shows no longer worked, now that so many more had just been added. I woke up scared, I went to bed scared. My heart raced all the time. Now, before I went onstage, I would bargain with myself like a scam artist. I would say, in a whisper, after I had crunched that mint, "I promise you, Sarah, I *promise you* that if you get through this one show, just this one show, I will never, ever make you do this again. I promise. If you can get to the end of this show, I won't ever make you do another one. You will never have to go onstage again for the rest of your life." But it was a lie. There was always another show. And another one. And somewhere along the way I kicked the liar that was conning me into these false bargains in the face. Betrayed by the bad deals handed to me by my broken self, I knew I had to find another way out.

In the midst of this mental state, which I believe was madness, the only thing that made obvious sense to me was to trade one terror for another. To get out of this fear, I needed to be split in two; I needed to have the surgery.

"I can't stand this any longer!"

—Alice in *Through the Looking-Glass*

I had lunch with Marti Maraden at her house to discuss the run at the Winter Garden. I watched her doing the dishes after lunch as I tried to figure out what to say, how to say it, and when to say it. Suddenly I blurted out, "I'm in terrible pain. My back hurts all the time. I don't know how I'll be able to keep going with another run when this one is over. I think I need surgery." She was quiet and still for a while. She studied me closely. I watched as she skillfully turned off her director self and made room for the warm, maternal nurturer that she also was. It wasn't a strategy, or false; it was a decision to reorient her priorities, with no warning, in that precise moment. I was a child, and she saw me as one. I told her that I needed to go to see a doctor as soon as possible, because I could hardly get through the days. She encouraged me to see an orthopaedic surgeon.

The next week I got on the train to Toronto, with a plan to finally get myself free. I went to a respected doctor I hadn't seen before, Douglas Hedden at the Hospital for Sick Children. Dr. Hedden, a kind, soft-spoken, gentle man, took me into his office after examining me. We looked at my X-rays together. He said that it was clear that the curve of my spine, which was now more than sixty degrees, needed surgery. I felt a wave of relief. The thing I had spent the last four years dreading was now my ticket to freedom. The surgery wasn't urgent, he said. It could be done early the next year if necessary. I quickly told Dr. Hedden that I was in unimaginable pain, that it couldn't wait that long. My back hurt all the time. I could barely walk. I was in the middle of a play right now, and I couldn't do another show. *I couldn't do one more show.* It just simply hurt too much. Dr. Hedden took a long time before he spoke. He looked down and quietly told me that scoliosis sometimes caused muscle spasms but it didn't normally cause terrible pain. When it got as severe as the case I had, it could eventually have a calamitous effect on other organs.

Lungs could become compressed, et cetera. But usually the curve of
the spine itself wasn't so painful. After another long pause he said,
"You know, I once had a patient who had scoliosis and he played baseball. And he really, really needed to stop playing baseball. He said he
was in a lot of pain. That may have been true. But what was definitely
true was that he really, really needed to stop playing baseball. Do you
know what I mean? He just had to. And so I wrote him a note saying he
couldn't play baseball anymore. Would you like a note like that?"

I looked down, embarrassed, and grateful. I nodded. "Yes. I would like
a note like that."

"And," he said, looking at his schedule, "we can do the surgery this
year. The soonest we can do it is November. But I'll write a note that
says you need to stop acting in the play immediately."

I could barely get the words out to thank him.

I don't remember what the note said. It wasn't a lie. It was beautifully
constructed. It said what I needed it to say but it didn't say anything
that was false. I'm not sure I've ever felt gratitude as piercing and transformative as I did when I held his note in my hand on that train. I took
that note back to Stratford with me and it made me free.

(There was a follow-up meeting with my father to get his consent
for the surgery. Recently, when I made contact with Dr. Hedden
again, he reminded me of this meeting, which I had forgotten. He
wrote: "I must admit there is one moment that I think about from
time to time. It was when we were discussing the surgery and going
through the risks and benefits. I asked your father what he thought
and his answer was something like, 'well it's her decision, seems like
she has been making her own decisions all along.' It spoke to the
empowerment of children and trusting them to make good decisions
[well most of the time]." I was happy to be reminded of this, and to

hear his perspective on the freedom my father afforded me, despite all its obvious pitfalls.)

I did one final agonizing show, showed the doctor's note to stage management and Marti, and left my panicked understudy, Christina, to pick up the pieces of the mammoth part in one and a half arduous days of rehearsals.

For the next week or so, I feigned being in enormous pain. My cousin Sarah insists to this day that there was real pain in there as well, and it's possible that there was, but I couldn't believe my own body because I knew how desperate I was to further my more important agenda of getting myself free of the play. My aunt, thinking I had simply become bored and wanted to go back to Toronto to live with Corey, as I had offered no other excuse other than my sudden onset of pain, seemed upset with me, barely making eye contact with me in those last days. There had been a future in which I stayed living with her and Sarah and they would take care of me, and our summers of reading and laughing would go on and on. They had floated this idea, more than once, during the happier days of rehearsals, when all I wanted to do was continue to work in theatre and stay with them, coddled and taken care of forever. Now this possible future was dying around us, and I felt, for a time, not only that my Auntie Ann didn't believe my pain but that I had been cast out of her small collection of treasured things. Sarah came to my bedroom every day to put bags of frozen peas on my back and sit silently with me. I could sense that she knew something else was going on, but I could feel that she was also aware that something in me needed to be tended to, even if it wasn't the thing I was pointing to, and she nurtured me anyway. It made me feel lucky, loved, and unbearably guilty.

With the news that I couldn't continue the show and was due to have surgery in November, the run at the Winter Garden was cancelled. I won an award of $500 for best newcomer to the Stratford Festival.

I made sure I wasn't in town during the ceremony, and when I got the award money, I cashed the cheque and left the money in an envelope in Michelle's dressing room with the words "For Katie's carpet" on it. I couldn't look anyone in the eye. I had cost them their winter income. The run at Stratford continued, with my understudy performing the remaining ten shows. Without even realizing it, I had made it through fifty-eight of sixty-eight shows.

Marti and the stage manager asked if I could come and watch with them in the stage manager's booth to celebrate the final show. How strange it was to suddenly see the show from the outside, to see the fabulous spectacle of it, to see how innocuous it was, instead of witnessing it from deep inside a nightmare. It truly was a delight to children.

After the curtain came down, I walked backstage with feigned difficulty. Douglas Rain, who usually disappeared as soon as the show was over, was there, waiting for me in the wings. He stretched his arms out wide, tears falling down his face, and hugged me hard and long.

This sudden dissolving of his armour in the face of the only disingenuous moment I had had with him crushed whatever was left of me. Years later, I wonder if he knew exactly what was going on. I wonder if that hug was for the hidden story that no one else would hear for many years.

About a week before the surgery was to take place, I was sent for a battery of tests at the hospital as part of my pre-op protocol. The curve in my spine was now more than sixty degrees. I was told that my lung function was significantly compromised by the scoliosis. I felt instant relief at this finding. It hadn't been due to a lack of work ethic, or a moral failing, or a failure of talent that I had needed that mic to be heard in the balconies. As it turned out, my lungs and diaphragm, constrained as they were by my twisted body, simply couldn't make sound travel that far. As I sat with Dr. Hedden that day, with an X-ray of my deformed spine lit up behind him on a light board, I began to feel the real fear of the surgery that had been obliterated by my fear of the stage and the pressing necessity to use the operation as an escape hatch. I trembled in my seat as he told me what to expect and what to prepare for the following Thursday. The surgery would take ten hours. I would be in the hospital for over two weeks. I would be unable to participate in regular life for months. He also told me the risks, which, though uncommon, included paralysis.

As I was about to leave, I turned back to him and asked if he had ever had a patient become paralyzed or die from the surgery. He looked me steadily in the eye and told me that he had performed this surgery every Thursday for years, and that he had never had that happen to one of his patients. He took a pause and said, "And I can tell you that if either of those things happened, it would change my life, too." I knew that he meant it, and I felt certain that I was safe in his hands. Years later, when I spoke to Dr. Hedden again, I reminded him of his words to me that day and told him how much they had meant to me. He said that he remembered the conversation. Just months before, a colleague of his had had a terrible outcome with a patient in an OR. He said, "I was speaking the truth. I had seen how it could destroy a doctor."

A few days before the operation I had a dream that my long blond hair had been sewn into my back during the surgery, and that when I awoke in the hospital I couldn't move my head forward with the hair stuck in my back. My face was pointed permanently skyward. The very next day I walked into a hairdresser's, and got a pixie cut.

The hospital wouldn't let Corey stay overnight with me. I was fifteen, and as I was a minor, only immediate family were allowed. This was horrifying to me, as Corey *was* my family as I defined it. He was who I lived with now and the person I loved. He was the person who now took care of me. The idea of him not being allowed to be present was terrifying to me. After much negotiation I got clearance for him to be in the recovery room. For some reason, it was my greatest fear that he wouldn't be there when I woke up from the surgery. I became obsessed with this one detail; I perseverated on it. I was terrified that my dad would be there when I woke up and would be unable to hear me due to his impaired hearing and his general lack of attunement.

On the day of the surgery, as I was wheeled into the OR, a young anaesthesiology resident stayed by my side, talking to me, connected and kind. I remember a gruff old anesthesiologist suddenly appearing and yelling at a nurse about my IV or something being wrong. I remember him shoving a mask over my face without telling me he was going to do so. I remember panicking and screaming, "This is all a lie! I don't need this surgery! I lied!"

And then I remember darkness. And I remember a tiny pinprick of light pulsating at the end of that darkness. I remember counting in the dark, unable to hear or feel or see as I counted, far into the thousands, and watched that beating prick of light. I remember having the thought: "This is what people see when they die. That is the tunnel with the white light."

During the surgery, I was later told, I had an episode of very severe bronchospasm, possibly an allergic reaction to something in the humidifier placed in my breathing circuit. They had to stop the surgery for an hour. They had to go out and tell my dad and my aunt in the waiting room that they had stopped the surgery and that I was having a severe episode. My dad told me later that he had been so upset he had vomited. He thought, from the gravity with which they shared this information, that I was going to die.

When I woke up after the ten-hour surgery, Corey was not there. They couldn't find him. (He had fallen asleep in another part of the hospital, terrified and exhausted after arguing repeatedly with nurses who had not been given the information that he had permission to see me.) When I opened my eyes to the blur of the recovery room, grey, full of beeping machines, nurses passing in front of my vision, my dad was there. I told him I was thirsty. I told him I was sad that Corey wasn't there. He understood every word I said. Even in my haze, I was astonished by his ability to hear me so clearly when he needed to.

The nurse pointed out a morphine pump that was in my hand. She told me that I could press the button anytime I felt too much pain and I would get more morphine in my IV. It was shaped like a cylinder, and hollow in the centre. Instinctually I placed the hollow part on the protrusion of my rib under my chest, thinking it would hold the pump upright if I could place it exactly right. It fell over immediately, rolled a bit, and then came to a stop, in a straight line. There was no protrusion anymore. The rib had moved. That part of my body was now level, even. I was in a different body now. I felt myself smile, and then I fell asleep.

Later, when I had been moved to a ward room, Dr. Hedden came in to see how I was doing. I told him I felt I had been conscious for the whole surgery, locked in my body, unable to feel any sensation or hear or see, but I had been counting the whole time. He smiled. He told me I had woken up earlier than patients usually do. I had still been in the OR when I started speaking. They had been discussing *Road to Avonlea*, the show I was in as a child, while they washed up after the surgery. I had suddenly said, in a clear voice, "Don't watch it. It's a shitty show." I had given them a start, he said. (I remembered his face, looking a bit alarmed, appearing over mine, comforting me, talking me back to sleep as the gurney was moved out of the OR to the recovery room. I could feel every bump of the floor in my brand-new spine, my torn-apart-and-put-back-together-again body.)

My Auntie Ann stayed with me in the hospital for two weeks, sleeping on the small couch by my bedside. Every half an hour or so, throughout the night, I'd ask her to change the position of the hospital bed, to alter the place of pressure on my spine. After five days of this she went to stay at her son's house to get a few hours' uninterrupted sleep, leaving my siblings to watch me in shifts, but I called her and begged her to come back. The morphine was wearing off, I was going into withdrawal, and the strain of vomiting felt as though it was ripping the stitches in my back. She roused herself from her only unbroken sleep in many days to come back and be by my side.

Twelve years later, as she lay dying of cancer, I visited her in the hospital and reminded her of this time, and commented on how exhausted she must have been, staying there day and night with me and knowing I couldn't let her go for even a short break. She said, smiling, with tears in her eyes, "I told you I would never leave you." I didn't know anyone could have meant this so literally. (Her daughters did the same for her in those last months of her life. She was rarely alone, and the perfectionist-level care they gave her was full of insight, creativity, calm, and intelligence. It is a learned art, this virtuoso caregiving, and she had taught it masterfully.)

When I got back to the apartment Corey and I shared, he had decorated it for Christmas; there were red-and-green plaid flannel sheets on the bed, and a small blinking Christmas tree stood in a corner of the bedroom. My cousin Sarah stayed with us for a few days, cooking and cleaning and caring for me.

For the first few weeks, a nurse came in a couple of times a week to help me shower. Then, towards the end of December, my dad picked us up to go to his house in Aurora for Christmas. I lay in the back seat and every bump in the road felt as though it might break apart all the new nuts and bolts in my spine.

With my short haircut and gaunt face after the surgery, I looked eerily like my mother in the final weeks before she died of cancer. My brother Mark told me later he found it hard to look at me, as I looked so like her in the throes of cancer, lying on the couch in the same house she'd suffered in.

In my stocking was a mechanical claw, placed there by Mark, so I could reach things from my lying-down position on the couch, which I remained in for most of the holiday. At the bottom of my stocking I found, wrapped in tissue paper, three miniature figures of Alice, the White Knight, and Humpty Dumpty. I thanked my dad without looking at him and placed them on the mantelpiece, where they remained, collecting dust, for years. My dad also gave me a short black dress. He said, awkwardly, as I held it up, "I thought . . . when you get better. It would look really sexy." Everyone looked away.

And then, when the epic of Christmas was over, Corey and I went home to our strange and quiet life. We were two parentless teenagers, with a major surgery to recover from. I tried to get used to living in my new body, which, among other changes, was now inches taller than it had been when my spine had been crooked. Corey and I had relied on a steady diet of takeout food and Alphagetti up until this point in our lives together. One day, Corey decided to show me *GoodFellas*, his favourite film at the time. As I watched it, he made a tomato sauce, looking up a recipe in *The New Basics Cookbook*, which I had bought that year but never used. I had a kind of Smell-O-Vision experience as I watched the characters make tomato sauce in the film while Corey made the same meal in the next room. This became a ritual. Corey would put on a favourite film and teach himself how to make a dish from the film at the same time. In these long months, when I could hardly move, Corey learned the art of cooking. (He would, in later years, go to chef school, work as a professional cook, and eventually become a restaurant critic and then a food reporter.) I couldn't move without pain for a long time. I read all of Charles Dickens, thought about writing books one day, and fantasized about being mobile enough that I could one day walk down the street to the hardware store to buy a nail. I had no idea what I would do with this nail, but the idea of being strong and mobile and free enough to get there to choose the nail was exhilarating to me.

She went on growing, and growing, and very soon had to kneel down on the
floor: in another minute there was not even room for this, and she tried
the effect of lying down with one elbow against the door, and the other arm
curled round her head. Still she went on growing, and, as a last resource, she
put one arm out of the window, and one foot up the chimney, and said to her-
self, "Now I can do no more, whatever happens. What will *become of me?"*

—*Alice's Adventures in Wonderland*

The plan was to go back to school when I got better. The plan was to
try to get into Oxford. The plan was derailed by the Conservatives in
Ontario winning the provincial election in 1995. When I could finally
walk and resume a life, the one I walked into looked nothing like the
one I had been heading towards before my surgery. One of the first places
I went on my own after months of convalescence was a meeting of the
International Socialists. I'd seen a poster on a lamppost. As everything
in the outside world had taken on a new shine after I'd been cooped up in
our dark apartment for months, I now noticed things like posters on
lampposts. This led me through quite a few meetings with various
Marxist organizations before I ended up at the Ontario Coalition Against
Poverty and found a community of activists who took me in, embraced
me, and educated me. So many of the conversations in my life now
revolved around justice, labour, and fighting the exploitation of the vulnerable, and my own difficult experiences as a young child began to seem
small and inconsequential compared with the suffering I was learning
about and now saw first-hand. After a year or so, at a dinner at John
Clarke's house (John is the charismatic, brilliant founder of OCAP),
someone asked me about being an actor as a child, and I reluctantly
recounted some of the early experiences that had haunted me from the
productions *The Adventures of Baron Munchausen* and *Road to Avonlea*.
Where I thought I would find eye-rolls in the face of my undeniable
privilege, I found empathy, understanding, a weaving of important political context, and a generous holding of my more troubling experiences.

I dove into a life of activism, helping to organize protests against cuts to welfare and healthcare and the attacks on the poor that the Conservatives presided over. Seeing first-hand the decimation of the already impossible lives of the most vulnerable people I had ever encountered made the idea of going off to university to *think* when there was so much to be *done* seem frivolous at best, and at worst offensive and selfish. My life became a series of meetings, protests, and conferences, imbued with the camaraderie of people who had dedicated their lives to justice. I had a community I was proud to be a part of, a place in the real world, and a purpose after many months of not even being able to move. This was so much more than my fantasy of being mobile and strong enough to go to the hardware store to buy the imagined nail for the unnamed project. In those activist years, full of conviction and purpose, I lost Corey, I lost school, and I gained a wild and practical education in direct activism.

Sometimes, during those intense years of organizing, I would be asked to speak at rallies or press conferences. I never felt I could say no, so I would write out my remarks, study them closely, and resign myself to weeks of not sleeping before I had to take a stage in front of people. Whenever I was asked to go onstage for any other reason, like an awards ceremony for film and television, I most often either said no or I said yes and then didn't show up at the last minute. I knew I would never again go onstage in any meaningful capacity. I had nightmares, many nights, that I was back on that stage again, forgetting lines, forgetting where I was, forgetting which side of the looking glass I was on.

I never told anyone the truth of what had happened in Stratford, until I met someone who had had an even more epic breakdown with stage fright than I. After my experience in Stratford, I had sought out and read any story about stage fright that I could find. There was Daniel Day-Lewis's famous walking off the stage during a production of *Hamlet*, Barbra Streisand forgetting her lyrics during a performance and then absenting herself from the stage for many years, Glenn Gould's resentment of the audience and his turning to the recording studio

instead of live performance, and the many other stories of terror of the
stage that I found at once comforting and fascinating. One of the most
famous stories was that of Ian Holm, who, when performing in *The
Iceman Cometh* in 1976 while arguably the most successful actor in the
English theatre, came onto the stage, looked at the audience, and said,
simply, "Here I am, supposed to be talking to you . . . there are you,
expecting me to talk . . ." He walked off the stage and didn't go back on
for years.

When I was seventeen, I was cast in *The Sweet Hereafter*, in which I
played a young girl in an incestuous relationship with her father.
Donald Sutherland was supposed to play a lawyer, Mitchell Stephens,
who represents the victims of a terrible bus crash, including my character, who has become paralyzed after the accident. At the last moment,
to my incredible good fortune, Ian Holm was cast to replace him. One
day, after rehearsals, we went out for dinner. I gently broached the
subject of stage fright. He told me his story in his own words. Of
course, fear of the stage had not been the only thing happening in Ian's
life at the time. He felt as though the rest of his world was crumbling
too. His paralysis onstage was partly a terror of the audience but also a
culmination of personal events that he felt might crush him. As he told
me his story, his eyes became haunted. The trauma of the stage fright
was still difficult for him to talk about, after all those years.

I told him my own story of stage fright. I looked into the face of the man
who would always, for me, be Charles Dodgson, who had loved Alice
Liddell in *Dreamchild*, who had been hurt by her, broken by her, and
I told him about how, as Alice, I had broken inside and then broken my
body to escape. When I was finished I said to Ian, "I wanted to tell you,
because you're the only person I know who might be crazier than I am."

He paused for a while and then said, with a smile, "No. You win. You're
crazier."

A year later, Ian returned to the stage as King Lear. Recently, after hearing of his death, a mutual friend sent me a photo of a postcard he had written her at the time. He wrote: "<u>LOVE</u> to Polley. Tell her I take off <u>all</u> my clothes in King Lear." I laughed. He hadn't just gone back onstage to conquer his fear; he was giving it the middle finger.

The night I told him about my stage fright, we talked about his performance in *Dreamchild*. I told him that I thought the best acting moment I had ever seen was in a scene in which he goes to say "I love you" to little Alice but stops himself right after the word "I." (This was, in fact, my father's favourite moment in film history, which I had absorbed and parroted.)

Ian said, "No. I don't stop at 'I.' The tip of my tongue touches the roof of my mouth to say the *l* in 'love.' Then I am interrupted."

I left that dinner shaking and changed. The weight of the secret of my stage fright had been bearing down on me, crushing me, and filling me with a hatred for myself. Now the story felt as though it was part of my life. (It wasn't until this moment, as I write these words, that I am struck by the fact that I first told the story of playing the part of Alice and breaking to the actor who had played, and defined for me, Charles Dodgson.)

I thought I might call my aunt and cousin afterwards. But I didn't. The lie I had told them stood between us now, as a kind of menacing obstacle. I fell out of touch with them for years, unable to conceive how I could face them without speaking the truth, and horrified by what I felt that truth made me.

About fifteen years after my breakdown, I told my cousin Sarah. She said she felt sick. Not because she was angry but because she hadn't known that I was in such psychological pain. Because I hadn't let her, or anyone else, help. This response astonished me. I had spent years fearing a conversation whose only threat was to heal me. When I told her how sorry I was for faking so much pain, she said, simply, "You *were* in so much pain."

In 2017, I received an honorary doctorate from McMaster University. My husband, David, had graduated from this university, and, given that I never graduated from high school, it meant a great deal to me to be invited to stand on that stage. But my stage fright had followed me throughout my life, never letting up. I would often curse myself for not finishing the run of *Alice*. I often wondered whether, if I had just completed those last ten shows I had committed to, I would still be locked in this anxiety, locked into these dreams of puberty gone haywire, at night.

I tried to think of what I could say, what I could contribute, to a group of students who had completed something that I never had. What did I have to offer? And then I realized that the only contribution I could possibly make was to share my terror, and to demonstrate overcoming it in front of them. I spent months preparing my speech. I went to a performance psychologist, Dr. Kate Hays, who worked with athletes and performers. I decided to tell, in excruciating detail, the story of my stage fright and how hard it was for me to be up there on that stage. I confessed in front of thousands of strangers how I had broken down, how I had lost control over the ends of my words, how I had gone mad, how I had rushed a major surgery to get out of it, how I had vowed to never go onstage again.

It was right after making this speech, from a stage in front of thousands, that my nightmares stopped. It has been years since I've dreamed of being on the Stratford stage, in that white pinafore, a mint in my mouth, not knowing the words. I even wonder sometimes if I might tell this story from that same stage one day. I see myself standing onstage, a misshapen, nonsensical world behind me, confessing the broken, terrified Alice that I was. I imagine that now I could look the audience in the eye and know that they were there to see the real me. Breasts and all.

"Oh, don't go on like that!" cried the poor Queen, wringing her hands in despair. "Consider what a great girl you are. Consider what a long way you've come to-day. Consider what o'clock it is. Consider anything, only don't cry!"

Alice could not help laughing at this, even in the midst of her tears. "Can you keep from crying by considering things?" she asked.

"That's the way it's done," the Queen said with great decision: "nobody can do two things at once, you know."

—*Through the Looking-Glass*

I have been "considering" this story (as opposed to crying about it), and writing this essay, for twenty-one years. The one (the considering) does indeed keep me from the other (the crying).

I recently revisited *Dreamchild*, that film of Lewis Carroll's (Charles Dodgson's) unrequited love for Alice Liddell, which was so loved by my father. As a grown woman, my father dead now for two years, I am gobsmacked by how differently I see the film on my own, compared to how I viewed it as a child sitting beside my father. I no longer see Dodgson as the innocent, the victim, who is unceremoniously spurned by the child Alice. In the scene that has lingered in my memory all these years, Alice splashes water in Dodgson's face while they row on that fateful day when he first spins the tales of Alice underground. Ian Holm, as Dodgson, flinches, his face shocked by the cold water, his heart shocked by the violence of Alice's rejection and mockery. I have carried around the memory of this moment in my head, with my father's sharp intake of breath on its soundtrack. I remember turning to him to see tears in his eyes. How could a child break a man's heart like that?

What I didn't remember was what preceded that moment: Dodgson stares at Alice in an unbroken, hypnotized gaze. He sees her beauty, he sees her innocence, he sees her magic. What he doesn't seem to see is how terribly uncomfortable he is making her. I find it agonizing now, to watch from little Alice's point of view. No matter how troubled and uninviting her countenance, his focus on her is unchanged, unrelenting, and detached from her experience completely. She can't make his oppressive staring stop, no matter what facial expression she uses, so she ultimately splashes him in the face, thus breaking herself free from the prison of the gaze she is trapped in. She isn't just uncomfortable; she is terrified. And his preoccupying love, or perhaps, more accurately, his obsession with her, prevents him from seeing just how monstrous he has become to her. Or, perhaps more disturbingly, he does notice and, preferencing his love over her feelings of security and safety, he decides not to care.

After Alice splashes him, her mother reprimands her. Alice says: "But he was looking at me."

It is after this bewildering exchange between Dodgson and his muse that he begins to tell the *Alice* stories, and we are supposed to feel, I think, that all is now right with the world.

Towards the end of the film, a grieving Charles Dodgson says to Alice Liddell, "I hope you'll always remember our little moments together, my dear. Time can blot out so many, many things."

She replies, "Oh I couldn't forget. Not even if I tried."

"It was much pleasanter at home," thought poor Alice, "when one wasn't always growing larger and smaller, and being ordered about by mice and rabbits. I almost wish I hadn't gone down that rabbit-hole—and yet—and yet—it's rather curious, you know, this sort of life! I do wonder what

can *have happened to me! When I used to read fairy-tales, I fancied that kind of thing never happened, and now here I am in the middle of one! There ought to be a book written about me, that there ought! And when I grow up, I'll write one—but I'm grown up now,"* she added in a sorrowful tone; *"at least there's no room to grow up any more* here.*"*

—*Alice's Adventures in Wonderland*

The
Woman
Who
Stayed
Silent

WHERE TO BEGIN?

A few years ago, I plugged in a search on Twitter. The following tweet came up:

"Wonder why Sarah Polley never spoke out about being assaulted by Jian Ghomeshi. #HerToo. She was the woman who stayed silent. Ask her."

The tweet was attributed to someone with no followers. It wasn't liked or retweeted by anyone. I felt as though I might be the only person who was seeing it.

Why do we write things about ourselves? To absolve ourselves of guilt? To confess? To right a wrong? To be heard? To apologize? To clarify things for ourselves or others? I've wondered all these things as I sit down to write this.

I've been writing and unwriting this essay for years now. It's difficult, when you've resisted telling a story for so long, to know where to start. Especially when it has haunted you to not tell it. When it has knocked around inside your brain, loudly in the middle of the night, asking why it didn't deserve to be told, asking you who you might have hurt by not telling it, who you might truly be, deep down, because of your decision not to.

This story starts somewhere. But I don't know if it begins twenty-nine years ago, when I was around fourteen years old, and a man in his twenties tenderly brushed a strand of hair away from my face. Or if it begins as a young teenager, when, lost and scared, something happened to me that I couldn't understand, and so a part of my brain hid it from me until years later. Or when I was thirty-three and, though I had found my adult voice with almost everyone else, I still behaved in a way that was deferential and ingratiating towards a man who had hurt me even though I wanted nothing from him.

I'll start at thirty-five. Because that's when the world started to know things that had remained hidden about CBC Radio personality Jian Ghomeshi. And it is when I started to remember.

THE CLUE

In October 2014, three years before the Harvey Weinstein allegations came to light, and before the #MeToo movement became a world-wide phenomenon, the *Toronto Star* ran a story about Jian Ghomeshi. Journalists Jesse Brown and Kevin Donovan reported that three women said they had been punched, hit, bitten, and choked by Ghomeshi. A fourth woman, who worked with him on his radio show, anonymously described harassment and assault at the hands of Ghomeshi. (She would later identify herself as Kathryn Borel.) The respected radio host, who proudly wore the cloak of a sensitive feminist man, had suddenly lost his job at the Canadian Broadcasting Corporation. In the days following the *Toronto Star* piece, more women came forward with similar stories, including actor and Canadian Air Force captain Lucy DeCoutere, who was the first to identify herself publicly. In an interview on CBC's *The Current*, she encouraged more women to come forward to tell their stories and to share their names, if they could.

By the end of October, the *Toronto Star* had reported that eight women had accused Ghomeshi of sexual assault and harassment.

Some people questioned why all the women sharing their stories now hadn't gone to the police long ago if they were indeed telling the truth. In response, the hashtags #BeenRapedNeverReported and #IBelieveLucy went viral, and millions of people, all over the world, used them to tweet the myriad reasons they hadn't gone to the police to report their own experiences of sexual assault.

Lawyer Reva Seth, writing in the Huffington Post about an encounter with Ghomeshi that she describes as violent, explained, "I hadn't been raped. I had no interest in seeing him again or engaging the police in my life. I just wanted to continue on with my life as it was. And even if I had wanted to do something, as a lawyer, I'm well aware that the scenario was just a 'he said/she said' situation. I was aware that I, as a woman who had had a drink or two, shared a joint, had gone to his house willingly and had a sexual past, would be eviscerated. Cultural frameworks on this are powerful."

On November 26, 2014, Ghomeshi was charged with four counts of sexual assault and one count of overcoming resistance to sexual assault. Two months later, three additional counts of sexual assault related to three more women were added. (Only one of the criminal charges was in relation to the first group of women who came forward to the Toronto Star.)

In the fall of 2014, shortly after the story breaks, I go to a post-election party at mayoral candidate Olivia Chow's house, my eight-week-old baby, my second child, attached to me in her carrier. I find myself with Bernie Farber (who I'd known for many years in his role as the chief executive officer of the Canadian Jewish Congress), talking about the Ghomeshi scandal.

I mention to him that I have known Jesse Brown for years, and when the women first approached him about the assaults, I had connected him with a few lawyers to get advice about how to break the story and avoid a defamation suit. All of the lawyers he spoke with advised him that he should not take the risk of printing the story. Jesse had called me after these consultations and said, "Sarah, I'm not looking for someone to tell me whether or not to print this story. I'm looking for someone to tell me *how* to do it."

I recount this story to Bernie, expressing my admiration for Jesse and musing that perhaps the only brave things one ever does are in opposition to sound advice. We talk about it for a while, and others join the circle of conversation, expressing their shock and horror at the things Ghomeshi has been accused of.

After some time, Bernie tilts his head sideways and says, "The strangest thing happened. A few days before the news about Jian broke, he finally got back to me about the Roma family I told you about."

Five months earlier, Bernie had sent me an email in which he asked for my help in getting a Roma family onto Jian's popular radio show, Q. The family were human rights workers who were about to be deported back to Hungary, where their lives would potentially be in jeopardy. Bernie was aware that I knew Jian, loosely. I agreed to pass on Bernie's request. Jian's response was not encouraging.

"thx. you can give bernie my email addy. (although there is no chance we could do this story anytime soon—show is booked solid) hope you're well. (are you well?)"

It was clear to me from knowing Jian a bit that this segment would never make it onto his show. Bernie heard nothing for months. And then, a few days before Jian is accused publicly of assaulting women, when he would have known his life was about to be blown apart (he had been in discussions for days about being removed from his job), he had suddenly responded to an old email about a story he'd seemed to have no interest in covering.

As Bernie looks off, as though trying to puzzle it through, I have the distinct sense of a vital but not immediately coherent clue being dropped into the middle of my life. This will change everything, but I'm not sure how. I don't know what it means, I only know that it has meaning. And I have the strong sensation that I don't want to know what that meaning is.

As Bernie continues to talk, I have a sinking feeling. I'm on the cusp of knowing something I don't want to know. I'm going deep inside myself. I have the sensation that I am becoming enveloped by darkness, with my tiny baby breathing in her sleep on my chest, unaware, I hope, of the racing of my heart. I say, "He's been looking at all my emails to him."

I leave the party, and as I walk the cold autumn streets home, I hear this over and over again in my head. "He has been looking at all my emails to him."

As I nurse my baby in the middle of the night, comfort my two-and-a-half-year-old after a nightmare, questions begin to form:

Why has he been looking at my emails? Does he think he might need them? Why? Is it because he thinks I will come forward? Why? Why would I come forward?

I ask my husband these questions out loud. We wonder together in silence. We are both puzzled and a little alarmed.

The next day I call my sister Jo and we talk about Jian and the allegations that he choked some of the women who have come forward. I say that I feel lucky he didn't choke me.

Jo replies that I've said that a few times since the story broke. She says she and my brother Mark have found it confusing. "Because he did choke you. Didn't he?"

I am dazed by the question.

I call Mark and ask him if he has a memory of me telling him that Jian choked me.

He says, delicately, that yes, he remembers me telling him that, years before.

My brother is a lawyer, and he chooses his words carefully. He is not prone to exaggeration or hysteria and tends to downplay things. I can't believe what I am hearing from him.

He says he has been wondering if I have been considering coming forward. He tells me to be very careful with this decision and to begin writing down absolutely everything I can remember before making it.

I start shaking. And then I start to remember.

THE PARTY STORY

Throughout my twenties and early thirties, I had a funny party story about my worst date ever. I left out my age when I told it. I left out the experience of the sex itself. I left out my hasty departure. I left out the real impact it had on me, including only that this terrible date was the reason I had remained so utterly monogamous in relationships and never had casual sex. By omitting these details, it was easy to convey this story in a funny manner, grossing people out with the details of the unbelievably stupid and awkward foreplay.

Here is the story I told, for years, about my date with Jian Ghomeshi:

I had known Jian, on and off, since I was very young. I was around twelve or thirteen years old and he was in his mid-twenties when I first met him, at a fundraiser for literacy. I met him again when I was fourteen and was the MC for another fundraiser, this time for the Canadian Peace Alliance. He was there to perform with his band, Moxy Früvous, which I loved at the time. While another band was performing onstage, we sat together on a back staircase. He told me I was doing great. He tenderly pulled a strand of hair out of my face, tucked it behind my ear, and gazed at my face, my lips, my forehead in a way that made me think he was going to kiss me. He didn't. But I was captivated.

Over the next two years, I would occasionally see Jian at events. He asked me to appear in a video for one of his band's songs, "King of Spain." I was thrilled beyond belief, dancing with him outside the Bloor Street Cinema. (I was thirteen so forgive me, world.)

A few years later, Jian asked me out on a date. We ended up back at his apartment. I was nervous. I had had two teenaged boyfriends before, but going back to a grown man's apartment was intimidating and strange. After he had played me some recordings of his music and cursory amounts of kissing, he said, "I'm into some pretty weird stuff, Sarah. Do you think you can keep up?" In the story as I told it, I would say, in an adult fashion, a simple "No." He proceeded to stand behind me and run his hands all over my clothed body at a million miles an hour, saying, "You're in hell, you're in hell, there's devil hands all over your body, you're in hell, it's the devil!"

In the story I told, I would give a slight cringe as I recreated my reaction at the time. I furrowed my brow analytically, as though studying an unusual specimen of worm in a lab. This always got a very big laugh. When all was said and done, Jian got out his guitar and played some of his own songs to me while naked. (A friend of mine now says that this should be its own offence.) I left shortly afterwards. The experience was so off-putting, I say, that I never again had a one-night stand. In fact, I never had sex without love after that, because I didn't want to risk having such a cringe-worthy encounter ever again.

When I ran into Jian a few months after that night, at some fundraising event, I told him I was sorry I hadn't returned his calls but I had lost his number. He yelled HORSESHIT! at me, clearly upset.

I told that story a lot. It got a lot of laughs. I just left a few details out.

I left out my age, at the time of the date, which was sixteen, and his age, which was around twenty-eight.

I left out what my true answer was to his weird "devil hands" routine and to his question "Do you think you can keep up?" I didn't say "No" with a strong voice. I said, "I don't know." Because I didn't want to seem weak or unsophisticated, and I didn't know what he meant. I didn't judge him analytically as I did when I told the funny party story. I was just intimidated and scared.

I left out what happened during the sex, which wasn't at all funny.

I left out that I took a taxi home, shaking, and finding myself locked out of my apartment, used the security guard's phone to call my brother. Hearing the shaking in my voice, Mark got into his car and jetted through the night and it felt to me as though he appeared, almost immediately, out of thin air. I left out lying in bed with my sister Jo, who was living with Mark at the time, and trying to calm my breathing. I left out telling Jo and Mark that Jian had hurt me, that he wouldn't get his hands off my neck, though I tried to pry them away and managed to say, while he briefly moved them away from my neck, that I hated having my neck touched like that and I didn't want him to do that again. He did it again. I left out of my funny party story that my neck hurt, I don't know how much, but a lot, and that I had clearly expressed that I wanted him to stop. I left out how petulant and furious he seemed afterwards and how the sex became painful after that. He bent my legs back over my head and wouldn't stop when it felt that muscles were being ripped and I cried out. I left out that I expressed that it hurt and wanted him to stop and he ignored this, looking at me with what looked like abject hatred. I especially left out the pity I felt for him, looking downcast after he was done, as though by expressing my pain I had pointed out he was some kind of freak, and how terribly hurt he looked when I wouldn't stay the night.

I left all that out because, honestly, it didn't occur to me to tell it. For me, it wasn't part of the story. It was the dark cavern in which my funny story happened. But I told pieces of it to my brother and my sister that night, and they collected me and held me as I shook like a leaf. For them, the story of a man's unwanted hands around my neck remained, even while I had managed to erase it from my own memory.

MAKING THE DECISION

I spent the next few weeks after I was reminded of that memory roaming the city, my new baby in the carrier, walking, hopping on streetcars, meeting or talking on the phone with anyone who would talk to me about whether or not I should come forward. It seemed that so many women were, either in the press or to the police. There was Lucy DeCoutere, who was bravely making her identity public, and who, when the time came, made sure she was photographed at the police station, disseminating the information that the police had treated her well, to encourage others to share their stories. There was a statement from the police chief assuring women that "if they come forward to the police, they will be treated with respect, they will be treated professionally and they will be treated with care."

He did not clarify that while the police might make this assurance, they were not the court system, a distinction that many of the women who came forward perhaps shouldn't have been expected to make on their own.

Everyone whose advice I sought said the same thing to me in different ways. I met with family members and friends who practise law, both defence lawyers and Crown attorneys, who chose their words carefully. They told me that if I was serious about coming forward I should write down absolutely every detail I remembered. That I should take days to do this, to make sure that there was nothing I was leaving out. They said that they believed me. They said that a court likely wouldn't. There were the emails, weirdly ingratiating ones, where I was asking Jian to host a charity event I was organizing or to have the Roma family on *Q*. Who would write these sorts of emails to someone who had assaulted them? In one email exchange, Jian tells me that he will arrange to have on his show the founder of a charity I am on the board of, despite his producer's lack of interest.

He writes: "you owe me. But we knew that already . . . :p"

And I reply: "Ah. You are the best. I shall provide you with my hot sister." (He had once told me he found my older sister Jo impossibly attractive.)

It's a dumb joke, but it's also a very strange one to make to someone who hurt you. Whenever I would see him over the years, I would assume a jocular, "one of the boys" tone with him, perhaps to avoid being a woman he could flirt with or prey on. But in the end, I can't explain why I would make that joke. I really can't. It's insane.

Over and over I heard the refrain: "I would have a very hard time recommending that someone I knew and loved come forward in a sexual assault case."

When I looked at the details surrounding mine, the emails I had sent him, the friendly interviews I had done with him over the years following the encounter, which would surely be held against the credibility of my accusation, it was hard to argue that, despite all this advice, I should just come forward anyway.

Until I consulted people about whether or not I should share my story, I had never felt any shame about my sexual past or about sexuality in general. But people I respected, lawyers I knew, even therapists, were now suggesting that many people read implicit shame into things that I had never considered in the least bit embarrassing.

"People will know that you lived on your own and had sex as a teenager and they will judge that."

"When people google you, this is the first thing that will come up."

"People will imagine you naked."

I was taken aback by the suggestion that other people's judgments would or perhaps should bother me. It had just never occurred to me. Should I be embarrassed that he had hurt me? That I had been living alone at too young an age? That bad things had happened to me? That I had a body? Shame and embarrassment were not my go-to responses on these matters. But now that shame had been introduced, it seemed, at times, to take up residence.

The biggest problem with my case, I was told, was the "recovered memory." Until my brother and sister reminded me that Jian had had his hands around my neck, against my will, I had not remembered it, and I had told the story of my date with him many times, to many people, omitting this important element. Judges don't like this kind of thing. People in general don't buy this sort of thing. I asked a close confidante who'd worked as a Crown attorney for many years what I should do. She took a great deal of time to talk to me, despite juggling kids and a demanding job.

"If I were the Crown on this case," she said, "I would have a very hard time bringing your case forward."

I asked her if someone could be called on to testify about memory and how fallible it can be when trauma is involved. She thought about this deeply, but still felt it would be a hard case to bring forward given the recovered-memory issue. I expressed my concern that I was leaving three women hanging in a court system that they were likely unprepared for, and that I might be able to offer some support by coming forward. She advised that my case would not lend credibility to theirs.

Another lawyer I know well said to me at the time, "You being ridiculed in court is not going to help them seem more believable." Once, at a gathering, I mentioned that I was worried I would make a fool of myself and seem like a flake. Another lawyer said, without equivocation, "I think you're right. I agree that's how you'd come across. You're making the right decision."

There was also the not small complication that I had told my funny-party-story version of my date with Jian, omitting the violence, to friends who were lawyers working at the firm now representing him. How on earth could I explain this if questioned?

My confidante who worked as a Crown attorney paused before I left her office and said, "The advice you get from lawyers about what to do here isn't necessarily going to be the same that you will give yourself as a woman, as a mother, as a political activist."

It was the first time someone had made this distinction for me, and it felt like an important one.

Only one criminal lawyer I know, Chris Murphy, advised me, without reservation, to come forward. He said, "Say everything. Say everything about your sexual past, say everything about the ways in which you were interested in him, all of your inconsistencies, and then be clear that you know that what happened to you was an assault." It was the right thing to do, he said.

I said I was worried about the repercussions it could all have on my life. I said, "I'm the mother of two little kids."

He said, "Yes. You're the mother of two little kids. That could be an argument for coming forward as well."

I talked on the phone with a woman someone I knew had put me in contact with. She had told a story that I had heard in bits and pieces for years about "a bad experience" with Jian. Though she was fairly certain she would not come forward, for a few weeks we tried to imagine what else we could do to support the women who had. We even imagined that perhaps we could come forward, not with our own charges, but simply to back up what the rest of the women were saying. When we looked into it, it became clear that was not how the system worked. In fact, it turned out, our speaking to each other about this at all could be considered collusion. (Later, this is exactly how the supportive text and email interactions between two of the complainants would be framed in court.)

The other woman and I stopped communicating and remained quiet.

I spoke with a friend who said there might be a political reason to come forward that had nothing to do with what the verdict in a courtroom might be. Perhaps the courtroom shouldn't be the focus. Perhaps the support I could offer was through writing about my experience. When I floated this idea past the lawyers I knew, they pointed out that if I came forward publicly with allegations, the police might ask me to come and make a statement, and based on this statement, take it upon themselves to lay charges whether I liked it or not, especially given my young age at the time my experience with Jian occurred. I should be very careful; I should refrain from talking about what had happened to me with anyone. Once a criminal charge was set in motion, I would be unable to stop the wheels of the justice system from turning.

The picture that had been painted for me of what could lie ahead would not leave me. When the lawyers I knew said they would never advise a woman they loved to come forward with allegations in a sexual assault case, it was for good reason. I was told that if it went to trial, it would take years. I was told it would be the most stressful thing I'd ever experienced. I was told that many people come close to suicide by the time the process is over. I was told that it would be very hard to protect my two children (then a toddler and a baby) from the overwhelming pressure of what would unfold in my life for the next few years. Needless to say, this seemed an irresponsible risk to take, not just for myself but for my children.

I made the decision to not come forward. Now, years later, I think I can finally articulate the reasons for my silence: I had too much information about what was going to happen to me and my family (I wasn't willing to go through the arduous and hostile encounter with the criminal justice system that I realized was required of me), my memory of what exactly happened all those years ago was only recently put back together, and, perhaps most important (and most painful and humbling to admit), I knew that I wasn't strong enough.

I often wonder: how many women *didn't* come forward with allegations against Jian Ghomeshi? How many *didn't* come forward with allegations against Harvey Weinstein? We will never know.

(I want to take a moment to point out that throughout this piece I will be using words like *alleged* in front of the word *assault* when it comes to talking about the Jian Ghomeshi trial. I have also, for the most part, refrained from using words like *violence* and *coercion* though I believe they should have a place in this story. I am using this language because Ghomeshi was found not guilty in a court of law and has always maintained his innocence and I was obviously not present for the interactions between the complainants in the trial and Ghomeshi.

As you can imagine, it pains me to include these qualifications, and to soften the language of this piece, as, based on my own experiences with him, I believe the women's versions of events—in terms of both what they say happened to them and how they behaved after the incidents they described. I do not personally believe the word *alleged* when I write it. But the verdict in the trial is a legal truth that I must include when writing this piece.)

Three of the women who came forward to Jesse Brown did not go to the police. It's possible that their main goal was to make sure that Jian was outed for who he was, so that he could no longer sit on a perch of fame and lure other women into the kinds of situations they had been in. Perhaps it wasn't their desire to see him behind bars, but rather to know that he couldn't keep preying on women so easily. I wonder, though: Did these women also avoid going to the police because they had been warned, as I had been, about what the criminal justice system had in store for them? Or was it because, like me, they were concerned that their memories were too messy, their behaviour after the alleged assaults too friendly, to give them credibility on a witness stand?

Many months later, I talked to a friend who had worked at CBC Radio during the scandal. I told her my memories of what had happened that night with Jian. I told her that I had decided not to go to the police or to share my story. She listened, quietly. At the end of our lunch she said to me, "I think that at some point your moral compass is going to kick in and you won't have a choice about what to do."

At the time, I felt this comment as judgment. Now, I'm not sure it was anything but someone finding words for the sticky truth I was living with. Some part of me appreciated her saying this to me, though it made me feel sick with dread that my part in this story was not over.

LYING AND LAWYER BRAIN

The trial was a nightmare for the women who came forward. The focus, as predicted, was the women's credibility. What else is there to focus on in the absence of forensic evidence? As is the right of every person accused of a crime, Ghomeshi was never required to take the stand. There was a crush of media around the trial, and it seemed to be all anyone could talk about, in Toronto at least. It seemed inevitable, to many outside the legal profession, that this would end with the satisfaction of seeing a once powerful man facing consequences for his violence. But while a great, unstoppable movement of women sharing their stories had begun, and it seemed that wide, systemic change would be an inevitable result of this momentum, the women, when they took the stand, were subjected to ridicule.

Holes in the women's memories became major problems for the Crown's case. The fact that some of them had had subsequent encounters with Jian after the alleged assaults, which they hadn't previously revealed, and had written him flirty emails and letters after the time of the alleged violence, were used to try to prove that they couldn't possibly have been assaulted by him. (Jian had kept hold of these letters and communications for years.) Lucy DeCoutere was made to read out the last line of a letter she had written to Jian after he had allegedly assaulted and choked her. The line read: "I love your hands." Compelling her to read these words felt like cruel theatre, the kind of knife jab that earns Jian's lawyer, Marie Henein, the praise of other lawyers when they describe her, admiringly, as "going for the jugular." It seemed unnecessary to add such a dramatic flourish to the cross-examination. The letter would have read no differently, but could have been a less humiliating experience, had Lucy not been compelled to read those words herself in front of a packed courtroom. Lucy swears that she hadn't remembered that letter until it was presented to her in court. Perhaps no one except a victim of sexual assault, or someone who is familiar with how people behave after trauma, could believe that it was entirely possible that someone who was assaulted could write this letter to their attacker, to try to normalize a terrible situation, or to make the attacker feel better for being rejected after the abuse.

It can seem perplexing from the outside, this pull that many women experience to make things better for those who have hurt us. The impulse to smooth things over to keep ourselves safe, as well as the constant messages many of us have received in our lives to "make things nice" no matter what harm has been done, can be so deeply rooted that it often results in behaviour that can later appear nonsensical to an outside eye. (The betrayal of oneself that results from this "making things nice" with an attacker can also make one bleed on a subterranean level.)

Dr. Lori Haskell, a renowned clinical psychologist who has written and presented extensively on the impact of trauma in sexual assault cases, writes: "Some sexual assault victims may continue to date their assaulters in an effort to neutralize the trauma or regain some control over an event that left them powerless. In fact, many reach out to their attacker again specifically to try to regain power in the relationship. While others explain that they believed he may acknowledge what he did and apologize."

When I look at my interviews with Jian on Q many years later, I am taken aback by my demeanour. I am bubbly and giggly. I try to make things feel normal even as he consistently tries to throw me off. In one interview he seems bored, looking up only occasionally from his notes with dead eyes. He sometimes mocks what I say in subtle ways, and I visibly flush with embarrassment.

In an interview for my film *Take This Waltz*, he asks me whether monogamy is natural. In a fairly undogmatic manner I suggest that I think it probably is. He brings it up again and asks me why I am suggesting that. Is it not just a cultural convention that has been imposed upon us somehow? I finally say that I feel I'm talking about something I don't understand at all, and I make fun of myself for being overly confident with my initial answer.

The film we are discussing is about someone leaving a relationship, so his question is not off topic, but he seems to relish diving into the most uncomfortable topics he can, ones that other interviewers haven't focused on during the extensive promotion of this film. He asks me about a scene where a character talks, graphically, about what sex with the main character would be like.

"Is talking about sex with someone other than your partner an act of infidelity?" he asks.

I smile. I answer the question as best I can. Inwardly, I hate these questions and I am deeply uncomfortable having this conversation with him. But I am good-natured, almost flirty, and happily diminish myself.

At one point I refer to myself as "completely oblivious to everything in the world, it seems." It's not just self-deprecation; it's self-flagellation. I am thirty-three in this interview, not a sixteen-year-old actress, and I haven't interacted with anyone, press or otherwise, in this flighty mode in a long time. I am, in interaction with him, no longer someone who makes their own films or has a voice. Somehow his very presence has taken who I have become away from me. To someone watching the interview, I would look happy to be there as well as deferential and almost obsequious. What I *don't* look like is a woman being interviewed by a man who assaulted her.

I manage to deflect or awkwardly navigate every uncomfortable question. He says, "Let me come back to the, talk about relationships in this film before I let you go . . . Do you still consider yourself a romantic? 'Cause I know you did, in the past.

"I guess it's because of the films you make but, I always feel like when I'm interviewing you it's really . . . I'm asking you about relationship and love advice."

I shriek, "I KNOW!" I laugh loudly and awkwardly.

"This is like the third time. 'So . . . tell me about love,'" he says, doing an impression of himself.

I try to keep the jokes going. I try to play along. I try not to succumb to how incredibly awkward this conversation is.

He ends the interview by saying, "I'd be a lot, a lot more critical of the film but you're pregnant so I have to go easy on you . . . I just can't be honest anymore."

I laugh uproariously, as though he has just made the best joke of all time. But I know him well enough to know that he is telling the truth. He didn't like the film and he wants to make sure that I know it. Nearly every inter-action I've had with him over the years, at fundraisers or parties or interviews, ends on an only partially buried, jagged note of meanness.

Later that year I did an interview with him as part of the release of my documentary *Stories We Tell*, which is about memory, my family, and revelations about my family of origin. In this interview, I am even smilier, even more of an ingénue, giggly and foolish, not presenting myself the way I believe I normally did at that time of my life.

He asks me if I'm uncomfortable doing interviews for a film so per-sonal. He says, "We're friends and we've known each other for a *loong* time. And approaching an interview like this I kind of go, well . . . I don't want to get too personal with Sarah, I don't want to make her uncomfortable . . ."

At which point my hand unconsciously goes up to my neck. A shadow passes over my face, almost like an echo of a memory has been provoked by his suggesting that he might make me uncomfortable. (Indeed, my neck has remained a no-go zone for everyone in my life. My kids do an impression of me screaming "DON'T TOUCH MY NECK!" Whenever anyone even accidentally brushes against my neck, I have a primal reaction of terror and fury, I believe ever since that night decades ago.)

At some point in the interview I talk about why I think we tell stories. I say that I think it is necessary to create stories to make sense of our bewildering lives, to create a narrative around them, to have something to grasp onto in the chaos. When I watch myself give this answer now, years later, I imagine that my subconscious is working on something: it is working on the story of what happened with him that night, it is working to make sense of it, it is working to normalize the current moment, and it is also working to hide the true story from myself.

Towards the end of the interview he says, "It's hard not to fall in love with you . . . and your honesty in this film."

As the interview wraps up I think to myself, "Wow. He didn't say anything mean this time." But as soon as the mics switch off he looks at me with an ugly, angry expression on his face and says, "Aw *FUCK*. I *thought* you were going to plug *my book*!"

He had sent me a copy of his memoir, *1982*, a few months earlier. I hadn't read it, but I had lied and said that I had. I didn't know that he had wanted me to sing its praises on his show. I feel an inexplicable feeling of having failed him, of guilt, and also, bewilderingly, fear. I apologize. I tell him that I meant to say something about it but I forgot. He is petulant and gives me a half-hearted goodbye. As I leave the studio I tell his producer, "I feel so bad about not talking about Jian's book." The producer rolls his eyes and tells me not to worry. "Jian plugs it every chance he gets," he tells me.

After every interview I do with Jian, people who have heard it ask me if I have had a relationship with him. He makes it seem that way with his questions. I make it seem that way with my overly accommodating demeanour. It sounds like flirting. It sounds like we are close. Or, perhaps it sounds like someone who has been assaulted trying to make everything okay.

I tell these stories because if I had come forward and said that Jian had hurt me, these interactions would have been used as evidence that he did not. I would have been made to seem like an idiot, like a ditz, like a liar. Any accusation of inconsistency or lack of credibility that was tossed at the women who were so mercilessly cross-examined in that courtroom could have easily been thrown my way as well. Had I not let years pass before telling this story, I'm convinced that I would not have felt that I could say everything. I would have concealed things. I would not have thought to offer stories of my embarrassing or inconsistent behaviour to the police or the Crown attorneys or the media. These omissions in the complainants' testimony sank the case and the credibility of those women in the eyes of the judge and many in the media.

I was shocked that some of my lawyer friends, who knew I had been hurt by Jian, took to mocking the way the women spoke at the trial, doing impressions of Lucy's police statement, and even going as far as to say that given that they'd lied on the stand, perhaps *they* should be the ones to go to jail. They said this to me openly, without reservation, while believing I had also been hurt by him. If I tried to defend them with the notion that many women who are assaulted may not tell the whole truth to cover up some embarrassment or, more likely, don't remember some of what happened during or after the assaults, I was met with variations of the argument that "to lie is not a good starting point. We can't just look at these cases with the starting premise of 'People lie.' It's not a good premise."

But people *do* lie. All the time. About all sorts of things. And I don't believe *lying* is the right word for the kind of inconsistencies that are common when someone tries to remember and relate the experience of being traumatized. One Crown I spoke with said that his focus is often on sifting through the dozen or so inaccuracies a complainant has inevitably told him about the surrounding details of an assault in order to get to the real story, even when he is fairly certain the complainant is telling the truth about the violence they have experienced. What, then, are we to do with the uncomfortable fact that people who have been traumatized do not often have a handle on the whole truth or are covering up some surrounding details of an assault out of shame or embarrassment? Are we trying to wedge the unruly reality of responses to sexual assault to fit into a rigid idea of truth in our criminal justice system? Is there any way to make room to accommodate the truth of the nature of this crime and the impact it has on people? What if lying is a sometimes unavoidable byproduct of what happens when someone experiences this kind of trauma? And what if much of what we are interpreting as lying is actually the blocking out of traumatic memory? Can our criminal justice system make room for this erratic but common human behaviour? All I know for sure is that we all occasionally have difficulty with the truth— especially when we are ashamed or traumatized. To say that we can't start from the premise that people sometimes lie even as they tell the truth is to ignore an important truth about human nature.

It was remarkable, seeing the lawyer brains overtake the human ones in people close to me. They believed my story, but they were still so attached to the supremacy of truth with a capital *T* that it was possible for them to mock these women and be furious with them for not being perfect witnesses.

After they lashed these women for their behaviour, I would sometimes hear these same people say, "But I'd love to get that asshole on the stand at a civil trial and cross-examine him." This seemed to demonstrate to me an incredible capacity for a kind of Orwellian double-think. They believed Ghomeshi was guilty of assault. But the details these women had provided—what happened before and after—weren't unassailably true. And that, in their eyes, made those women villains.

When I am at my most dismayed by this capacity within these lawyers to drain the empathy out of their bodies so efficiently, I remind myself of my experience walking through the Kingston Penitentiary in Ontario. I produced a miniseries at this recently closed maximum security prison in 2016. It was horrifying to walk the length of those rows of narrow cages, to see the way we lock people up in spaces too small for humans, with incessant noise and light, in a manner that one only hopes is looked back on, in the not too distant future, as barbarism. I remind myself that the lawyers I know are defending people who are facing this kind of animal-like future, and if I am to be honest with myself, I don't believe that anyone should be treated this way, regardless of guilt. This knowledge, of the lack of liberty that may lie ahead for people found guilty of serious crimes, makes the lawyers I know ferocious in the defence of their clients, and rightly religious about the principle of innocent until proven guilty. One former Crown attorney I know told me about being part of a process to put a man in prison and then later being confronted with evidence that he had been convicted based upon the lies of another person. This lawyer remembered, vividly, seeing this man stand outside the courthouse after being acquitted on appeal, taking a drag of a cigarette, and looking up at the sun as he took his first breaths of fresh air as a free man in many months. This image haunted him throughout the rest of his career. Thinking about this man, and knowing he had played a part in taking away his freedom for a portion of his life, brought him to angry tears, even as he told the story years later. He vowed to fight this kind of injustice for the rest of his life.

The burden of proof must be very high if we are to contemplate taking away someone's freedom. Of course I agree that no one should face so dire a consequence as going to prison if they are not proven to be guilty beyond the shadow of a reasonable doubt. My question is: do women who come forward in sexual assault cases need to be destroyed in the process of our looking for those shadows? It's a genuine question.

Elaine Craig, in her book *Putting Trials on Trial: Sexual Assault and the Failure of the Legal Profession*, quotes a woman who, after a year-long trial that resulted in the conviction of her attacker, said, "The bulk of my rape trauma is not the result of the sexual assault itself but of the brutality of the legal system. This trauma is difficult to understand for those who have not lived it."

Later Craig writes, "It is of course true that the adversarial nature of our legal system, and constitutional protections such as the right to full and fair cross-examination, mean that testifying as a complainant in a sexual assault trial will likely always be psychologically challenging and unpleasant. The criminal justice system is not designed to heal those who have survived sexual harm. But nor should it operate to effect a 'second rape.'"

Most of the lawyers I have spoken with insist that nothing should change in the way that sexual assault cases are tried, that defence lawyers generally behave very well in courtrooms and in accordance with Canada's very progressive rape shield laws (Craig's book disputes this claim), but that they would, once again, *never* advise a woman they loved to come forward in a sexual assault case. How they manage to hold both these beliefs simultaneously and confidently is endlessly fascinating to me.

The complainants who testified against Jian Ghomeshi described the experience of being on the stand as excruciating. Jian was acquitted on the four counts of sexual assault and one count of "overcoming resistance" by choking. When I read the following lines of Justice William B. Horkins's ruling, I was rattled by how relevant it was to my own case. I was also struck by this demonstration of the human tendency to judge reality according to our expectations rather than evaluating our expectations according to the way they match, or don't match, that reality.

"Each complainant in this case engaged in conduct regarding Mr. Ghomeshi, after the fact, which seems out of harmony with the assaultive behaviour ascribed to him. In many instances, their conduct and comments were even inconsistent with the level of *animus* exhibited by each of them, both at the time and then years later. In a case that is entirely dependent on the reliability of their evidence standing alone, these are the factors that cause me considerable difficulty when asked to accept their evidence at full value."

Later the judge writes: "The harsh reality is that once a witness has been shown to be deceptive and manipulative in giving their evidence, that witness can no longer expect the Court to consider them to be a trusted source of the truth. I am forced to conclude that it is impossible for the Court to have sufficient faith in the reliability or sincerity of these complainants. Put simply, the volume of serious deficiencies in the evidence leaves the Court with a reasonable doubt."

Grief and anger from the supporters of the women followed the verdict. But while a not-guilty verdict is not the same as proclaiming someone innocent, this is often how it is interpreted by the general population. "Not guilty" quickly became conflated with "innocent" for many people after the trial, and some now ascribed guilt to the women who had come forward, because of the inconsistencies in their behaviour and testimony. People who had remained quiet and polite during the #IBelieveLucy days now openly said that they didn't trust these women. People don't like ambiguity, however much it may hold a place in, and inform, their own lives. People like answers. The verdict served as an answer for many. Once I found myself in a heated argument on a streetcar with a complete stranger who had been ranting to her friend about the women in the case being "liars." I blurted out that if the women who had been in that courtroom were liars then so was I. I told her what I believed to be true based on the stories of the women who had come forward and my own experiences as someone who hadn't: that I believed there were likely others like us who hadn't come forward. The woman who had been ranting became quiet, and we sat in silence until the next stop where I got off, rattled by myself.

A few months later, Ghomeshi signed a peace bond and formally apologized to his former producer, Kathryn Borel, for "inappropriate" behaviour as part of having a sexual assault charge withdrawn. He never admitted to doing anything illegal, but it was the first and only time he had opened his mouth publicly to address the allegations since he was charged.

In 2020, Jian Ghomeshi re-emerged with a podcast on the Iranian diaspora, supported by a financier who has been quoted as saying he "never believed" the women. But so far, Ghomeshi has not resurfaced as a cultural figure in any major way; his two previous attempts at a comeback via another podcast and an essay he wrote for the *New York Review of Books* were drowned out by public outrage.

The legacy of Ghomeshi's acquittal is mixed. As recently as 2019, the journalist Robyn Doolittle referred to him as "the original #MeToo casualty." I wonder if, despite the nightmare the complainants endured, he was, perhaps, the first #MeToo victory. While he could not be convicted in a court of law as Harvey Weinstein was, he had to, reputationally and career-wise at least, face the consequences of his conduct towards women.

A couple of years ago, I sat on a panel discussing the #MeToo movement at the University of Toronto's Faculty of Law. Afterwards I met Linda Redgrave, one of the anonymous complainants in the Ghomeshi case, who had since identified herself. I didn't tell her about my own experience with Jian, but we talked for a long time. She had started an organization called Coming Forward, to support survivors of sexual assault and to educate complainants on how to prepare for the court system—something she didn't feel she'd had the benefit of. We talked at length about how brutalizing her experience of the court system had been, how much she had discovered after the fact about her own memories, and memory after trauma in general.

At one point in our conversation Linda said, "I'd like to be redeemed one day."

LUCY AND ME

In 2017, years after the Ghomeshi trial, I ran into Lucy DeCoutere after a screening of *A Better Man*, a documentary about violence against women. She was talking with a small group of people I knew. She looked at me, gently, and said, "I'm just talking about the Jian Ghomeshi trial. I'm not sure if you followed it at all."

My breath caught in my throat. I said, "Yes. I followed it very closely. For a bunch of reasons."

She said, "I think I know one of those reasons."

I realized in that moment that she knew. She had heard what had happened to me and she also knew that I had not come forward to support her. I trembled as I told her my memories of what had happened. I tried to explain why I didn't come forward. I said: "I had two tiny children. I was told it would drag on for years, that it would destroy me, that I would come close to suicide."

She teared up and said, "I didn't get any of that advice. No one told me any of that. And that is exactly what did happen. And no one prepared me for that. I'm only happy for the women who didn't come forward. I know there are lots of them. If you need to hear from me that I'm cool with it, I am. It's okay."

She gave me what I think is the strongest, biggest hug I've ever received and said, "I'm so sorry that happened to you. You were so young."
I gasped at her empathy as she held me in her arms, and I tried to imagine how the people who didn't believe her, who had mocked her, would process this moment of pure authenticity and selflessness if they could see it.

When I told a mutual friend about what Lucy had said to me, how she had hugged me, she cried and said, "Lucy is an emotional giant."

TELLING THE STORY

If I had told my story publicly at the time, here is what I would have wanted to say: I blocked things out, I hid things, I was ingratiating towards him, I didn't behave in any of the ways a "good victim" is supposed to behave. I don't remember a lot. A lot of the details I have laid out here I omitted at various points along the way. But I remember his hands around my neck. I remember him causing me pain. I remember saying no and trying to resist and that not being enough. And that, despite all my other lapses in memory and faults in my character, I know for sure.

I don't know if what happened that night would have resulted in a conviction. My guess is no. My memory may be unreliable on some of the details; my story has likely changed in increments I don't even notice over the years. But I know that he hurt me and I didn't want him to. I know that I asked him not to. I know that he didn't listen for a while, but I don't remember how long that while was. I know that I spent time trying to pry his hands off my neck and it didn't work until I was in a lot of pain. I know that I was a teenager and that he was much older. I know that I didn't call it assault at the time, or for years later, and neither did anyone else. I know that I was nice to him, always, after it happened, even ingratiating, and to watch my

interviews with him in the following years is a humiliation. I would
have said that I believed the women who came forward, because
their stories sounded so similar to my own; his behaviour and petu-
lance and self-involvement sounded so familiar. I believe those
women because the erratic way they behaved later, the inconsistencies
in their stories, the gaps in their memories, all reminded me of my
own behaviour, my own memory. For me, those inconsistencies were
as much evidence that they were victims of sexual assault as it was for
others that they hadn't been.

As I write this now, years later, I think of the advice that lawyer Chris
Murphy gave to me long ago. "Say everything. Tell the embarrassing
parts. Tell the truth." I don't think it's that easy to access the truth, or to
remember to say everything, but I'm trying now.

When the sexual assault allegations against Harvey Weinstein came
to light in 2017, I was asked to write an op-ed in the *New York Times*.
I wrote: "There's no one right way to do any of this. In your own
time, on your own terms, is a notion I cling to, when it comes to talking
about experiences of powerlessness."

I also wrote back then:

"I hope that the ways in which women are degraded, both obvious and
subtle, begin to seem like a thing of the past. For that to happen, I think
we need to look at what scares us the most. We need to look at ourselves. What have we been willing to accept, out of fear, helplessness,
a sense that things can't be changed? What else are we turning a blind
eye to, in all aspects of our lives? What else have we accepted that,
somewhere within us, we know is deeply unacceptable? And what,
now, will we do about it?"

When I sent a draft of the *Times* piece to a friend to proofread, she sent
helpful comments. She also wrote, "You don't have to submit this, you

know." She knew that the last question I had written was to myself, and that it was an unresolved one.

I also wrote this: "I hope that when this moment of noisy sisterhood dissipates, it doesn't end with a woman in a courtroom, being made to look crazy, as these stories so often do."

We had a trial run of the #MeToo movement in Canada with the Jian Ghomeshi case and #BeenRapedNeverReported and #IBelieveLucy. When the movement ran into a courtroom it was a train crash, engines on fire and gears mangled and shooting in all directions.

I've often wondered if the history of the Ghomeshi case explains why so few men of power in Canada were accused during the #MeToo movement when it seemed so many powerful men were losing their positions elsewhere. We'd already lived it up here, and it hadn't gone the way we thought it would. The most high-profile case in Canada post-Ghomeshi was addressed through a civil suit, where the complainants have more control, framing the question, asking for the remedy that is meaningful to them, and deciding when to start, move, and stop. It was unsurprising that the women in that case did not opt to participate in the criminal justice system, after what they had witnessed in the Ghomeshi case.

For so long, I had been holding my breath and waiting, nauseously, for Harvey Weinstein's acquittal, for the complainants to be ridiculed for "lying," for proof, once again, that the world hadn't changed as much as we had hoped it had. Certainly, watching holes poked in their memories and emails, and the attacks the defence launched on their characters and too-human behaviour, made it seem as though this case would go a familiar way.

When Weinstein was found guilty, alongside the surge of relief I felt that this case didn't end terribly for the women who came forward, I also found myself in possession of a profound ache for the wounds that the women in the Ghomeshi case, and in so many other sexual assault cases, still bear. They too walked through hellfire, but with no expert witnesses called to explain the effect trauma has on memory, no post-#MeToo jury to hear their case, no "watershed" verdict finale to be universally lauded for. I ached for the profound misunderstanding people had of their subsequent contact with the accused, and the derision of their typical behaviour after the alleged assaults took place. I ached for the judgment they endured, in so many legal judgments. I couldn't stop thinking about how the attacks they endured on their credibility were the same attacks that so many of us who have experienced sexual assault would be subjected to if we shared our stories, no matter how hard the truth of our assaults.

Law professor Melanie Randall writes: "[The] limited appreciation of the nature of traumatic responses is, undoubtedly, an expression of a broader lack of understanding of, and information about, the complexities of human psychology and human behaviour within the legal system. This failure is particularly sharp in terms of legal responses to sexual assault, as it is entrenched within the many myths about sexual assault, including conceptions of authentic and credible (read 'ideal') victims."

In Justice Horkins's ruling in the Jian Ghomeshi case, he wrote the following about one of the complainants not revealing information: "She said that this was her 'first kick at the can,' and that she did not know how 'to navigate' this sort of proceeding. 'Navigating' this sort of proceeding is really quite simple: tell the truth, the whole truth and nothing but the truth."

So many of us who have been sexually assaulted know that remembering the truth, knowing the truth, and telling the truth about it is anything but simple.

How extraordinary to think that the rest of the world may be beginning to know that too.

High
Risk

"How much did you bleed?" asks the soap-opera-hot doctor who lives two doors down from my house.

"You can check my underwear if you want," I say, defeated. "It's over there." My hand waves weakly towards the crumpled pile of clothes on the chair in the corner, in a gesture of "all is lost, I might as well disgust you." (I found out this new neighbour of mine was a doctor several weeks earlier when he moved into the semi beside ours and all the women on the street kept whisper-hissing towards my porch, "Have you seen the new hot doctor neighbour?" I did not know he worked as an obstetrics fellow in the hospital I am scheduled to give birth in and am currently bleeding in. I only ever imagined him working on the set of a soap-opera hospital, having illicit affairs with soap-opera nurses and such.) I watch him gingerly pick up my bloody underwear and look back at me. He's not my type, anyway. Too much face moisturizer.

I've been rushed by ambulance to Mount Sinai Hospital in downtown Toronto. I have called an ambulance for myself and waited, ashamed, as I heard the sirens get closer. Hearing emergency vehicles arrive for you is unexpectedly embarrassing. ("All this for me?") A fire truck arrived first, and the firefighters looked as hesitant as I was. I got the sense that a pregnant woman bleeding out was the kind of emergency call they prayed the ambulance would beat them to. We made awkward chit-chat as I told them not to bother coming up on the porch. One of them shuffled from foot to foot by the curb, looking anxiously down the street as the siren sound of the ambulance got closer. When the paramedics arrived, I insisted on walking myself into the ambulance. I asked them about their labour negotiations. There was a potential strike coming up. They asked me questions about my condition and I answered them briefly, but I was weirdly skilled at manoeuvring the conversation away from the terrifying thing that was happening to my body and back to labour strife. I stubbornly refused to lie down on the stretcher. They pushed me into the hospital in a wheelchair, and when we arrived at the obstetrics floor and they said to someone behind a desk, "She's thirty-three weeks, previa, bleeding," it seemed as though every person in my field of vision joined a sprinting parade behind my wheelchair and into a delivery room. Everyone was running down the hall. I held on to the armrests of the wheelchair for dear life. There were about eight people, staff doctors, residents, and nurses, in the delivery room, looking nervous and ready to catch something. That's when Soap-Opera Doctor appeared, out of nowhere, followed, it seemed, by some kind of key light that illuminated the sheen of his abundant face moisturizer.

I ask him if he wouldn't mind shovelling my walk when he's done his shift. He laughs lightly. An indulgent doctor laugh. Not my type.

My placenta is in the wrong place—it has implanted abnormally low, covering the cervix, the outlet for the uterus, making a natural birth very dangerous and making it probable that I will hemorrhage at some point in the pregnancy. Historically, placenta previa has been a leading cause of maternal death. It usually happens after multiple C-sections (when the placenta is all like, "Where should I implant myself? Oh, look at all that scar tissue! That looks cozier than where I'm supposed to implant!") or in women of advanced age. It generally does not happen to women in their early thirties during a first pregnancy.

I am, at this point, not surprised that things have taken a turn for the worse, as my pregnancy has been a screwball comedy for months, starting with a diagnosis of gestational diabetes (something else I have absolutely no risk factors for), followed by ripping of scar tissue left over from severe endometriosis as my uterus grew. As Soap-Opera-Hot Neighbour Doctor will tell me a few months later, "Add to all that your rods in your spine complicating a spinal block, you were basically a walking Royal College of Physicians medical exam!" (Thanks, Soap-Opera-Hot Doctor! Now move along the sidewalk and go home, or I'll find myself remembering that time I told you, in self-destructive surrender, to handle my bloody underwear.)

The gestational diabetes was my favourite pregnancy complication (I have begun to rank them at this point) because it at least made me feel macho to prick my own finger a few times a day, and I liked the weird introduction to it. The kind endocrinologist, who I was generally fond of, said something bonkers like, "You're going to hate me during the pregnancy because of what you can't eat but you're going to *looooove* me when the baby pops out and you realize you've basically been on a diet and don't look like you've had a baby!" I thought, Why do people assume that everyone wants to look skinny? And why would I want to look like I haven't had a baby? Having a baby has been my main goal for most of my life. Why would I want all evidence erased as soon as I give birth? She sent me over to the building next door as I was "just in time!" for the nutritionist's workshop on how to manage gestational diabetes. As my blood sugar numbers were very high, I would likely have to go on insulin down the road, but for the time being she was hoping that if I was very strict with myself, and followed the nutritionist's advice to the letter, I could manage the diabetes with diet.

I burst into a workshop room where twenty other crabby-looking pregnant women had just been informed they couldn't eat whatever the hell they wanted during their pregnancies and needed to draw their own blood three times a day in lieu of scarfing cupcakes. I worried for the peppy young nutritionist. She sat in the middle of the ring of famished, irate, heavily pregnant women. She looked as though she was surrounded by a pack of bloated, hungry wolves. There wasn't a single question that was asked in a non-confrontational way. One woman kept asking about twisters. "WHAT ABOUT A TWISTER?! ARE YOU TELLING ME I CAN'T EAT A TWISTER IN THE MORNING?

COME ON! NOT EVEN A TWISTER!" The group of women, who were mostly Asian, WASPy, or Black, had no clue what a twister was. Though I knew what it was, I initially had the good sense to stay well back from the fray. A Southeast Asian woman dared to ask what many were likely wondering. "I'm sorry. What is a twister?" She was met with a shriek of "YOU DON'T KNOW WHAT A TWISTER IS? FROM HAYMISHE'S! YOU KNOW! COME ON! WHAT IS THIS PLACE?!" The nutritionist, who clearly had not been on the job very long, acted politely curious about the exotic cuisine being discussed and asked someone to explain what a twister was. "It's bagel-like," I finally offered quietly, unable to stay out of any fray for very long. "Oh! You mean a bagel!" the relieved nutritionist exclaimed. "A TWISTER!! IT'S WAY BIGGER THAN A BAGEL!" was the response. "Oh, well," the nutritionist said. "You can only get away with half a bagel in the morning, so I guess a quarter of a twister would be okay. But that would have to be it! And it's probably better to spend your carbs on something more nutritious." I decided she was suicidal. Twister Lady was in a state of total combustion. "Give me that sheet!" she said. She grabbed out of the nutritionist's grasping claws the sheet of information about what could and couldn't be eaten and in what portions. The nutritionist went red as she tried to ignore the physical aggression and suggested we all practise pricking our fingers. There were moans. One woman screamed.

I couldn't stop laughing, but only because I hadn't registered what every other person in the room had. Not eating what one wants to eat when one is pregnant makes one angry. By the time dinner rolled around, David would have done well to go marry Twister Lady, who suddenly seemed like the paragon of rational thought in comparison with the person he was now living with.

I can't figure out why David can't cook in batches. I say this word a lot. Batches. My mom always had giant casserole dishes and pots on the stove full of food, enough to feed an army. That's the way I cook. I want to know I could invite someone over at the last minute, perhaps nine other people; I want to know there will be leftovers, that there is always home-cooked food around. David is tired of hearing the word batches *barked at him several times a day. He's a great cook, and since I've been put on bedrest at home he does pretty much all the cooking. He doesn't deserve my anger. But I'm angry because I'm hungry all the time, and nothing he can feed me will satisfy me. I blame the lack of batches. But the person who is really to blame is my mother, for dying. I'm hungry for my mother and it makes me angry and there is scar tissue ripping inside me making me scream and I might suddenly explode blood and I want a BATCH of something that is not diabetes-friendly that I can eat for days and days until there is no hunger anywhere inside me anymore so I can feel as though she didn't die, leaving me to figure out how to be a mother after only eleven years of getting to witness my own.*

The first time I felt the severe pain, we went to the hospital right away. I was in my fifth month of pregnancy and I was sure something was going terribly wrong, or that I was in labour. At that point, I knew I had a placenta previa, but I had been told it might move out of the way in time for delivery. The high-risk doc on call that night took me into an ultrasound room, his scrubs and cap still on after coming out of an operating room. From the conversation I overheard between the resident and nurse with him, and from my far too nosy questions, I put together that they had just come from a complicated C-section in which one twin had made it and the other hadn't. He looked at my ultrasound, decided that the pain was likely due to the ripping of scar tissue from my endometriosis, and added, "This previa isn't going anywhere. It will be a C-section for sure. This one is likely coming early. You need to stay quiet at home. If you have any bleeding *whatsoever* you must come directly to hospital, as we'll likely need to deliver you immediately."

David asked, "So I drive her to the hospital right away if there's any bleeding?"

"Oh god no," the doctor said. "Call an ambulance. There will be so much blood in the car you won't be able to drive."

We went home and lay awake, terrified. I didn't want to be anywhere but the hospital.

When I spoke to my own obstetrician a few days later, I mentioned that the high-risk doctor had told me there would be so much blood that David wouldn't be able to drive. Dr. Bernstein was quiet for a while, thinking. He washed his hands. He said, quietly, "I wonder where he had just come from." I told him he had just come from a stressful C-section in which they lost a twin. "Ah," he said. "So you caught the wave."

Dr. Bernstein has been delivering babies at Mount Sinai since 1975. He is a legend in Toronto. I have, more than once, met women who have been delivered by him, as have their mothers and their own children. He is funny, warm, wise, eccentric, always appears completely relaxed, and would generally rather talk about movies and books than pregnancy. He also gives the least uncomfortable pelvic exams and Pap smears I have ever had in my life. I dread gynecological exams; my endometriosis has always made them terrible experiences for me. Throughout my life I've reacted with pain, surprising and sometimes frustrating doctors. When I wince as Bernstein examines me, and involuntarily begin my customary wriggling away from the metal implements, he doesn't make the mistake of telling me "Relax" in a frustrated tone, an ineffectual technique used by so many doctors. He doesn't flinch at all. When I apologize for being overly sensitive, he puts out his arm to help me up to a sitting position and says, "I'd be far more sensitive. It's an unpleasant experience. Please don't ever apologize for having a reasonable response to something difficult. It's hard enough to train doctors to behave like human beings."

Beyond his general magic, Dr. Bernstein can look me in the eye and process, without imploding, what I am telling him about my pain and anxiety. This is something I desperately need right now. While I scream in pain at home, David has taken to pounding away at building the crib or making soufflés. He has joined a running team and started two courses and seems to be on several committees. He is staying positive and productive, as is his wont, while I want him to just sit with me. He cannot. The quiet makes my pain unavoidable, and as he feels it like a sledge-hammer to his heart, he must avoid the silence and fill it with as much activity as he can. I know that his avoidance comes from unbearable love for me and over-identification with my pain, so why does his constant activity make me feel so afraid and alone and angry? Why doesn't the knowledge that his need to keep moving comes from panicked love alleviate how devastated I feel?

My mother was always running from place to place; from the stove, to the phone, to work, to the laundry, to a fight with one of my siblings, to a party, to the vacuum. She was always so busy. And then she died.

I love Dr. Bernstein. So does every other woman I have met who has ever been in his care. He's the father you never had, the guardian angel watching over you and your baby, the constant calm bringer of light, reminding you that there is a world outside of your anxious pregnancy. At several of my appointments, when I express anxiety that things seem to be going off the rails, he says, "If I need to jump, I will jump. I'm not jumping right now." I can't imagine him jumping. Until he does.

At five in the morning, pumped full of morphine in the delivery room after bleeding and calling an ambulance, I wake up to Dr. Bernstein's face above mine, his eyes wide. "You're not going anywhere," he says. "Sorry. No going home for you."

I am so relieved to see him I want to cry. I even have a momentary, nonsensical hope that the baby will come right now, seven weeks early, so he can be there for the delivery. He is scheduled to be away when my C-section is booked. I have had an unsettling appointment with the surgeon who will be replacing him in which I was promised, "With this previa you'll need multiple units of blood, I'd bet my bottom dollar," and advised, "You might do well to go straight to general anaesthetic, since a spinal block may not work with your spinal fusion." He said all this without making eye contact. (Later, when I ask Bernstein if I should go straight to general anaesthetic, he says, "Oh no. You'll want to be there for that. Don't miss it. Be there if you can.") Maybe Bernstein will be here to deliver my baby after all. I have had a night of various doctors coming and going, disagreeing on whether they should continue to give me morphine to stop my contractions or if it is even effective, since my contractions have not stopped. The last guy who came in tried to give me more, and I stopped him, telling him there had been a debate about the efficacy. He explained to his resident in a stage whisper how one was to "deal with women" when they get like this. He had a hairy chest and a lot of chains peeking out from his scrubs, and later I learned he ran a side hustle doing post-birth vaginal cosmetic surgery. (He was a real gem and I was sorry to see him go.)

Dr. Bernstein stops the administration of morphine. The contractions continue, so painful I can't speak, but just part of the package at this point. None of this seems to be leading to labour. I'm moved to a ward on the high-risk pregnancy floor, terrified that someone might send me home. No one does. Dr. Bernstein looks visibly concerned, cracks no jokes, and has nothing to say about movies. This is him jumping. I like it.

I had wanted a baby, desperately, ever since I was sixteen years old and held my newborn niece Diane in my arms. Her thick mane of black hair spilled out over my arm, her eyes staring straight up into mine. She was alert in a way I'd never seen a human be. She saw everything. She saw through me. She saw through the ceiling of the room and up through the roof of the hospital and to the stars. Every time she cried, for those first few days of her life, I cried too. My heart had become tethered; a coiled mess of tangled threads caught me to her.

Within a week, I had one goal in life: to have a baby. I didn't care about a career or meaningful work or really anything except having a baby. As far as I was concerned, anything else that happened in the intervening years was coincidence, luck, or distraction. I was deeply aware of how unfeminist and perhaps unhealthy this singular, solitary goal of procreation was, but that had no influence on how fiercely I wanted it.

Shortly after Diane's birth, I began to have dreams that I had a baby, but it had been only half-formed in the womb, born too soon and misshapen. Sometimes it was half cat or half dog; sometimes it was so small it looked like it shouldn't yet be out of my body. Often in this dream, I had forgotten it in a basement years before and it was still down there, starving, neglected.

I believe this recurring dream was born out of my neglect of my little dog Mookie after my mother died when I was eleven, but also out of a sense that there was some essential flaw in my very existence that would make the healthy birth of another human impossible. I didn't believe I was capable of making something good. Nevertheless, I wanted a baby.

When I began dating David, I had just separated from my first husband. On our second date, I said to David, "I have absolutely no interest in having a relationship with anyone, but I want to have a baby right now."

He looked off, thoughtfully, and said, lightly, "Okay."

I laughed. He was serious.

After dinner, he pulled me by my hands down the middle of icy streets and I skated, fast, on my feet, all the way home, as he slid backwards in his shoes without faltering. Within three weeks, we were trying to make a baby, wildly in love.

A year later I became pregnant. On the first night after the positive pregnancy test, I had a dream about a small baby with a beautiful mane of black hair, like Diane's. She looked straight at me with her wide eyes, and then fell asleep. I loved her already.

Two days later, she was gone.

I went up north to a cottage and stared across the lake at an island. Seagulls floated back and forth across a rocky cliff face. Trees grew precariously, perched on the edge of boulders, their exposed roots clinging to their foundations. I thought of all the things that lived and died, every year, on that island alone. The loss of a life wasn't treated as a particular tragedy, just as the natural course of things.

I wouldn't get pregnant again for another four years.

Many nights in those years I lay awake wondering if the thing I wanted most would simply not be a part of my life. I regretted the inordinate and unseemly amount of luck I had had thus far. Why should I deserve to get the thing I most wanted, when so much had been handed to me?

My mother had five children. She never "tried" to have children. In fact, when she found out she was pregnant with me, she considered terminating the pregnancy. I was an accident, a child conceived during an affair. She was overly fertile.

When I was thirty-one I went to a silent meditation retreat in the country. For three days I didn't say a word as we were guided through sitting and walking meditation. During the last hour of the retreat, the meditation teacher told us all to choose a partner and tell them one thing that we had discovered from our time in silence. Without having consciously had the thought before the words came out of my mouth, I turned to my partner and said, "There is something wrong with my body. I need to find out what it is."

My mother knew there was something wrong with her body. She went to her doctor and told him about all kinds of symptoms that concerned her. Over several visits, he never really listened to her. He thought she was a hypochondriac. She died four years later, at the age of fifty-three. She had colon cancer, a very treatable cancer if detected early.

I made an appointment to see a fertility specialist from the car on the way home from the meditation retreat. Two months later, I sat in Dr. Kimberly Liu's office at the Mount Sinai fertility clinic and told her my history. Ever since I was a young teenager, I had experienced a lot of pain during my periods. I had thought I was an especially fragile, overly sensitive person, so I assumed I was just being weak when I had to lie in bed, sometimes for a couple of days, curled in the fetal position. Usually, the pain would get so bad I would vomit. That pain had, for years now, become a regular feature of my life, no longer limited to times of menstruation. My digestive system had also been affected. I had become conscious, in my early twenties, of mostly limiting my acting roles to ones in which I could express a lot of pain. I never knew which days I would be mired in physical struggle, and pain was something I knew I could always express. I had had ultrasounds, but the cysts that had been spotted on my ovaries had been assumed to be ordinary, benign "chocolate" cysts, not signs of anything more sinister. I described my symptoms in detail to Dr. Liu. As soon as I finished speaking she said she felt fairly convinced that I had a severe case of endometriosis and would like to book a laparoscopy as soon as possible.

Before the procedure, the anesthesiologist, Dr. Mary Ellen Cooke, came out to talk to me. She was chatty and funny and self-deprecating and she touched my shoulder as she spoke to me. She immediately put me at ease. She told me about novels she was reading and asked me if I had read anything lately she should catch up on. I felt as though I was having lunch with a friend, not lying in a busy OR with half a dozen people readying to perform a surgery. As she administered the drugs to put me to sleep she said, "Now, a lot of anesthesiologists tell patients to count backwards from ten. I like to tell people to think of the nicest place you can possibly imagine. Because I get the feeling that if you go to sleep feeling wonderful, you'll wake up feeling that way too." When I woke up, I did indeed have the sensation of lying on the quiet Mediterranean beach I had imagined myself on as I had fallen out of consciousness.

Dr. Liu told me that I had stage 4 endometriosis. I had large cysts on my ovaries and fallopian tubes and it had spread to other organs. My uterus was stuck to my bowel, which the endometriosis had also seeded itself on. "It was a severe case. We managed to get some of it, not all of it."

I said, "I thought I was just a wimp."

Three months later, I was pregnant. I was nauseous. My breasts hurt. I was tired all the time. These were good signs of a healthy pregnancy and I revelled in all of them. And when those feelings passed, at around four months, I became the happiest of happy pregnant ladies. As my body grew and my hips became fuller and my belly grew swollen, I felt as though what had always been missing had finally arrived. It was as though the absence of a baby within my body had left me gaping open, looking for the missing piece of myself for most of my life. I was finally whole.

I went to every workshop and seminar on breastfeeding and early childhood development I could find. I read every parenting book I could get my hands on. I lost myself in the extreme "attachment parenting" philosophy of Dr. Sears, who made me see mothers who put their babies down for five minutes or didn't breastfeed their children until they were four as neglectful. It would be years before I realized that I was taking advice from an evangelical Christian who had eight children. There is no one more susceptible to overzealous parenting advice than a motherless mother.

At around fifteen weeks, I was diagnosed with gestational diabetes. At my twenty-week scan the placenta previa was discovered. A few weeks later, the pain of the internal ripping of the scar tissue from my endometriosis began. And I was cast back to my dreams of giving birth to something half-formed, half-born, because my body and I were not worthy or capable of making something complete.

A nurse comes into my room on the first night in the high-risk ward. She is chatty and high-pitched and from Bulgaria. She puts a large rubber mat under me. I look at her questioningly. She shrugs and says, "It's so strange with placenta previas. Always with previas, it happens in the middle of the night! You hear the alarm go off, you come into the room, and the woman is just sitting there and the entire bed is *soaked* in blood! It's dripping all over the floor! Goodnight!" She gives me a cheery smile at the door. I turn to look at David, who has set up a camping mat on the floor. My eyes are wide with fear. He gives me a supportive smile, but it's hard to say anything that can undo the gothic Eastern European horror-movie bedtime routine we've just been treated to.

I was told, by a resident earlier in the day, that if I begin to bleed, I am not to push the button for a nurse, I am to rip a plug right out of the wall. When I ask why, I am told that it will set off an alarm and it will be all hands on deck to run to my room and get me into an operating room to deliver the baby as soon as possible.

That night, around three, I hear an alarm, many feet running, and the clattering of a hospital bed being wheeled quickly down the hall. "A previa," I whisper to David. He sleeps through the noise.

At seven I wake up to Dr. Bernstein in his running gear. I am groggy and disoriented to see him there without his white coat on, and I struggle to understand what he is talking about. He is full of unbridled enthusiasm. "It was Saturday night at the movies last night! Have you seen *Monsieur Lazhar?*" I manage to say a few inane things about Quebec cinema. He sees a copy of Buddhist nun Pema Chödrön's book *When Things Fall Apart* on my hospital tray. "No!" he says, and flicks the book. "Don't read that. Things aren't falling apart! Have a little faith!" He looks at David on the floor, still sleeping. "Where'd you find this guy?" he says. "Why is he asleep? Hey, David! Wake up!" David wakes up. After ten minutes of talking about movies and books, I realize that Dr. Bernstein is just there to let me know he is there. He already knows everything that is going on with me medically from the nurses and other doctors on the ward. But I swear my heart rate plummets to normal as soon as he is in the room. And I swear he knows it. I sheepishly tell him the Buddhist book isn't as depressing as it looks. He rolls his eyes. "Quite the title, then."

In the weeks before my mother dies, one of her more woo-woo friends brings a Buddhist monk to the house. He walks slowly, his footsteps not making a sound, down the hall and into a chair in our den. He sits there in his robes, smiling, as though it is the most natural thing in the world for him to be

sitting in our suburban atheist home in a La-Z-Boy. Thinking he is a recep-
tacle for all things woo-woo (which I am secretly quite skeptical of), I tell
him I have a special crystal that I got for my mom to make her better. I'm
thinking of a small malachite I have, which apparently absorbs negative
energies. He asks me if I will go find it and bring it to him so that he can see
it. I look all over the house for the malachite, sweating in a panic, but I can't
find it. I find an amethyst necklace instead, and decide to pretend this is the
one that will heal my mother, even though I know amethysts are really only
good for calming people down. (Skepticism aside, I've been learning a lot
about crystals from the woo-woo people on the TV show set I work on.) When
I return, the amethyst in my hand, I hear hushed, serious tones from behind
the now closed door. I realize he has skilfully redirected the child (me) so that
he can speak candidly and privately with the sick woman he is here to tend to.
When I slowly open the door, my mother wipes away tears, and he greets me
as though I am the main thing he has been waiting for. He looks at the crystal
necklace and smiles. He asks if he can hold it, and he looks at it carefully.
I can tell he is being kind, and that Buddhist monks perhaps don't know as
much about crystals as I thought. I feel embarrassed. When he gives it back
to me, I put it around my mother's neck in a show of caring for her, something
I don't feel right now, as I'm generally angry at her for making this illness
seem worse than it actually is. Two weeks later my mother will die with this
amethyst around her neck. I will feel guilty for years that I didn't find her the
right crystal.

I am safe here on the high-risk ward. The nurses are, for the most part, incredibly kind, funny, and nurturing. Three times a day, I am delivered a gestational-diabetes-friendly meal. Friends inquire as to how I am coping with all the disgusting hospital food, and I can't even pretend to not like it. This, more than anything else, makes them worry for my mental health, but I am happy as a clam, having food that I can eat delivered on a regular basis.

David wheels me down the hall and drops me off at a support group for women on the ward. One woman from China has a brother who has flown to Canada just to cook for her so she doesn't have to eat the terrible hospital food. (I keep my mouth shut about my beloved institutional cuisine.) Another woman shares that she has figured out how to punk the system and custom-order stuff from the kitchen. The facilitator gently suggests that we aren't allowed to do this, as there are too many patients to accommodate this kind of individual request. Before she can be shut down again the woman screams out crucial information, as though she is being dragged away from us to be jailed: "EXTENSION 225! JUST CALL DOWN! THEY WILL HELP YOU GET EXTRA CHEESE SQUARES!" The facilitator takes a deep, calming breath and asks how we are all doing.

Two of the women who have been sharing a room for weeks, a Jamaican woman and a Southeast Asian woman, both heavily pregnant, do each other's hair.

On the surface, all our lives couldn't be more different from each other. There are women here who have come as refugees, a woman who works in investment banking, a special needs assistant, a grocery store clerk, a lawyer. There are stay-at-home mothers, women who live in small towns, and women who live in the heart of the city or in the suburbs. Some women here have other children or partners and some don't. Some are rich and some are very poor. Every socio-economic background is represented here, and there are about seven different cultural backgrounds in this room alone. But all of us are fearful for our babies' lives. All of us are fearful for our own. Devoid of our accents and without seeing us, if you were to hear us speak with each other in this particular room about our present lives, about our fears, you would think we couldn't have more in common.

I ask if anyone else is fearful of being discharged before they give birth, of going home. They all nod. One woman, who wears a hijab and speaks little English, and who has the kind of beaming, all-encompassing smile that makes you ashamed to complain about anything, says that she is afraid to go home but is also desperate to get back there. She has three other children. Her youngest is still breastfeeding, or was until she was admitted with a placenta that has migrated into her bladder and will require a multi-team surgery when she gives birth. Her husband has never woken up with her baby at night before now, or cared for any of the other children. The social worker adds, "And they live far out in the suburbs, and he works long hours, so he only brings them to visit once a week, right?" The woman smiles and nods, and leans her head on the social worker's shoulder. The social worker gives her a squeeze. They know each other well by now. The woman says, "Yes, that's right. I don't see them very often. I don't know how they are doing, really." She keeps smiling as a tear drops suddenly out of her eye, surprising her. She is twenty-one.

I try to keep my panic about what is happening to me in context.

A few days later, I go to a breastfeeding workshop down the hall. I have an obsession with breastfeeding. Earlier in my pregnancy I attended a workshop run by a renowned pediatrician/breastfeeding guru with a floral scarf who openly shamed women who didn't breastfeed until their children were toddlers and treated the attendees to Unabomber-style rants about the evils of formula. He was around seventy and had been giving this talk for decades. At one point he muttered, seemingly to himself, "The bottle kills, the bottle kills, that's for sure. Very soon we will all be on formula from birth to death." He began with a slide that he'd entitled "Truth Number 1. It's All About the Birth." He encouraged an "ideal birth," which, according to his research, was one in which the woman was in a dimly lit room, alone except for another woman sitting silently *behind* her. Knitting. Then the mother would clean up from the birth herself. "Anything that disrupts the link between the mother and the baby after birth can lead to the mother rejecting the baby." (Behind him, on a screen, was a picture of a baby gorilla, refusing to latch to its mother's breast.) He didn't clarify whether he was speaking about humans or the gorillas behind him, and no one dared ask. When one woman asked whether an epidural could affect breastfeeding, he said, "It sure does. There are other, better ways to manage pain. If a woman has a natural birth, alone in a dimly lit room, there are ways that her thinking self can disappear and she can manage the pain in an amazing way. Unfortunately, natural births do not happen anywhere in Canada."

At one point I raised my hand and said, "Um . . . I already know that there's a chance I may have to have a C-section under general anaesthetic, which is obviously less than ideal for breastfeeding—"

"Yes," he interrupted me. "You can say that again. Way less than ideal. Not ideal at all." He suggested that I email him to discuss the matter further.

I detected the rest of the room quavering at the idea that they may also end up with C-sections and reject their babies à la the gorillas. (I had encountered this kind of fear in pregnant women before. In my prenatal yoga class I'd met women whose eyes bugged out of their heads as they talked about their seemingly singular attachment to a natural birth. Sometimes, when they talked about their elaborate birth plans, and how devastated they'd be if they didn't go as they expected, it seemed as though the birth was more important to them than the baby.)

Later, when I asked whether my gestational diabetes could affect breastfeeding, the guru said, exasperated, "God, is this you as well? Well that's . . . that can be . . . email me and I'll send you some charts."

I realized that Horror Show C-section Diabetes Lady was getting all her questions deflected to email so as not to put any ideas beyond natural dimly lit knitting births into anyone else's pretty little head.

Breastfeeding Guru went back to taking questions and reprimanding the women there who had to go back to work within the year, or who hadn't breastfed their older children for long enough. He said things like, "I know a lot of people want the father to do some feedings from the bottle. Because they want their bodies back, or they want their freedom, et cetera. Well, guess what? *You're having a baby.* There is no freedom anymore. None. And honestly, giving a bottle is not the role of the father."

I'm not an idiot, and I know this guy is loony-tunes and offensive on a number of levels. But he is a renowned expert on breastfeeding and my motherless self is completely susceptible to each and every way someone implies that I might fail at assuming a role I haven't had enough time to witness up close.

My mother did not breastfeed all of her children, as she found it difficult and painful, but she breastfed me. My siblings have told me this. In a photo of me at five months old, she wears me in a green corduroy snuggly, close to her body. It is one of the only clues I have of how I was mothered as a baby. I was held close. I was breastfed.

The breastfeeding seminar I go to now on the high-risk unit is very, very different. We are taught how to use breast pumps, which will be necessary if we are separated from premature babies. Many of the women here have already given birth, and have babies in the NICU. They cry, and apologize for crying. They are told that it's okay to cry. They talk about their babies' brain bleeds. The social worker and lactation consultant shift seamlessly away from the technical instructions of breastfeeding and into engaged, compassionate listening for these women who have been on bedrest, had traumatic labours, and are now visiting their tiny preterm babies, some not knowing whether they will live or die. I realize, quickly, that this workshop is a therapy group in a breastfeeding workshop's clothing. If it had been billed as a support group, it's likely that many of these women would not have come. One by one, the new mothers excuse themselves, as it is their time to either hold their babies skin-to-skin or to try, once more, to breastfeed.

I lie in my bed that night, scared that my baby will go to the NICU. I am also scared that my baby will not be born early and I will be sent home after I have felt so scared and depleted during this pregnancy, unable to assume the role of being a mother.

I have another concern. Because of my spinal fusion, an epidural or spinal block can be difficult to perform, and I've heard horror stories of it not working on women who have rods in their back, as I do. I've asked Dr. Bernstein if Mary Ellen Cooke, the anesthesiologist who attended at my laparoscopy, is available to administer the spinal block for my C-section, but I've received the message back that, given the complications of my spine, she feels a leading-edge anaesthesia ultrasound expert should be assigned instead.

I ask for a meeting with anaesthesiology to talk about the potential complications of my spine in relation to an epidural or spinal block. I ask the young anesthesiologist who may be there for my C-section if, before she administers the spinal block, she will use an ultrasound to look carefully at my spine, with its fusion and metal attached. She replies, dismissively, "I may if I have someone I'm training with me and I want to demonstrate. But I don't really need it." I start having dreams that the morning of my surgery arrives and Mary Ellen appears in the doorway of my hospital room and tells me that she will be there for the birth. I realize, when I wake up from one of these dreams, that Mary Ellen, with her fast-paced talking, incredible competence, self-deprecating humour, loud laugh, and obsession with novels, reminds me of my mom.

When I finished making Stories We Tell, *a personal documentary about storytelling, memory, and discovering that I was the product of an extramarital affair, I asked my father what he thought of it. He had this critique: "Your mother got a degree in philosophy from St. Andrews. She got a master's in social work. She was funny. She had so many close friends. She read voraciously. She was a casting director. She produced amazing comedy shows. In your film you've shown her only in relation to the men in her life and the children she had." He was right. My mother was a thousand things. I had omitted most of them.*

Most people who have lost a parent young miss them, in one way or another, for the rest of their lives. It's such a fundamental part of who I am, to be missing a mother, that I can't imagine the terrible anticipation of having to experience loss like that for the first time as a less adaptable adult. (I sometimes think that one of the things that binds David and me together is that we both lost parents young, and so we understand the intensity of a life after a bereavement in childhood.) But while the loss of any parent is devastating, I have yet to meet anyone who lived as warmly, loudly, and hilariously as my mother. When she left, she left me searching the planet for anyone remotely like her.

My mother woke up to read books before the sun rose. I would come into her room to snuggle after a bad dream or just as a matter of course, and she would be propped up in her nightgown, blasting her way through a novel, begging me to let her read "just one more page" before I interrupted her. (I would catch her stealing three or four more when she thought I wasn't looking.) She made breakfast, did the dishes, drove us to school, drove herself downtown to work. She worked as a casting director for much of my life, working with misogynist bullies who expected perfect work to be delivered on impossible deadlines. She came home after dark, usually with bundles of groceries weighing down her arms, unpacked, and made a full, well-rounded dinner and usually a homemade dessert. She would do this while juggling last-minute phone calls from work, many of them with audible shouting coming through the other end of the phone. She would clean up, catch up with her teenagers, put me to bed with books and stories, catch up on some work, and sometimes dress up to go to an industry function or party at night. Repeat.

I often look back at a particularly exhausting day in my own life and wonder how on earth she did so much more than I ever do, with no practical support from her husband, yet was always so full of laughter and capable of so much joy. Sometimes I feel inadequate when I compare my life with hers. Sometimes I wonder if she could have lived longer than fifty-three years if she hadn't lived at such a frenetic pace.

I think the frenetic pace was partly due to an insatiable appetite for life, and a genuine love of people, and in part because with no one to help shoulder the demands upon her, she had to live three days in one. I think she may also have been outrunning a childhood fraught with secrets and shame. The story of that childhood would be hers to tell, not mine, but I think that what was hidden throughout her life drove her forward and outward, her arms out-stretched, ready to embrace the whole world if it could keep the contradictions in her memories muffled.

She was adored. As an adult, I am still sometimes stopped on the street by people in their seventies or eighties who tell me how much they loved my mother, how much she made them laugh, how much she helped them and believed in them. One of her former colleagues told one of my siblings that they remembered her rushing into a meeting late one day, which was odd, as she was usually so organized and responsible at work. He noticed that her face was greasy-looking and sweating. He said, "Diane—were you just sunbath-ing?" She yelped. "Yes! I'm so sorry! It was just such a beautiful day!" She managed to pack these shards of joy into a life that was constantly overstuffed.

She left a gaping hole when she died. But I had never felt rage over it, or felt the need to fill it as acutely as when I was about to become a mother myself, and I was always hungry and she wasn't there to feed me.

One of the nurses tells me that she herself was a patient on this ward a few years ago. She had been working here for years, and then had a bleed with a placenta previa. Suddenly she was trapped at work with her colleagues tending to her. "It was so weird. I hated it," she says. "But I felt safe. And the only reason I wasn't a basket case before I was admitted was because I was here working every day, in case something happened." I tell her that I am very anxious. I feel like my body is a ticking time bomb that could explode at any minute. She says, "Yes. That is what it feels like to have a previa." She tells me that the anxiety is something I should talk to my doctor about. It's important that they know I am feeling this anxious. It turns out that many women on the floor with previas are on some kind of anti-anxiety medication.

The nurse on shift the following day asks about my contractions, checks the baby's heartbeat, and gently asks about my anxiety and how I am feeling. The other nurse has talked to her about it. The casual conversation I thought I was having was clocked and has become information about my care. They are, as a team, thinking of my mental well-being as their responsibility as well as my body and my baby. It makes me feel safe and noticed and cared for.

An amazing high-risk doctor who runs the floor, and who the nurses idolize (along with an incomparable bedside manner, she is also highly respected and widely published), comes into my room the next day and says, "Good news! I'm doing your C-section!" I say, "Oh my god, I'm so happy. Thank you. I've heard such great things about you!" She winks and says, in an almost lascivious tone, "Don't believe everything you read on bathroom walls." High-risk pregnancy doctors seem to have a lot of energy.

A nurse writes the date for my C-section on the whiteboard next to my bed. It will be three days from now. I'm surprised and relieved. It's way sooner than I thought it would be, more than a month before my original due date, but I'm so happy to have this pregnancy be almost

over, and with it this sense of my body being a threat to me and my
baby. Dr. Bernstein comes into my room, as he does every morning at
seven in his running gear, full of book and movie recommendations.
He says goodbye—he is going out of town the next morning—and
wishes me luck. He flinches a little when he sees the date written on
the board. "Wow. That's very . . . soon."

The morning of my C-section, I wake up to a soft knock on the door,
and Mary Ellen Cooke walks into my room. I am sure that I am dreaming. She puts her hand on top of mine and squeezes. "What a time
you've had," she says. "I'm sorry for all the confusion. I didn't want to
do your C-section because your spine is so complex. I wanted someone
with good experience with spinal ultrasound to do it, and to do a pre-
liminary consult where they looked carefully at your spine with an
ultrasound and could tell you what to expect. I'm old, and I'm not good
with ultrasound technology, but after about twenty emails back and
forth I realize that what should have happened hasn't happened. So, if
you're okay with it, I have a brilliant young person with good ultrasound skills who will assist me, and I'll do it myself." I nod, unable to
find the words to thank her for appearing like an apparition in my room.

Before I go into the OR, I ask the obstetrician if she thinks the baby
will be okay. She says, "Everyone's got their knickers in a knot about
this baby! I got a call from Bernstein this morning too! The baby is
going to be just fine!"

I go into the OR without David. He will come in later, when they finish
administering the spinal and are ready to begin the surgery. I say goodbye to David. I have left a note in his pocket telling him that he has
everything he needs to parent this child in case something bad happens
to me during the surgery. He will need confidence, I think. I hug him

tight, and say goodbye as well as I can, in case I die. I am strangely sanguine about this possibility, though in retrospect it makes no sense that I'm entertaining it at all. He doesn't find the note until months later, by which time I've forgotten that I ever wrote it.

The day before my mother died, we were all given a few minutes to be alone with her, so that we could speak with her and say what we needed to say. She was in a coma, her eyes rolled upward, her breathing sounding like a chainsaw. My father later recounted that he had told her that he would always love her and that he would never forget her. My brother Johnny told her it was okay to let go now, she didn't have to fight anymore. My brother Mark suggested to her that she think of one of her favourite comedy sketches, where a man is constantly frustrated because the last page of the book he is reading is missing. When I was left to sit with her alone, I told her that the amethyst around her neck would heal her and that she would be fine. I watched her in silence for a while, and wondered if the amethyst (which was the wrong crystal to heal her anyway) felt heavy on her now tiny, birdlike body, which struggled to produce each and every breath. Later, I realized that if she could hear me that morning, she heard an eleven-year-old who didn't know her mother was going to die, who didn't know how to say goodbye or even that she should.

The spinal block is administered by Mary Ellen, who fills the space with her warmth and chatter. She does it in collaboration with a young anesthesiologist who scans my back with an ultrasound. Before she puts the needle in my spine, she tells me I will need to help direct them to the right place. I am to say "left" if it is causing pain to the left and "right" if it is causing pain to the right. I yelp out directions a few times, the sharp pains in my spine guiding them to the right spot.

I lie down on what feels like a narrow board, my arms outstretched in what, Mary Ellen says, "we Christians call the crucifix position." A curtain hangs over my chest, separating me from the rest of my body. The obstetrician says, "Well, I'm going to go get scrubbed up and ready and we're just going to leave you here half-naked because that's how sensitive we are!" When she comes back in her scrubs and mask, she introduces me to a male doctor beside her. "Aren't I lucky to have someone this sexy helping me with your C-section! He actually delivers babies as a family doctor up in North Bay, but every now and then he likes to come downtown and see how the big girls play." There's that wink again. Who *is* this lady? She's like the Annie Oakley of ob-gyns.

David comes in and leans over me, cradling my face in both of his hands as they begin the surgery. He looks into my eyes, his face close to mine. There he is. He's not being positive or productive. He's not trying to outrun the moment. He's just suddenly still and right there with me. Just in time.

I don't feel the pressure I've heard described during C-sections. I feel intense pain. I feel my body being opened up. Mary Ellen immediately notices that I am in pain and looks down into my eyes. I say that I think I'm going to vomit. She strokes my forehead with a strong hand as she speaks quickly. "I can have you put out in seconds if it's too much." I shake my head. I remember Dr. Bernstein's words. I remember all the meditating I have been doing. I say, "No. I want to be here for this." She nods. She leans down into my face, holds my head firmly on each side, and says, gathering all my focus to her, "Okay. Almost a year ago today I was there for your surgery and I saw one of the worst cases of endometriosis I've ever seen in my career. Now you're having a baby and I'm so, so happy for you."

It's a Jedi mind trick. I am completely redirected. I look into Mary Ellen's happy, calm face and feel nothing except excitement and grati-tude. All physical sensation is momentarily suspended. I feel a *whoosh* of pressure and I hear a cry that sounds like sung melted butter. I see a perfect face beside me. Thick black hair. Wide eyes. Full lips, the top one overlapping the bottom. As soon as we lock eyes, the crying stops. Both of our eyes go wide. "Hi, Eve," I say. Eve's eyes close. There is a sucker punch to my stomach. I hear someone remark that it is my uterus "going back in." It raises the question of what the hell it was doing out, but I don't care about any of it. I don't care about the pain. Here Eve is. Eve is here.

Mary Ellen begins to speak quickly. She is looking over the curtain, concerned. The timbre of the doctors' voices has changed. Something is going wrong. But I feel as though the rest of my body is a thousand miles away. All I see is Eve.

There is a photo of me holding Eve on me in the OR, right after the C-section. Eve sleeps. I smile, serenely. There is a substantial amount of blood on the floor behind us. Later I learn that a blood vessel "went" and it was, in Mary Ellen's words, "touch and go there for a little while."

As I am wheeled out of the room I hear Mary Ellen say to one of her colleagues that she would like to have it recorded that she gave me a very generous dose of anaesthetic for my height and it did not accomplish the spread she wanted.

The baby isn't "just fine," as the high-risk doctor has (weirdly) promised me. I try to nurse Eve in the recovery room. It doesn't work. Eve is sleepy. A nurse tells me that if Eve doesn't latch on soon we will have to go to formula. Based on my experience with the floral-scarf breast-feeding Nazi, I hear this as "If you don't figure out how to get your baby to latch soon we will inject a fetid, evil potion that will leave your child without a soul, wandering a barren hellscape of a life, alone." Eve's temperature keeps dropping. When it evens out, we are transferred to a ward room, and the threats of formula cease now and forever. I try, all night long, to breastfeed. I can hardly move. David watches videos on hand expression, and as I can't get anything out when I do it, he does it. He has always been an excellent student, and now he can add "expert hand-expressor of breasts" to his list of eight hundred degrees. He tries to feed Eve from a tiny cup. I try to sit up despite the incision and recently separated muscles in my stomach and together we try to manoeuvre Eve into a hundred different positions supported by many different structures of pillows in order to breast-feed. Eve just sleeps or makes strange hiccupping sounds that alarm me. Something isn't right. The next day, when the nurse comes in to take Eve's vitals, she tells me that oxygen and temperature levels are low.

Eve is relocated to the NICU. I try to push away the thought that this must be my fault, for being so anxious, for secretly hoping I'd have more time to become a mother before going home with my baby.

David pushes me in a wheelchair into the NICU, with its bright over-head lights and constant beeping. I am looking for that face that made me know, for the first time I can remember, what *wonder* meant. There are dozens of babies in isolettes in here. With a jolt I recognize Eve in the middle of the room. There are tubes and an IV in Eve now, one in the nose, one in the leg, a whole lot of wires attached to various parts of my baby's tiny body, and an IV. Eve is curled up in the fetal position, fragile, wearing only a diaper, and looking like something that belongs back in my womb. I realize, now that I see Eve separate from me, that my baby is not quite formed, just like the ones I dreamed of having. I have failed my baby. Some deep doubt about my capability as a human is realized. David lowers the isolette with a small pedal so that I can see Eve at eye level without having to stand up.

My brother Mark appears, a pack of Maltesers, my favourite candy when I was a kid, tucked in his suit pocket. I had emailed him that we weren't ready for visitors yet, but here he is anyway. He doesn't say a word as he hands the red package of candy to me, klutzily, tenderly. I can't hold it together at this strange offering from our 1980s suburban childhood. He turns his gaze away from my tears to the small creature in the isolette. He says, "Oh. Perfect." I look at Eve again. He is right. Eve is perfect. Beautiful. My brother sits in silence with me for a long time, marvelling.

When I put my hands on Eve's body, through the holes in the isolette, I see on the monitor that the heart rate steadies and oxygen levels go up. I watch as the monitors confirm what my hands are telling me. My child needs and thrives by my touch.

The nurses call the NICU mothers "Mom." Always. It's a genius trick. They don't have to learn as many names, and the women there, who are separated from their children, are acknowledged, many times a day, as their babies' mothers. After I've been called "Mom" for two or three days, I start to wonder if I might actually be one.

I desperately want to hold my baby, whose breathing has worsened and who has now been put on a CPAP machine, a machine with a breathing mask which covers almost the entire tiny face. After a few days, I am allowed to hold Eve next to my skin. My entire body relaxes, for the first time in recent memory. I say to David, "It's like a thousand lemonades in the desert." No one explicitly tells me that my baby will be fine, and I have no rational thinking skills to speak of in my current state, so I hold Eve, each time, as though it's the last time. I am thankful for every second I have my baby on my skin. I am in a state of wonder every time Eve's eyes open. I try to capture these moments with every molecule I have, in case suddenly there aren't more of them.

On January 8, two days before my mother died, it was my birthday. She had been confused for about a week, not making sense, and then, for the last couple of days, not speaking at all. As I climbed the stairs to go to bed that night, she suddenly looked up from the couch on which she lay, her glassy eyes suddenly alert, her speech clear.

She said, "Happy Birthday. Goodbye, dear."

"Goodnight, Mom," I replied.

"Goodbye," she reiterated. "Goodbye."

I laughed at what I thought was a persistent slipping of her tongue. "Okay. Goodnight, Mom."

"No," she said. "Goodbye, dear."

I went upstairs to bed, brushing off the weird exchange. Those were her last words.

I haven't slept more than an hour at a time for a week and a half. I take literally the instructions to pump for twenty minutes every three hours to bring my breast milk in and hand-express for twenty to forty minutes after that. In the first few days we get only tiny drops of liquid. I say "we" because David is still doing the hand-expressing—to the lactation consultant's delight when she pulls back the curtain to a visiting tour of nursing students and pronounces, "And here we have a father bringing in the breast milk with perfect hand expression!" David grins. He loves being the perfect student. (It's irritating, how good he is at everything.) I sleep for about an hour and a half to two hours, hold the baby, pump, then hand-express while David holds Eve on his chest. Repeat. Once, as David wheels me down the hall to the NICU, he falls asleep while walking and we slam into a wall.

I am producing hardly any milk. The tubes we are delivering to the nurses are a tenth full at most. On the fifth day, I sob in frustration and exhaustion beside Eve's isolette. A nurse named Cindy sits down beside me and moves my chin so that my eyes are level with hers. She says, "This baby doesn't need you crying beside the isolette. This baby needs your milk. To get your milk to come in, you need to sleep. You need to eat. You need to sleep and eat for your baby." I go back to my room on a mission, eat a huge plate of food, and sleep for three hours straight. When I wake up, my breasts are swollen. My milk has come in. I fill containers full of milk when I pump. When I arrive in the NICU with full tubes of milk finally in my hand, Cindy beams proudly, grabs the tubes from me, and shakes them in my face, victorious. "See?" she says. She whoops. Her message is clear. This baby doesn't need a martyr. This baby needs a mother who is okay. Cindy puts the milk into Eve's feeding tube and scuffs the back of my head as though we are playing a rough team sport and I've just scored a spectacular goal.

But Eve is still not latching, receiving my milk only through the feeding tube. Many times, when I try to feed, a lactation consultant or a nurse is there with me, putting pillows under my arms, holding my hands in theirs, coaching me. They are teaching me to move the baby's head towards my breast instead of my breast to the baby's mouth. They are teaching me to nudge Eve's nose with my nipple so Eve smells the milk. I am learning how to use my wrist to move the little sleeping mouth onto my breast as soon as it opens. I miss. Over and over. They teach me to be gentler with myself, to stop raging at myself for what I haven't yet learned. Occasionally, Eve sucks lazily on my nipple, but it feels as though nothing is really happening.

On about the ninth day, I see Eve rooting in the isolette, mouth open, looking for my breast in a way that looks desperate, and I sense, strongly, that this will be the moment where the latch finally works. I ask Cindy if I can hold Eve, if I can nurse now, and she says not yet; Eve has to be examined by the doctor on her rounds first. I wait, watching my baby so clearly ready to feed. Just as she approaches Eve, the doctor is called to another baby. I say, panicky, to Cindy, "Can I please feed now? Eve is ready. Can the doctor see us first so I can feed?" Cindy says no, and keeps walking towards the other baby, joining three or four other nurses and respiratory therapists. I start to cry. I put my head down, defeated, as I see that Eve has stopped rooting. I've missed my moment.

I feel two strong hands on my shoulders. It is Cindy. She says, "Tell me." I say, "Eve was ready to feed. I missed the moment. Can I please try now?" She looks at me, then says, "I'm so sorry. This is so frustrating and so hard. You should be able to hold your baby right now. But I don't have time to help you do that because that baby over there is very sick. Much sicker than yours. And I need that doctor over there right now. We all need to be over there right now. I'm so sorry." She leaves. My breathing calms. I watch them working on the other side of the room on a baby who is much younger, much more fragile than mine. I see the mother's terrified face as she is ushered away and loses sight of her baby in the crisis that is unfolding. The one I didn't notice because of my own desperation. I put my hand through the isolette, so grateful for Eve's size and health. So grateful for the clear communication that both validated my frustration and explained clearly the reason for the limits on how I could be helped at that particular moment.

When Eve falls asleep, I leave to get something to eat. As I pass the other isolettes, I realize that my baby is the biggest, healthiest baby here. There are parents here whose babies have been in here for months, many who are unsure if their babies will make it. Like the baby near Eve, whose mother is gasping for air by the door right now, frantically washing her hands.

While Eve sleeps, I go to another breastfeeding seminar. A woman named Jack holds her one-year-old, Tess, while giving a talk to nursing students about the parent experience in the NICU. Partway through her talk, Tess nurses as Jack continues to talk to the group. Tess latches on easily as Jack stands there. Tess sucks for about five minutes and then effortlessly pops off and feeds on the other side. I am stunned by the ease with which this is happening. Tess was in the NICU last year, born at twenty-seven weeks. Now Jack comes to support parents with babies in the same unit. The women in the group talk about their babies' brain bleeds and the middle-of-the-night phone calls. They've been there for months. One of them watches me sympathetically as I shuffle slowly because of my recent C-section. She says, "Oh, I remember those early days."

I don't want any visitors. I don't answer emails or phone calls from friends asking if I need or want any support. But other women who have had premature babies, most of whom I barely know, keep showing up, unannounced. David and I will be sitting by Eve's isolette and women I vaguely recognize, who had babies in the NICU years before, will suddenly pull back the curtain around our little area and deliver food, ask if we want them to sit with the baby while we take a break, and offer valuable advice. It's like I am now a part of a secret club. (I now find myself running to hospitals when people I barely know have had premature babies, to offer the same unrequested support. I now know that you don't know what you need in such a situation; what is needed has to just appear, as these women with their practical offerings are now, as my brother Mark did with the package of Maltesers.)

The next time Eve roots, Cindy is there. She unhooks wires and untangles tubes and hands Eve to me. As Eve's mouth begins to open wide, I quickly use my wrist to move it onto my breast. I scream. Cindy claps. "That's it!" she yells. Eve has latched, feeding, mouth wide, the pulls strong, the telltale *click* in the throat informing us that milk is being produced and swallowed. Three other nurses and a lactation consultant gather around, clapping. I feel as though I have an army of mothers around me, cheering. They say, "Congratulations, Mom."

My sister Susy and my brother Johnny visit. While I breastfeed, David takes a photo of us all sitting together in front of Eve's isolette. It is a strange picture. Johnny sits beside Eve's tiny, premature head. Eve still has tubes attached, and is feeding on my breast. There is an IV bag and hospital paraphernalia all around us as we sit, smiling, as though posing for a normal family photo, my breast half-exposed. Johnny examines the photo thoughtfully. "This is a good profile pic for Grindr." I laugh for the first time in a long time. I laugh so hard I sob and pee.

As we are discharged, we walk down the hall, Eve in our arms. I look back at the hallway of the high-risk ward we've spent the last four weeks of our life in. I see the nurses and doctors gathered around the front desk for a group meeting. I hear someone suggest that it would be helpful for the mothers to have a "Bring Baby Home" workshop, to keep them thinking about the future and alleviate some anxieties that many of the high-risk mothers on bedrest have. I hold this image like a moving photograph in my mind as I walk away and they grow smaller in the distance behind me, their voices becoming dimmer as they make their plans for the future of this place, and I say goodbye to it, grateful for how it held me through the most terrifying days of my life, while they try to make it better still.

When I enter our house for the first time in almost a month, my baby in my arms, I am grateful for everything. Every shard of sunlight coming into the room, the soft chair and bed, the home-cooked food. I am grateful for Eve, beside me, on me, never apart from me. I stay awake watching my baby sleep, in awe, as I was in that first moment, that something this beautiful has come into my life, that I had a part in making this person. Every time Eve wakes up, I am stunned and thrilled to find that my baby is still there, the initial euphoria of entering our house with Eve in our arms never far out of reach.

A week after we bring Eve home, we go to an appointment with our pediatrician. He tells me that I look very pale, and remarks on the dark circles under my eyes. He asks how the C-section went. He wonders if I lost too much blood, if I should have had a transfusion. When he asks about breastfeeding and I tell him it is going well, he says, "A baby born at thirty-five weeks who is exclusively breastfed. That's quite an accomplishment. That is very unusual. It's a real accomplishment." He looks at me with some concern, and I wonder if he is measuring whether this accomplishment was worth the toll he knows it must have taken.

I break down. I break down because I am suddenly proud that we did something perfectly for this baby. I break down because the way he says it implies there might have been another option and no one ever mentioned there was, and in my sleep-deprived, torn-apart state I couldn't have thought it up myself. I sob because I realize I have almost killed myself in order to avoid a tiny bit of formula. I sob because I have been so inundated by information about breastfeeding from old male breastfeeding experts that I didn't even realize I might have been harming myself by being so pure about all this. Mostly I sob because he is so, so kind to see me and to say this to me, right now, when I so badly need to hear that I have done something well.

On Eve's first birthday, I take cupcakes to the high-risk unit and the NICU, Eve in a snuggly, attached to me. After I thank the nurses and lactation consultants involved in my care and prepare to leave, I notice there is a workshop on for NICU parents, run by Jack, the woman who ran the one I had been to the year before. She has become a good friend. At the workshop I breastfeed Eve, who pops on and off in five minutes, just as Tess did, to my astonishment, a year before. I hear the women gasp. "It's that easy?" one of the mothers of a baby born at thirty-four weeks asks. "Not right away," I say.

Eve grows and grows. Aila and Amy are born, both by C-section, each right on time, without incident. Mary Ellen has retired in the intervening years, but has left behind careful notes and I am now in the care of another magician-like anesthesiologist, Dr. Jose Carvalho, who has, because of my significant postpartum pain with my last birth, done an ultrasound of my spine well in advance of the surgery and walked me through how he will manage my specific complications. He also prescribes gabapentin, which has been shown in a small study by his group to reduce pain outcomes by reducing the anxiety with which a patient goes into a C-section, which is helpful for those who have experienced significant postpartum pain before. The time he takes with me before the surgeries makes my anxiety plummet, which I think is the idea, as this apparently directly affects how much pain I will experience in recovery.

After Dr. Carvalho administers a generous dose of anaesthetic in the spinal block, I am rotated side to side and then head down to help the medication spread in my spinal fluid. It works. I have no complications and I can walk within a day of the surgeries. Dr. Bernstein now openly refers to my first pregnancy as "waaaay out there." I am still in a state of shock that I made three whole people.

What was half-formed was not, as in my dreams, my children but my ability to see myself as a mother.

Two and a half years after Eve is born, I present my documentary about my family, *Stories We Tell*, to the Toronto Psychoanalytic Society at their Annual Day in Applied Psychoanalysis. If you are ever uncertain whether you have self-destructive tendencies, it's useful to know whether you would say yes to an invitation to sit on a stage while three hundred psychoanalysts talk about your family for an entire day. I didn't hesitate when I was asked.

I listen to panels (*panels!*) on my family and sit on a stage and am asked one loaded question after another by people who are professionally trained to see dynamics in my family that I can't, ones it would have taken me years of my own psychoanalysis to finally name. By the end of the day, my head is spinning. A woman at the back of the audience stands up and says, "I have a much less loaded question because I'm not a psychoanalyst. I'm just here with my husband who is an analyst. I just wanted to ask about your pregnancy, and becoming a mother, and how it affected your memories of your own mother."

I take a moment. This woman looks familiar. When I finally place her, I say, "That's a misrepresentation of your threat level. I believe you are the mother of one of the obstetricians involved in my pregnancy." Indeed, it is Soap-Opera-Hot Doctor's mother, whom I've met a couple of times as she walked by my porch while visiting her son. As she blushes, smug, self-satisfied psychoanalytic laughter echoes from every last corner of the lecture hall.

I take a deep breath and I answer Soap-Opera-Hot Doctor's mother's question. I say that I didn't know how much I missed my mother until I was pregnant. I say that I didn't know how angry I was at her for dying. I say that now that I've lived two and a half years with my child, and felt the intensity of our subterranean, inexpressible, and indelible knowledge of each other, I've gone from feeling that eleven years with my mother was not very much, not nearly enough, to knowing that to feel adored and cherished by a mother who was full of warmth and joy is quite a lot, actually. More than most people get in a lifetime. And because, as I became a mother myself, I was nurtured, for a short time, by a team of wise and skilled people at Mount Sinai Hospital (an incubator that finished off the work that my mother left undone), I've been able to remember, clearly, what was best in her, and to discover what was, in fact, fully formed in me.

Mad
Genius

Eve recently asked me to help find more "live-action comedies" to watch. I've been debating whether or not to introduce my kids to Monty Python. By the time I was Eve's age I'd listened to all their albums, watched all their movies. Then again, I'd also watched *A Clockwork Orange*, unsupervised, several times by the time I was seven. I'm constantly comparing the boundaryless childhood I had with my own children's, wondering if I'm protecting them enough, or if I'm being overprotective in response to feeling too vulnerable myself. When there were so few limits in my own childhood, every one I set down with my own children is the result of a lot of thought. There is nothing instinctual about these decisions for me. It's hard work, informed by the ever-engaging process of getting to know them, and myself in relation to them. Eve is now nine, the age I was when I acted in the film *The Adventures of Baron Munchausen*, directed by Monty Python alum Terry Gilliam. Eve has asked me about it in the past, and whether we can watch it together.

"Is it scary?" Aila, who is six, pipes up. "I'm not watching it if it's scary."

***

When I was four years old, I treated my junior kindergarten class at North Toronto Christian School to a raucous rendition of "Sit on My Face" by Monty Python. It was show and tell, after all, so I sang them my favourite song, which included the lines "I love to hear you oralize, When I'm between your thighs, You blow me away!"

I would later hear my parents gleefully recounting to friends that when the teacher and principal confronted them about where I had learned the song, they had feigned shock and horror and denied any responsibility. (My parents, by the way, were not Christian. They sent me to kindergarten at a Christian school only because the school was around the corner and their love—or perhaps need—of convenience outweighed their considerable cynicism about religion.)

I knew the song because among my father's most treasured possessions were the albums of Monty Python's Flying Circus. Over and over we would listen, as a family, to "The Lumberjack Song," "The Dead Parrot Sketch," and the "Argument Clinic." Over and over we watched *The Meaning of Life*, *Life of Brian*, and *Monty Python and the Holy Grail*. By the time I was four, I could recite most Monty Python sketches and scenes by heart.

In 1987, when I was eight and already a frequently working child actor, Monty Python member Terry Gilliam came to Toronto to do a screen test with John Neville for the title role in his new fantasy/comedy film, *The Adventures of Baron Munchausen*. He was auditioning girls all over the world for the part of Sally Salt, the Baron's trusty sidekick. The collective blood pressure in our house almost exploded over my getting the chance to meet Terry, let alone a chance to work with him. My dad worked with me for long hours on the English accent the part required, and though my parents had been wondrously hands-off with guiding my performances so far, my dad suddenly had performance notes for me when I practised my lines for the audition. In response, I refused to work with him anymore. If I was going to do this, I would do it my own way.

Terry was giggly, fun, rambunctious. He reminded me of the kind of disobedient, unregulated child I had avoided in school in order to keep out of trouble. During my screen test I was delighted to notice that he treated me no differently than John Neville, the acclaimed actor who was seven times my age.

When my mother got the phone call that I had got the part, I saw her cover her mouth in what looked like a mixture of shock, excitement, and fear. I witnessed in my father a pure, unmitigated elation, which was simultaneously exhilarating and daunting. In that instant, I knew that he had never felt as proud of anything in his life as he did of my accomplishment in getting this part. I also knew that there was nothing I could ever do in my life to make him that proud again. I had been cast in a movie directed by Terry Gilliam, in which Eric Idle, another former Monty Python member, would also perform. The pinnacle of my success, and of my father's pride, had been reached. I was eight years old.

Production would begin in three months' time in Rome, primarily at the legendary studio Cinecittà, where Fellini had made his movies, as well as two locations in Spain. I began counting down the days until my departure. My Grade 3 teacher said, "You must be excited about going to Italy!" I said, "I'm trying to think of it as just two weeks to wait until it's only two weeks."

Our apartment in Rome was in a tiny little square called Largo dei Librari, just off the Campo de' Fiori. From our living room window, I could reach out and touch the facade of a very small grey church, centuries old. There was a pervasive smell of antiquity in the square, as though mould had been caught under layers of stone centuries ago and was now breathing through the cracks in the plaster. A tiny store across the street sold small chocolate ice cream balls, and I would eat them on the rooftop garden of our apartment while overwatering (and no doubt destroying) a perfectly tended garden planted by the landlady. Almost every night, for the first month of rehearsals, my mother and father and I ate dinner in the same small restaurant in Campo de'

Fiori, courtesy of my per diem. Every night I ordered scampi, which I would busy myself with for an eternity, trying to get every last tiny morsel of meat free from its shell. When I got bored, I would follow around a musical trio of an accordionist, a violinist, and a guitarist, who would play on the terrace every night, hoping for tips from tourists. They would happily include me as part of their performance, as would the waitstaff, who would smuggle me extra desserts as I followed the musicians around the restaurant.

As a North American child, I was not used to being out late. Back home in Toronto, on the rare occasion that my parents had taken me out with them at night, I had felt unwelcomed by other adults. In Italy, being a child felt like a revered, enviable state. The look on the face of the average adult upon seeing a child was one of unreserved delight. I felt included in the world in a way I hadn't before, and dread at the thought of returning to the reality of a child's diminished status back home. Sometimes the trio of musicians would show me down into the basement of the restaurant. They'd have a secret door opened for me that led to ancient catacombs.

On days off, my family went sightseeing. We went to the Pantheon, the Colosseum, Piazza Navona. We had at our disposal a driver and a stretch limo Mercedes. My siblings all came over on first-class tickets, and my parents bought leather jackets for everyone with my per diem. We were a middle-class suburban Toronto family, and this glamorous life we suddenly found ourselves in the middle of was a shock to our family's system, although not an unwelcome one.

The cast included Alison Steadman, Bill Paterson, Eric Idle, Jonathan Pryce, Oliver Reed, and a seventeen-year-old Uma Thurman, who was appearing as Venus in her first major film role. As we rehearsed, I felt that I was always, in Terry's eyes, just one of the actors, never a child, never treated with condescension. And always, his insane hyena giggle would greet me whenever I said or did something he found funny. Eric

Idle was also immediately kind to me, spent enormous amounts of time playing games and singing songs with me, aghast as he was that an eight-year-old knew so many of the rudest Monty Python songs by heart, including "Sit on My Face," which he wrote the lyrics to. Every now and then he brought me cassettes of unreleased Python material as gifts.

As we went into production, things quickly began to fall apart. Terry was erratic, a dreamer, someone who didn't live in the world of "logic and reason"—just as the Baron himself didn't. I would overhear the crew complain that plans, months in the making, would suddenly be replaced at the last minute with wild, ambitious impulses that put enormous pressure on the crew, the budget, and the schedule.

There were many special effects in the film; scenes of battle, exploding bombs, space, and moonwalking. As we were about to shoot a sequence involving explosives, Terry led me down a route I was to run through the set of a bombed-out city. I was to go through a corridor of half-destroyed structures, duck under a log, then run up a staircase to the ramparts, where I was to hurl rocks and scream at the Turkish army who were bombing us from the other side of the city walls. I was told there would be explosives going off as I ran, but I wasn't concerned. It would all be perfectly safe, I was told. I was given two cotton balls to put into my ears, in case the sound was too loud for me. After Terry yelled "Action!" I began my run as instructed. Blasts of debris exploded on the ground around me, accompanied by deafening booms that made me feel as if I myself had exploded. The log I was to run under was partially on fire. The gigantic blasts continued and shook everything around me. I ran, terrified, straight into the camera, tripping over the dolly tracks. Terry laughed and looked perplexed. "What happened?" he asked, as though I had just run screaming from a slow-moving merry-go-round. I couldn't breathe. It didn't seem possible that this could have been the plan, that things hadn't just gone terribly wrong.

But they hadn't. This was the plan. And I had just ruined the take. I was mortified. It took a long time to reset the take, and while Terry didn't show any frustration about the delay, he also didn't seem to notice how scared I was.

I had to do it again. I had to do it until I got it right. This time, before action was called, I went cold with fear, shaking. I could feel my heart thumping in the pit of my stomach. The blasts were deafening, terrifying. It felt like the world was collapsing underneath my feet, explosives going off in places I had just run right by. I felt as though I would be swallowed up whole by the torn-apart earth around me if I didn't run fast enough. In my panic, I now ran too fast for the camera to keep up with me. We had to do it again. During the next take, I wasn't running fast enough, my legs now as heavy as lead. I sobbed in my father's arms in between takes and pleaded with him to intervene, to ensure I didn't have to do it ever again. His arms in that moment felt safe. He held me close, soothing me. But when an assistant director came over to say they needed another take, my father said, with genuine remorse, "I'm afraid they have to do it again, love. I'm sorry. There's nothing I can do." And so I ran the gauntlet of explosives again. And again. And again.

There were many subsequent scenes in which explosives were used. They became a regular feature of my life, though one I never acclimated to. I began to stuff the cotton balls I was given by the special effects team deeper and deeper into my ears, hoping to drown out the sound just a little more. Sometimes it would take days to fish out the remnants of all the cotton balls I had pushed deep into my ear canals in anticipation of the explosions. I came to love the sound, so loud in my ears, of the tiny threads left behind by the cotton balls as they were pulled out, and I would compulsively fish around in my ears for them, even when they weren't there.

One scene involving explosives took place in a rowboat, which was placed in a giant tank of water to mimic the sea. Jack Purvis, Eric Idle,

Charles McKeown, Winston Dennis, and I were seated in the rowboat behind Angelo Ragusa (John Neville's stuntman), who sat
astride a large Arabian horse. As I remember it, in the scene, in which
the Baron is attacked in the water by cannon fire, a series of smallish
explosions were to go off beside the boat, followed by a larger explosive. As this last explosive was so powerful, it was placed deep underwater at the bottom of the tank. On the first take, the small explosions
scared the horse and it began backing up into us. Angelo forced it to
jump overboard into the water to save us from being trampled. As
the horse hit the bottom of the tank, its hooves pulled the larger
explosive up from the bottom of the tank. As it surfaced, it detonated
quite close to me.

I remember not hearing anything, Eric's terrified face, the crew looking
panicked at the edge of the tank. I remember a hard, crushing sensation
in my chest, and being carried towards an ambulance as the crew looked
on, alarmed. I remember many suction cups attached to my body as my
heart was monitored in a hospital, and my ears being examined. A nurse
pulled cotton out of my ears—both the new balls I'd placed in there
before the scene and the unretrieved little pieces of other balls that had
been buried in there for weeks. I remember that even when all the cotton had been pulled out, everything still sounded dim, muffled, and
would remain that way for a week or two. I remember that the doctors
were kind, that my parents were told there was nothing wrong with me,
and that I went back to work the next day.[1] The scenes with explosions
continued, each one terrifying me more than the last.

We shot quite a few scenes in that same giant tank of water, one in
front of a backdrop of a beautiful sky. We floated there, wetsuits under
our costumes, for long periods of time, shivering with cold, our wetsuits insufficient to keep us warm in the chilly water. Once, we shook
with cold in the tank for several hours, until Eric Idle yelled at Terry,
and I was taken out early. In another scene, I dangled from an anchor
from the underside of a boat that had become the Baron's hot-air

balloon. I was attached by a harness to a crane and hung high above the ground in the parking lot of the studio. I was very scared and at one point I screamed as I heard a loud ripping sound that I thought was my harness coming loose. It turned out to be a minor rip in my dress, but I became petrified of falling. Terry giggled at my fear, telling me I was fine. "Don't worry!" he yelled up. "We can't afford to lose you!" (I learned to hide my fear.) One day, my father told me he had over-heard Terry say to someone that his own daughter had inspired the character of Sally Salt and he would have cast her to play the part but he knew how terribly difficult the production would be and he didn't want to expose her to that difficulty. (It's unsettling to think this might have been true, and, to be honest, I have no idea if it was or if it was my dad's conjecture reframed as anecdote.)

The hours were crushingly long sometimes. I was under a Canadian union contract, but a representative from my union never once showed up on the set to check on me. One day, after many months of long hours and a gruelling production, I came into work staring at the ground, not an ounce of energy left in me. Terry asked me what was wrong. I wasn't my usual self, he said. I told him that I was tired. I was unable to stop the tears falling down my face. He asked me why I was so tired. He asked me what time I'd gone to bed the night before and what time I had woken up that morning. After I told him, he did a quick mental calcula-tion and said, "Well, you got seven or eight hours. That should be enough." He didn't say it meanly, it was just clear that he couldn't, for whatever reason, see how exhausted and burnt out I was. I spent many hours that day shooting a scene in the cold water of the ocean, shivering until a transportation driver intervened and carried me off set, wrapped in blankets, and into his warm car. Someone told me he was fired after that, though I have never verified what happened to him.

I started drinking coffee. A lot of it. When my dad was with me on set, he was fine with it; if my mom or my Auntie Ann (who sometimes acted as my guardian) was with me, I snuck it from the craft services truck. If

I had coffee in me, I knew I could do what was asked of me, even if my body was resistant. My heart might beat too fast, but at least I wouldn't fall asleep standing up.

One day I saw Uma crying behind a set piece. I had heard a few men jokingly talk about how drunk Oliver Reed had been the night before and how he "wouldn't leave her alone." I didn't know what this meant, but I was very aware that there was a vast distance between how scared and angry her eyes were and the jocular recounting of whatever had happened that I was hearing on set. One day on set I saw Oliver stomp, very hard, on her foot. She cried out, and tears filled her eyes. Because no one seemed surprised or tried to intervene, I thought it must have been a joke that had gone wrong. If it was a joke, I thought, adult jokes seemed scary, and I wanted no part of them.

(Many years later, I was more than a little dismayed to read in the *Hollywood Reporter* Terry's reframing of the dynamic between Oliver and Uma as he reminisced about the shoot: "She was all of 17, and I thought, 'Well, you can't beat this for Venus, that's for certain.' It worked out brilliantly. She was wonderful. When one thinks about it, there's Ollie Reed who's a real terror—a great actor but terrifying as a person—and she's a 17-and-a-half-year-old girl holding her own against him. I think her first scene was the rising in the shell. . . . I was so impressed because she could deal with Ollie, and it created a great relationship between the two of them because I think he was besotted with her.")

There was chaos, almost daily. Between the problems with the bond company, the producers, the studio, and Terry, the production always felt on the brink of disaster. And the chaos didn't stop there. A crew member became trapped between the legs of an enraged elephant during a battle scene and had to be rushed off to the hospital. A tiger, playing the Sultan's pet, tore through the set and crew.[2]

One night I awoke in my bed in the middle of the night to the sound
of an explosion. I ran, screaming, into my mother's room. There was
another explosion. My mother tried, fruitlessly, to calm me down, telling me that it was only a car backfiring. I didn't know what this meant;
I couldn't process what she was trying to tell me about the mechanics of
a car suddenly exploding and making such a terrifying noise. I only
knew that I was being assaulted by the sound of explosives again, as I
was so often during the day at work. My mother was unable to calm me.
It says something about her habitual patience and warmth that I was
alarmed, several hours later, when she became impatient with me and
told me she had to get some sleep. I had never experienced anything
but comfort from her when I was upset, at any hour of the night. She
didn't tell me that night that she felt sick, but I knew something in her
was changed. Soon after, my mother returned to Toronto, experiencing
the first waves of the cancer that would take her life three years later.

For a short time, my Auntie Ann took over my care, and on days off we
would knit or play Consequences, a storytelling game, for hours and
hours until the sun faded behind the ancient buildings outside our window. It wasn't until I was an adult that my Auntie Ann confessed how
frustrating it had been, after she had been so excited about living in
Rome for a few months (she already spoke fluent Italian), to sit in a
darkened sound studio during the week and just stare out the window at
the city all weekend long, unable to explore it or even go outside. I asked
her why she didn't make me go sightseeing with her, the way my parents
had on weekends. "Because you were a child and you were working
long hours, and you were exhausted and wanted to stay inside. You
needed nothing more asked of you."

After the production moved to Spain, I came down with an illness that
had me vomiting and feverish for days. I listened, through a haze, as my
aunt fought with my father, insisting that I couldn't work until I was
better. My father explained that the production would be moving to a
different location the very next day, and there was no choice but for me

to work. My father won. The next day, legs shaking, fever raging, I ran with hundreds of people out of the gates of the town, in the last scene in the film. The war against the Turks, which is the main struggle of the film, had been won. I had to look happy. And I did, between rounds of barfing. I saw my aunt crying, waiting for me off-camera with a blanket to wrap me in when the scene was finally over.

In my Christmas stocking that year I had found a palm-sized pink and green keyboard. It was a little plastic square with tiny cheap buttons on it that made musical notes. I would bring it to work with me and keep it in my hands right up until they rolled the camera. I could pretend I was somewhere else when I tried to make music, somewhere other than in a giant battle scene, or about to submerge into a freezing tank of water, or in a giant mob of a wartime scene, or about to run through explosions, or in a dusty studio filled with desert sand on my fifteenth hour of work that day. One day Eric, who was watching me closely as I played on my tiny little cheap keyboard, said, "Do you have a real keyboard?" I said, huffily, "This *is* a real keyboard."

The following weekend, Eric called my family and asked if we could come over to his apartment. When we got there, there was a brand-new synthesizer keyboard for me with a bow on it. And Robin Williams. I didn't know until that moment that Robin Williams was to play the part of the King of the Moon. I was a huge fan of *Mork & Mindy* and I felt weak with happiness to get to be in his presence. I spent the day with Robin and Eric. Robin programmed himself doing different voices on all the effects keys, so I could play whole songs entirely in his voice. That day we walked around Rome, ate gelato, and went to the Vatican and St. Peter's Square while Robin did impressions of the Pope and kept me laughing all day. From that day forward, both Eric and Robin seemed to have an agenda to make light moments for me. When it was possible, when the world around us wasn't exploding and crumbling and freezing, they made up games for me, sang songs, and treated the set as a playground.

And then: a miracle. Production was shut down. The film had gone wildly over budget; there were vicious fights between the producers, the studio, and Terry. It was finally time to go home. I was suddenly safe back in my suburban Canadian home, away from the mayhem, thrilled to be back at school and to never work again. I had asked for photos of my bedroom to be sent to me in Rome, which I had stared at longingly for months. And now here I was, back home in my small room with my floral wallpaper, my books and stuffed animals, my old frayed bedspread.

I was devastated to receive the news, just three weeks later, that an agreement had been reached between the producers, Terry, and the studio. The production resumed. I went back to Europe, and it was months before I would come home again.

When the film was finally released into the world, it came out with a deafening thud. It was a bomb for the ages, right up there with *Heaven's Gate* in terms of ill-fated, budget-bloated failures. One of the most expensive movies that had ever been made had become a victim of political wrangling and vendettas at the studio. The film was too closely associated with outgoing executive David Puttnam, who was leaving Columbia Pictures on bad terms, and the release was purposefully botched. I was stunned that after about $46 million spent, horror endured and survived, and a pretty great movie made, a production's fate could be reduced to the outcome of a petty studio squabble.

For the German release, I was invited to Munich. One of my stranger press obligations was to appear in *Stars in der Manege* (Stars in the Circus), an annual televised circus in front of a live audience in which celebrities performed circus acts. For my act, I hid in a large basket. Plácido Domingo ordered a woman into the basket with me and then stuck five swords through it. The other woman and I, twisted up together in the small basket, guided the swords slowly and carefully past our faces and legs through to the other side. Plácido then removed the swords, opened the basket, and the other woman jumped out, unscathed, to thunderous applause. Then, shocking the audience, who had not known I was in there, I popped out after her. Plácido Domingo sang me an aria from three feet away. Not knowing who he was or what the hell was happening generally at that point, I assumed he was lip-synching to a very loud recording. I had just never heard anyone sing so loudly. This, by the way, is the closest I have come to the experience of being on an acid trip.

After the circus performance (which my mother couldn't attend at the last minute because of her increasingly severe cancer symptoms), my father and I were ushered into a car. Autograph seekers mobbed us. They had no idea who I was or what I was doing there, but I was part of the show and so they wanted a signature on their programs. As we got into the car, people started reaching into the car after me, and in a panic my dad closed the car door on someone's arm. At that moment, I was inoculated against wanting to be famous.

Terry Gilliam came to Toronto for the Canadian release of the film. My father called him and arranged a dinner for the three of us at Terry's hotel. My father was delighted to have this time with Terry, and took over the conversation with jokes and theatre stories. I sat there, sidelined and fuming. At one point my dad went to the washroom, and Terry said to me, "Let's go on an adventure." We snuck through the hotel's kitchen, trying not to be spotted, went through any door that said "Staff Only," and broke as many rules as possible in a twenty-minute period. We found our way into a ballroom and played the grand piano together, Terry grinning at me. It was a silent, kind acknowledgment of how I had been cut out of the adult conversation at the table, and an empathetic solution to an awkward problem. Finally, we went back to the table, to rejoin my bewildered father.

I confronted my dad on the way home about monopolizing the conversation. "*I* was the one who worked with him for eight months. *Not you!* You never even let me get a word in!"

My father was mortified, and apologized profusely. He asked if he should set up another dinner with Terry. He promised he would let me speak this time. I rejected the offer, but I've always remembered how he took responsibility for this infraction. It is possible that it stands out for me because he never took responsibility for what he didn't protect me from on the production itself, but I think it's mostly because it was a striking offering of apology and non-defensiveness that took me aback. It made me feel at once grateful for the acknowledgment and guilty for confronting him.

When I was in my mid-twenties, I met a nine-year-old actress on a film set I was acting on, who I will call Sandra. Sandra's mother, who I will call Jessica, clearly had big ambitions for her kid. Like almost all parents of child actors I've met, she made jokes about being an "evil stage parent" in order to create separation between herself and the stereotype she was aware she might be cast in. It was clear that Jessica got a lot out of the success of her very talented child. She had wanted to act herself when she was younger and was now a stay-at-home mom who managed her child's career. She became a helpful part of the crew on set, pitching in wherever she could on the low-budget production we were working on, and I liked her. I had many conversations with her about being a child actor, which sometimes became awkward when I said things she didn't want to hear.

One day, she emailed me to let me know that her daughter was very close to landing a part in Terry Gilliam's new film, *Tideland*, which would be shooting in Canada. Was there anything I could do to help or put in a good word for Sandra? I gagged when I read the email. I told

her how big a mistake I thought it would be for Sandra (who I happened
to be very fond of) to work on a Terry Gilliam production. I told her
again the stories I had told her already about my experiences on *The
Adventures of Baron Munchausen* and how lightly my safety and sense of
security had been taken. None of it got through to her. Her excitement
at the opportunity for her child continued unabated. In a panic, I finally
wrote to Terry about my experiences working with him, hoping it might
spare another kid from the kind of traumatizing experience I had had.
Here is our email exchange.

Hi there Terry
I hear you're making a film in saskatchewan this summer. i hope
you have a great time - there are some great crew people you'll
probably be using from Winnipeg who got into making films because
of you. (it's actually pretty bizarre - i worked out there this winter
and at least 5 people told me that Baron Munchausen was the film that
made them choose to be in film.)
I guess i just wanted to touch base and share a few things about
my experience working on that movie. I know you'll be working
with a young girl and i realize we've never had a chance to talk
about that time - or i guess i mean i haven't communicated to you
what my experiences were, or how i remember them now, or how
i feel they affected me. I know you've heard varying reports (i can't
remember who told me that) and i realize that it's not really fair for
me to not communicate it all to you directly. especially since the only
people who i hold responsible (and who, by definition, were supposed
to be responsible) were my parents.
Basically, I remember being afraid a lot of the time. I felt incredibly unsafe. I remember a couple of trips to the hospital after being
in freezing water for long periods of time, losing quite a bit of my
hearing for days at a time due to explosives, having my heart monitored when one went off relatively close to me, etc. I remember
running through this long sort of corridor where explosives went
off every few feet, things were on fire, etc. i cried hysterically in my

dad's lap and begged him to make sure i wouldn't have to do it again, but I did. I think i did it quite a few more times. I remember the terrifying scene where we were in the boat and the horse jumped out and ended up surfacing a plastic explosive that went off right under my face. i remember being half trampled by a mob of extras and then repeating the scene several times. i remember working very long hours.

i know i had some fun as well, but it's pretty much obliterated by the sense of fear and exhaustion and of not being protected by the adults around me. And again, the adults who should have been there to protect me were my parents, not you. This of course took some time to arrive at. I admit i was pretty furious at you for a lot of years.

what i went through is nothing compared to what many kids in the world suffer. but it certainly was unusual for a middle-class kid in toronto and it hardened and isolated me for many years i think. it also created a pretty substantial lack of trust in my parents (again, not your fault, but a byproduct of the experience).

this - contrary to how it may read - is not meant to be a guilt trip. you were always fun and fascinating and you gave me a ton of confidence. you're a genius and it was a privilege (no matter what my age) to watch you make a great film. I think that film was hell for you too and you had enough responsibility just keeping it going without having to be a parent to someone else's child. I believe that you felt that if there was something that was particularly traumatic to me that my parents would have informed you and pulled the plug. of course this is what should have happened on many occasions. i don't think my parents were monsters by any stretch of the imagination. i do think, though, that you can't underestimate how in awe of you people like them can be. i think they were so shocked and thrilled to have their daughter in a Terry Gilliam movie that they couldn't see past that. they didn't want to be an annoyance or an inconvenience to anyone and it must have been daunting to imagine holding up 100 people for your kid.

so here's my point. who knows who you'll cast and what their parents will be like. my suspicion is that you might need to be constantly analyzing whether you would put your own nine-year-old in the positions you'll be putting this kid in. because it's entirely likely that the child's own parents will be (for whatever reason) incapable of making the right call. this is a huge responsibility but i'm starting to think (from watching other kids and parents) that this is a fundamental part of the job when you're working with kids who should really be in school anyway.

here's some unsolicited advice:

try to keep a close eye on the mood of the kid, ask them a lot of questions about how they're doing, if they want to stop doing what they're doing, etc. if they seem uncomfortable, afraid, take it upon yourself to make the call as to whether or not it's best to stop or keep going.

if there are water scenes in this one - make sure it's warm!!!! if there are explosions in this one - i really can't emphasize enough how much better it would be if you could do reaction shots separate from the explosions themselves. I still duck when a car door slams too close or too loud.

i know it's probably a sucky way to shoot it - but it might save you another e-mail like this one.

sorry for the babbling. i just realized i wasn't doing either of us any favours by not letting you know this stuff. and i really think you're a decent person so hearing this might have an impact without being too alienating (i hope).

good luck with the film. i know it'll be brilliant.

sarah polley

He wrote me back the very next day.

Sarah,

Ever since I started this Canadian project your name has been at the forefront of most of my Toronto conversations. Every potential crew member I interview ends up including you in the chat. You are ubiquitous. How many people get that adjective thrown at them? I also hear you are about to start your first film as director. Congratulations. You've done brilliantly. You've continued to be a wonderful actress and I'm certain you'll handle the directing business just as well.

As far as the scars of *Munchausen* go, I had no idea that they were
that deep. What always impressed me from my side of the camera was
how professional you were . . . always prepared and willing to dive
into anything, no matter how difficult, that we organized (possibly
that should read, disorganized). In fact, I started taking for granted
that you could always be counted on, unlike some of the adults. You
seemed so focused, I had no idea you were having such a terrifying
time. For what it's worth, we were always concerned to make things
safe for you (you were too valuable to the production to allow anything
to happen to you). Although things might have seemed to be dangerous, they weren't. The only time events got close to trouble was when
the horse jumped from the boat. We all were terrified, however I knew
that Angelo Raguzzo [sic] was one of the most brilliant horsemen I had
ever seen and that he would make sure none of you in the boat were
harmed. Nevertheless the explosion was a fuckup and I apologize.

One thing I'm curious about. Can you tell, when you see Sally
in the film, in which of the shots it's you . . . and which ones are your
double? Do you remember that the shots of you in the boat were right
at the edge of the tank with stuntmen in the water next to the boat?
I only ask, not to minimize your bad memories, but to try to understand the differences in the way you and I remember the events . . .
especially since you were so young and impressionable and sensitive
and yet seemed to be so wise and about 30 years old.

Luckily, for the girl in the film we are starting, there are no
physically dangerous or terrifying scenes. I grant you there are some
disturbing ones for adults but I don't think so for her. Like you, she is
in every scene. It's her film. She's nine years old and has been acting
since she was four. Extraordinary! Luckily for her, I'm much older
now. And a lot more tired. Possibly a bit more wise as well. And I will
take to heart your suggestions.

Thanks for making contact. Hopefully, next time I'm in Toronto
we can manage a dinner together. I'm curious to learn who you are now.

Terry

hi terry

thanks a lot for getting back to me. i do know in retrospect that
many things that terrified me were not as terrifying as they seemed
then. (and i definitely remember that the boat was in a tank.) - and i'm
pretty sure i know which shots were the double. however - it does raise
a question of what i remember vs. what happened. it's like this with
photographs. whole memories get built around them, which is sometimes a reflection of a general sense of things as they felt at the time
as opposed to what actually occurred. so i'm willing to accept that my
impressions may have been unlike what an adult might have. i think
that's sort of the point. it wasn't a good environment for a kid because
there were things that could easily be interpreted as dangerous without
actually being dangerous. i think it's harder to make those distinctions
as a child, and i didn't have a lot of support in trying to make them.
the really traumatic things that happened are distinct memories
that gave me nightmares well before the film came out so confusion
between what the stunt double was doing as opposed to me didn't
really play into my bad memories i don't think.

i really appreciate you responding. i wasn't sure how you'd react.
i hope the film goes really well. i'd love to get together when you are
next in toronto. i've really appreciated this exchange.

Sarah

In the end, Sandra wasn't cast in *Tideland*. Another child was. When
she found out that her daughter did not get the part, Jessica went
into a state of grief so irrational that she turned to me for comfort. She
was devastated by, among other things, the fact that Sandra's university education would now not be paid for. She mentioned in her email
to me that Sandra herself didn't seem at all upset by the rejection.
I suggested to Jessica that she might want to take her cues from her
daughter in terms of how to react to the news that she wouldn't be
in *Tideland*, which I believed was actually a great stroke of luck.
Until this exchange, I hadn't realized how deep the delusional roots
were in many parents whose children work in film. Even faced with

a first-hand account of a terrible experience, Jessica was able to justify risking putting her child, whom she clearly loved, in harm's way, and then, when that didn't come to pass, turning for comfort to the person who had warned her against it.

When *Tideland* was released, the *Globe and Mail* published an article called "Twinkle, Twinkle Little Star." It was about *Tideland* and its ten-year-old Canadian star Jodelle Ferland. It also touched upon Terry Gilliam's past use of a Canadian child actress, and speculated that perhaps it was no coincidence that Gilliam had used a young Canadian girl more than once.

The writer, Gayle MacDonald, wrote, "Filmmakers like Gilliam keep coming to the Canadian talent trough for child actors because our kids, by all accounts, tend to be easy to direct, manage and mould. Chalk it up to our easygoing, accommodating national character."

Unsettled by MacDonald's framing, I asked for Terry's permission to publish our email exchange as part of an article I wrote for the *Toronto Star* in response to MacDonald's piece, and, to his credit, without hesitation he agreed. (One of the things I still admire about Terry is this lack of fear, this lack of an instinct to hide and protect himself from exposure or attack. I think most people would have refused to let their emails be published this way.) I wrote the following conclusion to the piece:

At a film festival event a few weeks ago, I saw Terry for the first time in 17 years. We had a friendly chat and spoke about Jodelle. He said, "She had a great time, you could tell she really loved it, she knows this is what she wants to do, and she was happy to be there . . ."

"Then again," he said, "I remember thinking the same thing about you . . . that's why I was so surprised to get your emails." He looked confused.

It would have been difficult for anyone to see how unhappy I was at the time. Like many kids, I was eager to please and good at adapting to difficult situations, storing them away to unpack later. When it came time to publicize

The Adventures of Baron Munchausen, I spoke glowingly of Terry and making the film.

In every interview I've read with Jodelle Ferland, she talks about shooting Tideland as a very positive experience. Though she is still a child, I think it's important to respect her impressions of her own film-set experiences, as they stand now. Yet, based on my own experiences, I'm curious about whether her impressions will change. Perhaps I'll drop her a line in a decade or two to find out.

I wrote this conclusion to the article in another time, in another political climate. Here's what I left out: When Terry first saw me at that film festival event, he grabbed my shirt "playfully," turned me around, tried to pull it up and said, "Come on—show me the scars! Where are the scars?!" I actually have a really long scar on my spine from scoliosis surgery, and, not understanding that he was speaking in metaphor, I said, "Um. It's right there."

I asked him how Jodelle Ferland had fared on set. I told him I had called my union to ask them to visit the set often to check on her, given my own experience with him. He laughed and said, "They came once or twice. She was great and we worked overtime a lot. No one paid much attention!"

I felt sick to my stomach. Despite my emailed pleas to him to be careful with children, a big part of me knew, deep down, that he was a writeoff when it came to taking any responsibility. But I was furious at the adults whose job it was to protect this kid. I was angry that I had called our union, told them that a child was heading into a potentially dangerous situation, that I had been put in harm's way many times by this same director, and yet they had done so little to make sure Jodelle was okay and not working long hours that their absence had been noticed even by Terry.

I had shown my dad the emails with Terry when we had originally exchanged them, and he had had a typically intellectual, removed response. We'd had conversations before about the terrible times on *Munchausen*, so he wasn't particularly surprised or offended. But when my piece was published in the *Toronto Star* and his friends read it and expressed how upsetting he must have found it, he became embarrassed, and then angry. He was horrified at being portrayed as a stage parent who had let his child come into harm's way, and he suddenly denied that any of it was true. After listening to a tirade about how angry he was, as he drove me home from a family dinner one night, I told him that it would be meaningful and perhaps even transformative if he would just apologize and admit that he hadn't protected me the way he should have. He said, "Well—I'm sorry. I'm sorry you feel upset and remember things that way and that we have such different memories of what happened." I told him that that wasn't an apology, got out of the car, and slammed the door. It was the last conversation we would have about it directly, but years later, as I cared for him after a surgery, he watched me, drugged on Demerol, and said, "You're a marvellous girl, you know. Considering you never really had a mother. Or a father." I turned away from him and wiped my tears away before he could see them.

When I was in my late twenties, an assistant director on a film I was acting in said to me, "Our special effects guy really wants to introduce himself to you, but he's scared you might hate him. He did the special effects on *Baron Munchausen*."

Later that day, when I reintroduced myself to special effects icon Richard Conway, who I hadn't seen since I was a child, his eyes filled with tears. He said, "I'm sorry. I'm so sorry about what happened to you on that movie."

I replied, in earnest, "What *did* happen to me?"

"A lot of things happened. A lot of things went wrong," he said. "Everyone in my job carries around an image that haunts them of something that went wrong at work. For me, it's the look on your face as you were carried out of the water tank and into the ambulance after the explosive surfaced so close to you. You were crying. No—you weren't crying. You were screaming, actually. You were hysterical. Screaming in terror."

We were silent for a long time. He said, "When the smaller explosives went off and the horse spooked and backed up towards you and the rider took it overboard, I yelled at Terry to cut. He refused. He just yelled at me, reached past me, ripped the detonator trigger out of my hand, and set off the explosive himself. And you were leaning over and it went off very close to you."

As Richard and I got to know one another better, he suggested we watch the movie together. "It would be a kind of exorcism, maybe. For both of us." Neither of us had watched the film in many years, fearful of how it would make us feel. One evening after wrap, we watched it together at the hotel. During the scenes that had been most terrifying to shoot, my breath caught in my throat. Richard, hearing the click of my breath stopping, said, "Can we hold hands?" I reached for his hand and held it tight. During the scene in the boat, I felt him squeeze my hand harder, and turned to see tears streaming down his face. "I'm so, so sorry," he said. I hugged him, so grateful for the apology, even though I didn't think it was his to make.

At one point, as the Baron and Sally make their way up into the sky on their way to the moon, we found ourselves marvelling at the artistry of the film, the hand-painted backgrounds, the meticulously crafted analogue illusions. As the Baron and Sally sail through a sky of perfect clouds, Richard said, "I spent weeks with my crew making those clouds by hand. No one gets to do anything like that anymore. No one gets to feel what it's like to create a magic image with your own hands.

Since CGI, it's all a lost art." We watched as Eric Idle, John Neville, and I climbed along the edge of a perfect crescent moon, watched horses and fish and scorpions materialize out of the stars, watched as we were swallowed whole and stayed intact in the belly of a sea creature, watched Uma and John Neville waltz into the air of an underground palace dotted with fountains. We watched together in wonder, holding hands until the end.

In 2018, when Terry was in the middle of a firestorm of controversy over comments he had made about the #MeToo movement, someone tweeted out the old email exchange between Terry and me as evidence of his subpar character. In response, Eric Idle, who I hadn't heard from since I was a child, tweeted a response:

"She was right. She was in danger. Many times. It was amazing we never lost anyone. It was me, her and Jack Purvis in the back of the boat. The explosion scared the horse which backed into us, and the brilliant rider took it overboard."

She was right. She was in danger. Many times. I read these nine words over and over again. Someone *who was there* was appearing from out of nowhere to confirm my memories and verify my version of events.

I swear it was around that time that I stopped ducking for cover when I heard the sudden noise of a car door slam.

SALLY: *Baron Munchausen isn't real, he's only in stories.*
BARON MUNCHAUSEN: *Go away! I'm trying to die!*
SALLY: *Why?*

BARON MUNCHAUSEN: Because I'm tired of the world and the
world is evidently tired of me.
SALLY: But why? Why?
BARON MUNCHAUSEN: Why, why, why! Because it's all logic
and reason now. Science, progress, laws of hydraulics, laws of
social dynamics, laws of this, that, and the other. No place for
three-legged cyclops in the South Seas. No place for cucumber
trees and oceans of wine. No place for me.

Because he was so childlike and full of genuine wonder, it was hard
for me, for many years, to see how responsible Terry Gilliam was for
the terror of being on that set. And so I blamed my parents more than
I should have, or perhaps I just didn't distribute my anger fairly to
include Terry. I'm struck by how many times in my emails to him I
make sure to tell him I don't hold him responsible and lay the blame
at my parents' feet. I think, at the time that I wrote these emails, I
didn't hold him responsible because I didn't think he *could* be. The
whole concept of "mad genius" that I had absorbed involved a necessary abdication of responsibility, empathy, and conscientiousness in
favour of erratic flashes of brilliance that I assumed had to coexist
with an obliviousness to other people's pain. On the back cover of the
book *Losing the Light* by Andrew Yule, which chronicles the disasters
of the *Munchausen* production, Terry is quoted as saying: "I think my
priorities are right. I will sacrifice myself or anyone else for the movie.
It will last. *We'll* all be dust." For so long, a certain glamour has come
along with this single-minded pursuit of a great film at any cost.

And yet no matter how much I thought about him over the years, Terry
still stubbornly lived in my memory primarily as someone who was
brilliant and who had also had that look in his eye that is most precious
to children: the look that immediately says, "I'm glad you're here."
Because he had never really removed himself from a state of childhood
himself, he was just like a playmate with a very large stash of expensive,

dangerous toys. It sometimes just felt like our playdate had careered wildly out of control, and I just didn't know who I could turn to, to tell on him when things got too scary and too many rules had been broken. *He didn't seem to have any parents.*

I think the truth is that I let Terry off the hook in part because, even as a child, I had bought into the glamour of the idea of the *enfant terrible* director, the out-of-control mad white male genius—a mythology that has dominated the film industry's understanding of what brilliance must necessarily look like. I have, throughout my life, witnessed many crews and read many film writers go out of their way to interpret the out-of-control dysregulated behaviour of certain men as a symptom of genius, or a colourful detail to make the story of the making of a film more interesting. In my years as an actor, I often saw young white male filmmakers even putting on *false* eccentricity and temper, as though that would make them more credible as an artist. It's so pervasive, this idea that genius can't come without trouble, that it has paved the way for countless abuses. As an adult, I find myself wholly intolerant of the fetishization of this archetype of genius, having seen, first-hand, great works made by decent, conscientious people, and having witnessed sharp impatience with female or BIPOC filmmakers who show any similar signs of irresponsibility. Terry lived for so long in the film world's imagination as a "mad genius" whose madness and recklessness somehow elevated his work. As the Baron says, when confronted with reality: *"Your 'reality,' sir, is lies and balderdash, and I'm delighted to say that I have no grasp of it whatsoever."* It's a wonderfully seductive line, but one that only a privileged white straight man could live by without devastating consequences.

(I believe there is reason to hope that these accepted norms of behaviour are beginning to change, at least within the film industry, as post-#MeToo standards begin to be enforced, and as expectations grow that people will be treated with more respect and dignity.)

I don't blame my parents as much as I used to, understanding more now how hard it would be to stand up and stop an enormous production under dire financial and time pressures, even if it was for the sake of a child. As the years go on and Terry makes more and more comments that demonstrate not just a childlike incapacity for understanding grown-up problems but a willful dismissal of movements that seek to claim equality and acknowledgment for past harms, I see him, and the role he played in the mayhem we were all trapped in back then, differently. I see it in the context of a cultural phenomenon of what many white men have been allowed to get away with in the name of art. Though he was magical, and brilliant, and made images and stories that will live for a long, long time, it's hard to calculate whether they were worth the price of the hell that so many went through over the years to help him make them.

Recently, my brother Johnny told me a story that my mom had shared with him years ago. She was on the set of *The Adventures of Baron Munchausen* with me, holding me in her arms. She had seen an ambulance parked at the end of a route I was to run down. She told the production team that she refused to let me do the shot. She described me being literally lifted out of her arms by an assistant director while she cried. As I ran down the route, explosives went off all around me, and she saw my small body disappearing into the chaos. My brother said that when she recounted the story, she kept saying, "They took her out of my arms. They grabbed her and lifted her right out of my arms while I cried."

I am glad to know this story. Glad to know that she had fought for me, glad to know that she had tried to say no, glad to know that there were moments I didn't remember or wasn't aware of (perhaps many of them) when my parents hadn't fallen like dominoes in front of the challenge of protecting me. Even if it had been just that once, my mother had tried not to let me go. And even if this story she told (which I have no memory of) never really happened, she had at least felt the necessity to construct it. Perhaps that shouldn't count for much, but it does.

In 2008 I acted in a movie called *Mr. Nobody*, directed by the great Belgian director Jaco Van Dormael. He was, in a sense, the opposite of Terry Gilliam in every way, apart from his similar childlike wonder, imagination, and visual genius. We worked short hours. Crew members brought their kids to set. Jaco cared deeply about his collaborators, knew them and their families intimately, and had saint-like reserves of empathy. Within a few weeks of long conversations, Jaco and I knew a lot about each other's lives.

In one scene, I was to sit beside another actor in the front seat of a car while a fire effect was blasted towards the windshield to create the impression of a car accident. Jaco and the cinematographer, Christophe Beaucarne, would be behind us in the car, getting the shot from over our shoulders. I found myself shaking before the shot, as I do before almost any special effects shot I have been in since I was eight years old. Jaco, perhaps noticing my shaky body language, asked me if I would like to see the effect before we shot it. Would I like to see him get into my place in the car while the fire effect happened, to know that it was safe? I nodded. He got in, the fire was blasted. It looked safe, but I could feel its heat even from where I was standing, quite a few feet away. I nodded again and headed for my place in the car. Jaco said, "Sarah, you are so pale." I shook my head. I knew it would be fine. He had done it himself. He would be in the back of the car. There was really nothing to fear here. He said, "Are you scared?" I said, "Very. But I know it's okay and I want you to get the shot." He told me that he didn't want me to do it if it was going to scare me. I told him I'd feel terrible if I didn't do it when it was a risk he himself was willing to take, alongside the other actor and the cinematographer. It would be absurd for me to refuse to do it. "All of you are fine with it," I said. He put his hand on my shoulder and said, gently, "But none of us were in *The Adventures of Baron Munchausen* when we were children." I was silent for a while. He said, "I'll find another way to shoot this. You're not going to do this."

I felt deeply ashamed and told him so. He said, "If this film is everything we want it to be, maybe, if we are very lucky, it will affect two or three people for a little while. The only thing that is *certain* is that the experience of making it will be with all of us, it will become a part of us, forever. So we must try our best to make it a good experience. It's the most important thing." He put his arm around me, ushered me away from set, and found a new way to shoot the scene. As we walked away from the set, something in me that had been stuck came loose.

So much of coming to terms with hard things from the past seems to be about believing our own accounts, having our memories confirmed by those who were there and honoured by those who weren't. Why is it so hard for us to believe our own stories or begin to process them without corroborating witnesses appearing from the shadows of the past, or without people stepping forward with open arms when echoes of those stories present themselves again in the present?

A few years ago, I travelled back to Rome. I sat on the cobblestones at the far end of Largo dei Librari. The store where I used to buy my little chocolate ice cream balls had closed a long time ago. Now there were tables and chairs filling the small square, and tourists eating in the open air. I looked over their heads to the apartment we had lived in for those months in 1988. The air in the square had the same smell. Centuries old. Romantic and disgusting. As though something was rotting, beautifully. I wondered if the tourists could smell it too.

The other day, Eve again raised the idea of watching *The Adventures of Baron Munchausen*. Eve is now the exact age I was when I made the film. (Aila declined to join us. "Maybe when I'm nine.")

As we watch, I find myself, many times, grateful for the comparatively predictable, boring nature of my children's childhood. At nine, there have been no great adventures for Eve, and no great traumas. After ten minutes of fires and explosions in the film's opening, Eve says: "When you made movies, back in the olden days, did they paint in the fires and explosions, or were they actually there, for real?" When I say they were real, Eve gasps. "I wouldn't have wanted to be in movies back then. It looks scary." Eve is captivated by the film, and finds it hilarious, mesmerizing, and strange to see how much we look alike. Halfway through, when the characters' lives are in danger for the eighth or ninth time, Eve gets scared and wants to stop watching. Just before I press the power button, Eve grabs the remote from me and says, "Actually let's watch to the end. I have to know if it turns out okay."

It does. When we arrive at the last scene, there I am, smiling in a crowd of hundreds of people. The war is won, the adventure over. Sally Salt can now go back to her regular life, and the Baron says goodbye, giving her a rose (somewhat reluctantly) to thank her for being such a loyal sidekick.

If I try, I can conjure up the feeling of what it was like to shoot that last scene; that harrowing day, when I was so ill and forced to work anyway. But the memory loses its power in the presence of my child's delight at having discovered a joyful ending, worth waiting for.

Dissolving
the
Boundaries

When my third child, Amy, is nine weeks old I have a dream. In the dream I am walking on a beach in Prince Edward Island. Eve, who is six years old at this time, holds my hand. The white sand stretches beyond us into the distance, where the beach melts into soft dunes, long grass growing precariously off the edges and swaying gently in the breeze. The sun is shining, the sky an impossible periwinkle blue. Eve looks up at me with a face full of joy. Later in the day, we find ourselves in a narrow hallway in a dark, claustrophobic hotel and decide we were better off outside.

Later in the dream, we go to a red sand beach. The sun is hot and orange and lower in the sky. I can't make out where the sand and cliffs end and where the boiling, menacing sky begins. My child is still beside me but with a heavier expression. Eve is not exactly unhappy, but we both feel trepidation now; the feeling of uninhibited freedom we had on the first beach is gone. We are both conscious that our togetherness has an added importance and weight now that our surroundings have abandoned their previous perfection. I hear the words "dissolve the boundaries" over and over again.

When I wake up from the dream, I say to my husband David, "I wish we could go to PEI. If we could get on a plane right now, I would."

As soon as the words escape my mouth I realize what is going to happen. This is the kind of far-fetched wish that David hears as a challenge. "Let's do it," he says. He goes to his computer, and despite my half-hearted protest that he be practical, he figures out a way to get us to

Prince Edward Island the next day, through two connecting flights on points.

This plan, to jump on a plane to PEI the very next day, makes no sense. David begins his first position as a professor at a law school next week, after almost a decade of work on a doctorate. We are sitting in mountains of laundry from a car trip up north that we returned from just last night, and we have a plan for every day of the next week before our two oldest children begin their school year.

This is exactly the kind of squishy scenario that David sees as an opportunity to prove we are alive by doing the most irrational, spontaneous thing possible. He has always been romantic like this, since we first met briefly, when we were fourteen years old. It's one of the most thrilling things about him, and it can create a kind of havoc that I sometimes struggle to enjoy.

I send off apologetic emails to friends and begin the brain-jamming process of packing for five people. We have a tiny new baby, we've never travelled with all three children, and we have other plans. This isn't like me, to go along with a spontaneous plan like this. I usually like to rehearse, in my mind, all the possible ways things could go wrong when we travel. When we go anywhere, in fact. But I know that we should go on this trip. There isn't a doubt in my mind. I feel uncomfortable admitting that this uncharacteristic certainty I am in possession of is owing to the dream I've had.

I've been paying attention to my dreams lately. After twenty years in psychoanalysis and psychotherapy, I'm used to noticing them, their smoke signals from the past drawing my attention to burned-out wreckage in a distant forest of the mind, packed and buried under years of debris, still smouldering. But lately I've also started to see dreams as guides, pointing the way forward. A dream brought us this third child who lies beside me now, as I imagine writing this, a newborn nursing through the night, opening her eyes occasionally, sensing it is not day yet, and then going back to sleep.

We had made a firm decision a couple of years ago not to have a third child. The two children we already had were full of energy and challenges to our endurance. But one night I had a dream that a beautiful little baby named Amy watched us walk away from her small cot in a hospital room, wondering who we were and why we had to leave her behind. I woke up crying nonsensically that we couldn't leave baby Amy. And now, Amy is here, and the energy we lacked before we have somehow mustered, and the frenetic energy of our older two children has been quelled somewhat. Amy has calmed us all down, and made us superstitious. While we may have been cynical before, now we try to read the stars, knowing what they brought us.

I take a break from packing for the trip to PEI and check my email. A friend has sent me a link to a new posting from the CBC Archives entitled "When PEI Welcomed Road to Avonlea's Sarah Polley." I shudder, both at the memory and at the eerie coincidence of her sending this to me now, just as we have decided to go to the Island. I watch the clip, an almost thirty-year-old news item about my visit there to promote the TV show I was in, which was based on some of Lucy Maud Montgomery's books, including *The Story Girl*. At the time, it was the highest-rated show in Canada, topping *Hockey Night in Canada*. I was often recognized when I walked down the street, on my way to school or out with friends. I found it agonizing. From the age of ten onward, I tried to avoid being noticed. When I was a teenager, my desire to disappear became even more pronounced. I wore baggy clothes, hunched myself over, and kept my eyes firmly on the ground. (For the most part, this never really changed.) I avoided groups of adolescent girls, especially. Groups of wholesome-looking girls, home-schooled, virtuous, or overly innocent, were sure to be fans of the

show and would ask me for autographs. Groups of girls like me—
cynical, brutally honest, uncompromising—would be sure to laugh
at me. Many times I'd pass a group of girls on a busy street in downtown Toronto, notice I had caught their attention, and quicken my
pace. "SARAH!" I'd hear yelled from a distance. I'd turn around and
they would laugh. I didn't blame them, particularly. It's what I would
have done at that age. But it smarted to be so intensely associated with
something that didn't represent anything about who I was.

By Grade 8, the precocious kids at the arts school I attended had long
since stopped being impressed that I was in a television show. My boyfriend, who wore a cape, fashioned himself as a kind of suburban Jim
Morrison, and was playing Hamlet in scene studies, said to me one day,
"Someone asked me the other day if I thought you were a good actor,
and I said, 'I don't really think I've ever seen Sarah act.'"

The activity that took up every waking hour I had for eight months
of the year was not thought of as acting by my peers. It was just an
embarrassment.

When I was in Grade 9, one of the Grade 12 students asked if I would
take part in a skit for the school assembly. It was thrilling, being called
upon by one of the older cool kids. The day before the assembly I was
informed that the skit was entitled "The Top Ten Things About Going
to Earl Haig Secondary School." I would be number ten, and when I
appeared onstage, the plan was for a bunch of kids in the audience to
throw peanuts at me. I pretended I was sick the next day, to avoid the
humiliation, and I was later berated for letting down the student council.

These weren't traumatic events, and as I look them over now they
read like a list of minor sob stories. I tell these stories only to illus-
trate that it was not modesty or a tendency towards shyness that made
me uninterested in fame at the time. The notoriety I received for the
show I was in actually humiliated me.

I stare at the CBC footage of my childhood visit to PEI. I am twelve years old. I look tired. "She confesses it's tiring," the voice-over says. I look tired in almost every interview I gave as a child. I say the right things, the nice things I am supposed to say. But I can see in my eyes a weariness, a wateriness, and a sense of betrayal. As the CBC clip says, "The crowds built all weekend." Everywhere I went, there were hordes of people. I participated in some kind of parade where I sat alone in the rumble seat of an old-fashioned convertible and waved at the crowds. I sat in shopping malls for hours as people lined up for my autograph; I would look up and see them hanging over the balconies and nauseously try to calculate how long it would be before they would reach me. I gave readings at Green Gables, the fictional home of Anne. Busloads of tourists crowded in to hear me read passages from *The Story Girl*, the book upon which the series was based, and get autographs. There were always questions from the audience, and once a little boy asked, "How come on the show you look so pretty and now . . . you don't?" I tried to laugh it off and come up with a witty answer. Before I could, the publicist, who was also my guardian for the duration of the trip, leaned over and whispered into my ear, "Makeup. Say it's because of makeup." This is the answer I gave and instantly felt bad about.

One day, the publicity team took me to a beach so I could have a break between the press obligations. I took a long walk by myself, taking in the extraordinary expanses of undeveloped white beach in Cavendish. There were lots of people there that day, sunbathing, splashing in the waves, and building sandcastles with their kids. When I had almost reached the far end of the beach, I heard a shuffling noise behind me. Many of the people I had passed on my walk had risen and followed me like silent zombies.

I've told this story a few times in my life, when people ask me if I've ever been to the Island. I've always been sure, while telling it, or the stories of the crowded autograph sessions and the parade, that I have been exaggerating somewhat. Surely it wasn't that big a deal. Surely there weren't that many people following me. I exaggerated a lot when I was a child, and as a result I have a sometimes fatal mistrust of my own memories, which leads me to interrogate them fiercely. As the years go on, I now veer towards minimizing things, and I've always felt sure the trip to PEI could not have been as overwhelming as I remembered it. But when I watch the CBC footage I realize, with some dismay, that I have not been exaggerating. One segment of the clip is in fact called "P.E.I. Fans Follow Sarah Polley Around the Island."

I felt like a circus animal in those days, a curiosity trotted out to make other people's children happy, while I lived in a house that was in constant squalor, motherless, and often working thirteen- to fifteen-hour days. While that period of my life was not a happy one generally, the PEI press tour—as I tried, half-heartedly, to appear innocent and happy and in the midst of a perfect Edwardian childhood—stands out as particularly cringe-worthy in my memory.

And now, strangely, I want to go back. I've had a dream, followed by the strange coincidence of this footage coming my way.

I write a post on Facebook asking friends if they have any recommendations of places to stay in Prince Edward Island. My friend Jackie private-messages me. "You're going to PEI? Really? Won't that be kind of . . . irritating?" I make a joke about being too old and haggard after having three children to be recognized anymore. She says she doubts it, and deep down, I do too.

When we check in for our flight, the attendant behind the desk takes our passports. Eve yelps, "We're going to PEI!"

"The birthplace of Canada," the attendant says, smiling, without looking up.

Eve looks up at me. "What does that mean?"

"He means Confederation."

"It's where Canada was born!" he says as he cheerfully affixes the tags to our luggage. He widens his eyes at Eve, trying to elicit excitement. "The birthplace of our nation!"

"So Canada was born there?" Eve says, looking up at me, confused. "How does a country get born?"

"Well, a bunch of white dudes sat around a table. They decided there would be a country. They decided there would be a Canada. That's what it means."

"You can decide to get born?"

As in all of these Big Question conversations with Eve, I know my answers will be inadequate. I know I will do my best. I know that later on I'll have moments of regretting both what I have said and what I haven't said. And it is the great privilege of my life to be invited into these conversations at all. I am conscious of not wanting to shatter the image of a Good World that can only really exist in a lucky, privileged childhood. But I also feel it is important to be as honest and thoughtful as I can. Any other strategy would be a failure now anyway. At six, Eve is already starting to sense hypocrisy, falsity, and exaggeration. Once, as I yelped and applauded a somersault Aila was showing me, Eve said, "That reaction you're having on the outside isn't the same as the one you're having on the inside."

So when Eve asks me, while David is checking us in, "Was Canada being born a good thing?," I try to find the truth of what I believe in a nanosecond, find words for that truth that Eve will understand, while juggling three bags, a crying newborn strapped to my chest, and a three-year-old who keeps attempting to bolt for the security lineup.

"I used to think it was only good, because it was important for us to try to rely on each other and not the United States. But now I know that Canada was really, really bad for a lot of people. Especially Indigenous people."

I can see, in my peripheral vision, that I am getting a frosty look from the check-in attendant. I've seen that look before. When people love their country, they don't like to hear it criticized. He stops interacting with us as he prints out our tickets and hands them to us without looking up.

As we near the security gate, Eve eyes the uniformed personnel nervously. Eve is obsessed with the idea that at any moment an arrest might be in store, and always tenses up around people in uniform. A small finger beckons me to bend down to ear level. There is a whisper in my ear:

"You know how you were a little bit, or almost kind of famous from TV and movies?"

I'm taken aback. At this juncture in our lives, I don't have the sense that Eve is aware of this at all. I stopped acting years ago, and stopped directing films when I started having kids. Eve and Aila know that I acted when I was young, and are vaguely aware that I wrote and directed films in the past, but they've really only known me as a stay-at-home mother, or a mother who writes while they are in school. Eve must have heard this from someone at school. Maybe a teacher. I feel a flash of unease as I consider this.

"Um. Sort of. Yeah," I respond.

"Well," Eve says, grinning a little, keeping focused eyes on the security person, "that would be a really good excuse to not get arrested if you got in trouble for something."

On the plane, the baby mercifully sleeps. Eve is obsessed with "making new friends" and sits in the row across the aisle from us, engaging a teenaged girl in constant conversation. When I suggest that the new friend may want to relax and sleep, Eve gives me a "Yes, Sergeant" flick of the hand, an officious nod, opens an *Ivy + Bean* book, and begins reading out loud in a full voice. I'm not sure this provides any kind of respite for the teenager in the next seat, but there's not much I can do from two seats away. Aila watches Peppa Pig on the small screen attached to the seat in front of her, and I contemplate how to talk to the kids about the fact that I will be known in PEI. People will stop us on the street. It may be confusing to them, and I want them to be somewhat prepared. (I seem to have to learn, over and over again, that whatever problems I prepare my children for will always be a little to the left or right of where the problem actually lies. And the problems I am anxious about will generally turn out to be fine. The real problems are almost always surprises that can't be prepared for.) I decide not to say anything.

As we disembark at the tiny airport in Charlottetown, we walk down the metal stairs from the plane and onto the tarmac. I keep a firm grip on both of my older children's hands while the baby stays asleep in her carrier. David manages the bags behind us. As we enter the airport we see a small crowd of people, looking expectantly at the passengers, anxious to catch a glimpse of the person they are here to take home. I smile, and am surprised to find myself trying to make friendly eye contact with anyone and everyone. I think, subconsciously, I may be trying to remedy the grumpiness I always displayed as a child when I was recognized. (Many times I've had adults my age tell me how rude I was to them when they recognized me as a child on the street. I somehow feel now that I should make up for that. It has always made me feel guilty to think that I wrecked other kids' days back then by not being the happy, romantic girl they saw on TV.) But any reconciliation on that front between my imagined public and me is impossible, because not one person recognizes me.

I stand and wait for our luggage, taking in this unexpected turn of events, as David goes to change the baby's diaper and Eve and Aila climb the giant shiny Cows Ice Cream cow statue.

Aila is singing, "There's NO people like SHOW people, they smile when they are LOW!"[3] She sings loudly, out of the corner of her mouth. It creates a forties movie star effect. She is somewhere between Ethel Merman and Mae West in her mannerisms. A few people look over at her, laughing, as they collect their luggage. My friend Rick taught Aila this song as a joke. "It suits her perfectly," he said, smiling at me. All my friends know that my worst nightmare would be to have one of my children become a child performer.

In all the years I acted as a child and directed as an adult, I met only one or two former child actors who were not in some way, at some time, gutted by the experience. For the most part, people who acted as children, particularly the ones who had success, have a hollow sadness about them as adults, their lives faint echoes of the booming triumphs of their childhoods. Many kids adore performing, and why shouldn't those kids perform—particularly in children's theatre groups or school plays? But why any parent would put a child, for any substantial length of time, in an environment that was designed with a profit motive, making the prioritization of their child's well-being an impossibility, has been, for most of my life, a mystery to me.

I've often been approached for advice by the parents of child actors, as someone who came out of the experience "successfully" and therefore evidence that it may be a good direction for their own child. As soon as I begin to imply that the reason I came out of the experience without major addiction issues was sheer luck and privilege and that waiting until adulthood might be advisable for *any* profession, or begin to recount some of the more damaging experiences I had as a child, I am met with combativeness, defensiveness, or a turning away. It has always given me a jolt to realize that most parents of child actors really don't want to hear the truth from someone who has lived it. Only twice has this not been the case, out of dozens of conversations with parents. The exchange usually goes something like this: "But he *loves* it so much! *He* wants to do it." To which I reply something like: "Yes—and lots of kids want to be firefighters or doctors too. But they must wait until they are no longer children to assume the pressures and obligations of adult work."

It's something our society made up its mind about a long time ago: *children shouldn't work*. Why this principle doesn't apply to an industry known for its exploitation and self-serving nature bewilders me.

(I should add that I have met a couple of former child actors recently who do look back fondly on their time in front of a camera. They both came from very difficult, abusive, or restrictive backgrounds and so, despite the stresses, film sets actually served as a welcome outlet, and an escape from other, more unstable environments.)

When I first got the part in *Road to Avonlea*, I was nine years old and I had already landed the role of my dreams. That was the part of the Black Joker in my elementary school's production of *No Big Deal*, a musical comedy about a deck of cards, written by the Grade 4 drama teacher, Mr. Gotlieb. The Black Joker had all the best jokes. He was funny and mischievous, and while it wasn't the lead role, he was certainly the most dynamic. (Think the Fool in *King Lear* but with more pathos, shorter ditties, and the vocabulary of a nine-year-old.) When I found out that I got that part, my body filled to the brim with butterflies and I shot out the school doors on a burst of adrenalin, yelling the good news to anyone who would listen.

A week later, when I was offered the lead in a TV show based on a famous book, my parents' image of themselves as atypical stage parents was put to the test. They didn't outright pressure me to take the part. But when I said, "But I really want to be in *No Big Deal* instead," they avoided eye contact and my dad muttered something about not wanting me to regret it for the rest of my life. Perhaps he was right. Perhaps I would have not only regretted it but blamed them later for letting me turn away from such an enormous opportunity.

And yet something in me protests that by then I already knew I hated acting professionally, and so did they. (I had had, by that point, the traumatic experience of working on the epic disaster of *Baron Munchausen*, which had soured me on the idea of acting professionally.) I was, by the age of nine, desperate to be a "normal kid." In my mind, "normal kids" (keep in mind my "normal" was white middle-class Toronto) went to school every day, and their big news was to land a part in the school play. But what nine-year-old is going to dismiss their parents' suggestion that they will regret something for the rest of their life? What nine-year-old isn't going to feel guided by their parents' elation at the news that they have just landed the lead in a big TV show? What nine-year-old doesn't notice the slow turn of their parents' heads as they try to hide their disappointment that their child might choose something else?

After I was cast, the producers proceeded to search for child actors for many of the other parts, and they decided to hold auditions for some of the roles at the elementary arts school I attended. For days, kids lined up in the hallway. They would stand and chat together nervously outside the makeshift audition room that had been set up in the library.

As I walked by them, I envied them, their easy camaraderie. I longed to be auditioning with them for one of the smaller parts that wouldn't take me away from them and this amazing school for most of the year.

My contract kept me bound to the show for six years. During the production of the first season, my mother died after a three-year battle with cancer. The following week, I had to go back to the gruelling hours at work. (I was told, when I was working on the show, that my parents had agreed to an arrangement proposed by the production in which I could work any amount of overtime so long as I was paid for it. This would have been prohibited by my union, and I was told more than once that we were not allowed to speak openly about it. Everyone looked the other way.) Kevin Sullivan, the show's producer, later told *People* magazine, "Sarah had been living and dealing with her mom's illness for a long while. And Sarah is a pro. Going back to work the week after her mother died helped take her mind off things." It sounded, from his version of events, almost as though I was given a choice. (I wasn't.)

The experience of being a child on that show was generally fraught. I watched a kid get fired, publicly, in front of dozens of adults, for "misbehaving." I literally heard the phrase "You will never work again!" screamed at a twelve-year-old who was goofing off in the background during a take. He cried, and actually, as far as I know, he never did work again in film or television. I can't even find a trace of him on the internet. I watched other kids "punished every day for being children," as my friend Zachary Bennett, who also starred in the show, says. I learned, quickly, to not be a child. I hit my marks, I knew my lines, and I was irritated when other kids tried to be playful with me or joke around. I knew I couldn't be thrown off my focus, and I wasn't.

A crew member in his forties or fifties stalked me for two years, starting when I was twelve. He would follow my van home and stare at me. More than once I woke up with a start on the highway at night to see him there, driving his truck alongside the van I was sleeping in. Just before Christmas he showed up at my house in the country when I was alone to give me gifts, including a heart-shaped necklace. One day, he told my tutor Laurie, who was staying close to me at all times in those days of his stalking, that her car tire was flat. When she went to the parking lot to investigate he found a moment with me alone in a corner of the sound studio. He asked why I hadn't thanked him for the gifts he had given me and openly professed his love and his "struggle with his feelings." He often stood in my line of vision during takes, staring obsessively at me with his ice blue eyes, wrote me romantic letters and phoned me, upset, when I didn't show up to a wrap party because I wanted to avoid him.

I ran between the set and the trailer where I would try to cram in my schoolwork. I wanted to be a writer. I wanted to go into politics. I wanted to go to Oxford. I needed to excel in school to accomplish these things. I was terrified that this acting thing would get in my way.

When I was thirteen, the producers didn't renew my contract by the deadline, in effect freeing me from my multi-year contract. I was elated beyond measure, sobbing with happiness, free as a bird. A week later my dad picked me up from school and delivered the bad news that he and my agent had decided to invoke the "pay or play" clause in my contract to get me paid regardless of whether the show continued, but now that the producers had decided to pick up my contract, it kept me bound for another two years. I felt my stomach lurch and cried all the way home.

My work on the show continued. I felt tired. I felt used. I began to have major anxiety about learning long monologues, sometimes with only a few days' notice. I developed a violent, visible twitch in my right eye, which caused irritation to directors, and many nights I con-templated downing a bottle of my mom's old morphine pills, which I kept beside my bed. Death seemed less scary at times than having a camera trained on me and failing in front of a group of adults.

There were other obligations as an actor on a successful children's show. Twice, when I was still a child myself, it was a child's dying wish to meet me. I went to meet these children, both of whom had cancer, in their hospital beds. The smell of their rooms, of the chemo, reminded me of my mother's recent illness. I tried to be someone other than who I was. I tried to smile. I tried to say nice things about the show. I tried to be the person they knew from TV. And both times I was left frustrated by my underlying gloomy disposition and its distance from who they wanted to meet. It was hard to be so close to death when my mother had died so recently and to feel that I was supposed to be a balm to someone facing it. It was even harder to feel that I had failed them.

Once, I went to the Hospital for Sick Children for one of my regular appointments to track and brace my scoliosis. As I passed a common area, a mother approached me, asking for an autograph for her daughter who was having brain surgery at that very moment. She fell on top of me, weeping. I held her tight. I felt like I might collapse under the weight of this sobbing woman, under the weight of the grief of these parents and these terribly sick children. But in retrospect, they were moments I was privileged to live, tangible evidence that the many hours I spent on that show were not totally wasted. For some people, the show was important, and even though I couldn't understand why, I realize now that that importance was, for them, very real.

A year or so later, a girl awaiting a lung transplant asked to meet me. I spent a couple of hours with her and found myself forgetting the strange premise of why I was there. I liked her. A lot. She was funny and kind and she had a wry sense of humour about her own terrifying predicament. I would have liked to be her friend. The year before my mother died, we had moved from a suburb of Toronto to Aurora, a town which was an hour and a half by bus and subway from the school I went to, and I was never at school long enough to really maintain friendships throughout the year. I was under the impression that this girl would live, that we would talk often, but maybe I just didn't ever ask anyone what her prognosis was. One day I called her to check in, and she was gone. Her father sent me a T-shirt with her face on it. I sat alone in my room for a long time.

I did occasionally have some reprieve from the isolation. When I was at my lowest, as my dad withdrew even further into himself in his grief over the loss of my mother and the house we lived in became more and more filthy, there was always someone (my on-set tutor and guardian, Laurie, some of the actors, a cinematographer, a wardrobe assistant, a makeup artist, a continuity supervisor, a driver) who took it upon themselves to get me from A to B. They'd take me to their house for a weekend, set up a fun adventure or hold me in their arms, and the world would feel, for a moment, bearable. Twice I went to San Francisco to stay with Mag Ruffman and her husband, Daniel—Mag played my aunt Olivia on the show—and the world, for those weeks, felt magical, light, and full of childlike adventure.

During the months when I was working and unable to see my friends, my Grade 7 French teacher, Ms. Huismans, would sometimes set up weekends for me at her house. She had two small children of her own and she seemed to put an extraordinary amount of energy into making these weekends absolutely perfect for me, sometimes even arranging for another girl from my class to join me so I wouldn't completely lose touch with school friends.

When I was around thirteen, my Auntie Ann and cousin Sarah moved from Quebec to Stratford, about two hours away from us, and when they would visit every now and then, the house was cleaned from top to bottom while I was at work. (On one visit the morphine pills disappeared from my bedside table.) Good people kept showing up, even if just for a moment, just when I was ready to break.

After I finally got out of the show, I only signed onto productions that had a complex edge, or the possibility of playing someone approximating who I really was. When I acted in a small part in Atom Egoyan's *Exotica* when I was a teenager, I remember the exhilaration of speaking dialogue that sounded like me. Though the character had a very different life from mine, I played myself through her, with all my cynicism, all my questioning and my low tolerance for bullshit. When I saw the film, there I finally was. In theory, I remained uninterested in acting, but as great parts in independent films came my way, I ended up forging a different kind of acting career, and I eventually started making my own films.

Every once in a while, someone recognizes me only from *Road to Avonlea* and is unaware that I have done anything else in the intervening years. It's an ugly feeling, a feeling of erasure of everything I did to escape it. I once met Bibi Andersson, the great actor from Ingmar Bergman's films, and I told her that her performance in *Persona* was one of my favourites of all time. She scoffed, avoided eye contact, and said, "Well, it was a good film." I understood her apparent rudeness only years later, when I realized that to be recognized only for something you did when you were very young, at the beginning of your career (even if it was a great film like *Persona*), can feel like a kind of negation of everything you have done since.

When I was on bedrest in the hospital with a high-risk pregnancy, a junior anaesthetist resident came into my room to change my IV. He struggled with my too-small veins for a while, irritated, as he tried and failed to insert the IV into several different places. At one point he looked up and said, "You're an actress, right? From a really long time ago? In that show about Avonlea? Whatever happened to you?" As if on cue, the IV backed up and exploded blood all over both of us.

We wait on the curb at the Charlottetown airport while the agent from the rental company pulls around our minivan. Aila looks around, dismayed. "*This* is PEI?" We had described the ocean to her, but not the airport. I think she probably assumed that the plane would just land smack-dab in the middle of a pristine beach.

We drive down a two-lane highway that takes us almost directly to the cottage resort we are staying at on the north shore. We pass white barns with red trim, and tiny old churchyards with small clusters of headstones. I'm taken aback by how familiar they look. I try to place them in my memory. And then I realize that they look familiar because they remind me of the exteriors of the sets I grew up on. I lived much of my childhood in a replica of this place, entering and exiting the skeletons of these kinds of buildings, erected for the show in Ontario fields.

A friend of mine once described the *Avonlea/Story Girl* stories as "nostalgia for a time that never existed." Lucy Maud Montgomery wrote *The Story Girl* shortly before leaving PEI. She moved to Ontario where she was married to a mentally ill, abusive minister and suffered from severe depression. She eventually took her own life. I have often wondered if the books she wrote about PEI became something idyllic for her to escape to. While Sara Stanley (the character I played) has tragedy in her past—she becomes an orphan, like Anne of Green Gables—the picture it paints of Edwardian life on PEI is nostalgic in the extreme. I've always felt somewhat offended by the glossy portrait the books paint of Canadian history. Montgomery's books are of a fictional, glorified, all-white past, and millions still lovingly embrace this history she put forth of the Island, accepting its erasure of the people who gave it the name that she herself liked to call it, Abegweit, a European mispronunciation of the Mi'kmaq word Epekwitk, which means "Land cradled on the waves." PEI is Mi'kmaq land.[4]

As I moved into my teenage years I came to see the show as a grave injustice in and of itself. While parents and children came up to me, often, to tell me that watching the show together every Sunday was an important family ritual for them, it became clearer and clearer to me that the show not only lacked a political backbone and had almost no diversity, but after it was taken on by the Disney Channel, it had more and more of a "family values" agenda. And as I got older, I became angrier about some of the things that had happened to me in those first years on the show.

Shortly after my own mother's death, a scene where my character cries about her dead mother was shot, requiring me to produce emotion about my character's mother's death. (Which was odd, since my mother in the show had died years before, and the father had died in that very season.) Scanning through the series, it isn't hard to find multiple scenes in which I cry about a parent dying, shot in the months after my mother's death. Needless to say, I gave a great performance as a little girl who had just lost a parent.

Later, perhaps capitalizing on this useful trove of grief, a scene was also written into the show in which my character described all the things she missed, specifically about her mother. It gutted me to say these words. I was trapped in the prison of that monologue about missing my mother's hands and forgetting the sound of her voice, unable to escape images of my own mother, unable to resist the obligation to do my best work, which required using my own grief for the show's purposes. Mag Ruffman held my hand as I said these words, crying as hard as I did, even when the camera wasn't on her. As I walked off the set, destroyed, when the scene was completed, a few technicians who I had known for years stood there, stock-still, with tears in their eyes as my own sobbing continued, uncontained. One of the grips, who had always been paternal towards me, gave me a hug and said, "I couldn't listen to that. I had to walk away. I'm so sorry." He looked at the floor, as though ashamed to have been made complicit in this strange emotional exploitation. I lay back on a pile of sandbags and stayed there for a while, all my tears gone, washed away for years to come.

Kevin Sullivan, again providing his own odd analysis, was quoted later as saying the scene "was specifically written for Sarah to mourn her own mom. Sarah gives a very touching performance considering the reality behind what you see on screen."

I had never asked for such help in mourning my mother. And as it turned out, it was far from helpful. Because some of the first tears I had shed about my mother's death after the day she died were in aid of a performance, I was unable to produce genuine tears of grief for years to come. Crying about my mother felt false, poisoned with the feeling that these tears had been used to further the agenda of a TV show rather than to genuinely express the loss of her. It was decades before I was able to cry about my mother's death without feeling disingenuous about it.

The pain and sadness this left me with gradually twisted itself into anger. I started to see injustice everywhere. The technical crew, who generally showed me more compassion and kindness than anyone else on set, and who clearly had far more experience and expertise than the people they worked under, had no meaningful say in the show's creation and were treated with noticeable disrespect by producers and some of the show's directors. Many of the crew worked such long hours that they would talk about falling asleep and swerving off the road, or not seeing their children at all during the week because they left for work so early their kids were still sleeping and returned home long after they had gone to bed. I saw elderly background performers moved unceremoniously out of lunch lineups to make way for the show's "stars," including myself, after they had spent twice the time outside as everyone else, in thin period costumes, in sub-zero temperatures. Sometimes even the food they ate was different from ours, cheaper and less healthy.

I became aware of a pecking order, one that I was near the top of, at least superficially. When I behaved in a bratty manner, no one held me accountable. But no one in charge seemed to care if I became so exhausted from work that I spiked a fever, or that I didn't get time off after my mother's death, either. Daily, I was fed a toxic concoction of coddling and neglect, which, unsurprisingly, did not bring out the best in me.

When I was a teenager I became more politically active, I think in part because of what I had witnessed of the hierarchical, insidious structure of the set I worked on, which I realized was a microcosm of the world beyond. I became something of a problem for the show. I went to a television awards show in Washington during the Gulf War, and several US senators were in attendance. I wore a large peace sign necklace that had belonged to my mother. I was asked, by a representative of the Disney Channel, to take it off. I didn't. Shortly after this I was told, over the phone, by an executive at the Disney Channel that when promoting a show for Disney, I was not to make political statements. They weren't "a political company," he said. Afterwards, at every opportunity, I told journalists this story about being "censored" by Disney. By the time I was fifteen, the producers could no longer pretend I wanted to be part of the show and they began to write me out. When I was in my twenties, Kevin Sullivan, perhaps after reading too many interviews where I talked about my bad memories of the show, ran into me at an industry event and said, through gritted teeth, "You had a good time on that show, Sarah. We all did."

After being locked into the show between the ages of nine and fifteen, I felt claustrophobic in the film and television industry, constantly pressured by it whether I was working or not. This stayed with me for decades. Up until very recently, whenever I had any degree of success at anything, I found myself behaving in ways that indicated that I unconsciously resented it, pushing away people who were only trying to support me and, in some cases, trying to find my way out of obligations. As soon as I felt other people wanted me to work, I became irrationally filled with a sense of dread at the idea of doing it. I always had the instinct to try to get myself free, no matter how attractive the opportunity. I felt this for as long as I can remember, with both acting and directing, and I often wonder if any other success I may be lucky enough to achieve in life will similarly feel like some kind of proxy noose around my neck, spun and woven in my childhood. When I first had my own children, I found myself treating any professional obligation that took me away from them as a stage parent or an authoritarian producer, even if it was something I myself had chosen to do. I suppose the idea of missing their childhoods to be on a film set, after I had lost my own, has been unbearable to me.

Finding my way to this truth about myself took a very long time. I have no idea why the incredible agent and manager who started representing me when I was seventeen, Gaby Morgerman and Frank Frattaroli, still represent me to this day after I set any career they built for me on fire. I feel lucky that they hung in there as I walked away from star-making roles they had miraculously put me in the running for, and then away from opportunities as a director, without accurate explanations.

Recently, when it started to become clearer to me that this need to extricate myself from any potential success came from feeling tangled in these vines sprouted in childhood, I called Gaby and Frank to explain what I finally understood. They have spent years having to extricate me from things when it was too late to pull me out of them, and trying to find explanations for my behaviour that I didn't have myself. When I told them I felt I finally had a handle on the childhood origins of this desire to Houdini my way out of anything threatening success, Gaby simply said, "Oh. That makes sense. Well, we all get older and understand ourselves better."

We arrive at our small cottage on the north shore. A cottage with separate bedrooms isn't available until the next day, so the five of us cram into a little room with two twin beds, set up the Pack 'n Play for the baby in between them, and then spend an hour killing bird-sized mosquitoes against the walls. We count fifty-two of them. The woman at the front desk had mentioned there had been a "salt-water hatch" earlier that week because of all the rain. I lie awake, wondering if we've made a big mistake.

Later, as I nurse Amy to sleep for the third time that night, I look over my sleeping children's bodies, out the window and across the bay. There is a single large reddish star, low in the sky. I think I might be seeing Mars. I feel the rhythmic tugging at my nipple and look over Amy's dark, soft hair into the night. I think, "If only I hadn't dropped out of school, I'd know if that was Mars. If only I had a proper education, or in the absence of that, a dedication to learning that was more rigorous, more disciplined, I could have learned more about science rather than be so intimidated by it. I could have . . ." At some point in this self-flagellating monologue, I must soften my inner voice and let myself off the hook, because I fall asleep, Amy still nursing.

The next day I walk down a perfect, unbroken beach with Eve and Aila, as Amy sleeps in her carrier, attached to me. Eve says, "One day can we walk all the way along the Great Wall of China?" I say that I'd love to. "Can we train for it now?" Eve asks. Aila builds a sandcastle and Eve and I walk together, for a long time. I look at Eve; I look at the beach, which melts foggily into the distant cliffs. I say, "This was my dream, walking with you." Eve says, "So this is your dream come true." I nod. We walk a long, long way down the beach until Eve jumps up, exhilarated, having found a "shark tooth." It may be a coyote's tooth, which would be extraordinary enough, but Eve has decided it is a shark tooth and this is what Eve needs to believe. At some point it slips out of Eve's hand and it can't be found. Eve is devastated. I don't think I have ever seen grief like this in any of my children before or since. (To this day, as Eve drifts off to sleep, I often talk about walking along this beach and finding that shark tooth, and I see the outline of a sleepy mouth curl into a smile in the dark.)

As we walk back to where we came from, we see Aila, running towards us in the distance. Her bathing suit is bright pink and she is brilliant, popping colour in the sunshine, the blue sea behind her. She has always looked like a cross between an angel and an emoji, her blond hair whipping behind her, her face utterly taken over and transformed by whatever she feels. Now she has her sad face on, and it takes up every inch of space. She says she feels left out. She says she wants alone time with me. I take her hand, and as Eve runs off to look again for the shark tooth, Aila and I jump in the waves together, holding hands and laughing. It's as though I can see this moment in Super 8. I can already sense how I will feel when I remember it years from now. I'm nostalgic for the present, mourning its passing even as it happens. Aila listens, for a moment, to the seagulls, which fly low around us in the surf, the water lapping her knees. After a moment of absorbing the sound of their cries, she lets out a shriek that sounds identical to a seagull. A few people walking by laugh at how uncanny it is. She does it again and again, the impression improving with each shriek and provoking more laughter from the passersby. I make eye contact with one of the women who is laughing. I shake my head and shrug, smiling. I look down at Aila and think, *She would be a great actress.* I immediately laugh at myself for having the thought. But it is in this moment that I suddenly understand what it is to see talent in your child and want the world to see it too. I would be incredibly reluctant to let my kids act professionally until they aren't children anymore, but only because I'm lucky enough to know better. In the blink of an eye, in the shriek of a seagull, I understand the instincts of a stage parent. We stop for lunch at a fish and chips stand on a pier that we have been told is the best on the north shore. As we approach, we see three girls, all wearing hats with long red braids attached to them, standing among the picnic benches. They are wearing Edwardian dresses and are clearly here to visit Green Gables, to imagine themselves as Anne. They fit the bill of the classic *Road to Avonlea* fans. When I see them, I instinctively put my head down and busy myself with retying Eve's shoe. When I glance up, I'm horrified to see that one of them has spotted me. She is smiling. She points, and her friends light up too. As the familiar, ancient dread of being recognized winds its way through my body, I realize their gaze is not on me but just behind me. I turn and look behind me, where Aila is singing a song from *Frozen* at the top of her lungs: "LET IT GO! LET IT GO! CAN'T HOLD IT BACK ANYMORE!" I look back at them, and they have turned away from me. I have, again, not been noticed. I smile at David, and wink at him, happy that this perfect day has not been ruined.

A few days later we go to Cavendish, true Anne of Green Gables country, where Lucy Maud Montgomery lived some of her formative years and where Green Gables itself is, with its busloads of tourists and young girls, hungry to see the fictional habitat of their fictional heroine. I have that strong memory of the beautiful beach here with the human zombies. I want to see if it is as I remember it. It is a rainy day. I see several girls dressed in period costume and I find myself purposefully making eye contact with them and smiling, thinking this might be a kind gesture, given the disappointment of their rained-out day at the beach. I'm trying to meet the eyes of that kind of wholesome girl who I used to run and duck for cover from. I'm trying, ridiculously, to be part of their tourist experience.

But I begin to wonder if my disingenuous prediction was right. Perhaps I really am too old and haggard now to be recognized at all. They look at me in passing, as their eyes travel somewhere else, but nothing clicks. It takes me far too long to realize that they are too young to have seen the show I was in. These thirteen-year-olds are not the same thirteen-year-olds from almost thirty years ago. There is even a new show now. A new Anne. Some part of me hadn't registered the passing of time. Not when it came to this chapter of my life, which haunts and remains so vivid for me. It has taken me far too long to realize that I am invisible, unknown to them. It's finally over. I turn to David. I smile so big I feel as though my face might break. Eve catches my expression and says, "Whoa. You must really like rainy beaches."

Besides the tsunami of relief, I feel something I don't have a name for yet. I call my friend Rick, who is my best friend/rabbi/only solid parent I've had since I was in my late teens, and find myself naming it. "This part of my life is officially over. After years of wanting to escape the prison of that recognition, I definitely don't miss it, but something in me feels a small sense of loss or confusion. I think I'm actually *trying* to be recognized by these people. It's so pathetic. What the hell is going on? I mean, it's only two percent of what I feel, but it's a damning two percent!"

Rick says, "Human beings are basically a disaster."

"There is truly nothing more humiliating," I lament, "than realizing some part of you, even if it's small, *wants* to be recognized by a bunch of wholesome schoolgirls you thought you were avoiding."

"Congratulations," he says. "You're a human."

In the car on the way back to our cottage, I tell the kids about the Tenant League, a militant agrarian movement in PEI in the 1800s. I learned about it in a bridging course I did at the University of Toronto a few years ago. I'd always wanted to do a degree in Canadian history, and I learned this story from our passionate professor, Thomas Socknat, who made the story come alive in his dramatic telling of it.

After years of clearing the land and cultivating it, the settlers in PEI were still paying rents to absentee landlords in Britain. The Tenant League was formed to support farmers who began to refuse to pay their rents. When the sheriffs came to arrest those farmers, neighbours would blow tin trumpets to alert supporters across the countryside. Sometimes dozens of people would answer the trumpet calls and arrive to surround the farmer in question, preventing his arrest. Finally, British troops were called in, but most of them were Irish, and when they arrived many found themselves siding with the tenant farmers. Though the rebellion was ultimately crushed, and the history of the Tenant League remains largely unknown in Canada, it had a profound influence on the Island. To this day in PEI, the acquisition of land by non-residents is highly regulated.

I marvelled at this story when I learned it, captivated by the image of those tin trumpets blasting over the fields, calling forth the solidarity of so many. Though I'd spent a childhood frolicking in period costumes in fake PEI fields and thought I'd had enough of the province's history to last me a lifetime, I realized that there were many other histories on this island worth learning.

The next day we walk another beach. And the day after that, another one. Because no development is permitted on these beaches, they look as though they are from another time, before everything was ruined. My kids say they never want to leave. I don't either. I am free from my past here. I am free even from my sleep deprivation. I nurse baby Amy all night, but being outside in the sea air makes fatigue feel impossible. And the kids are never bored, never run out of ideas for things to do and play, with such a vast expanse of space always in front of them.

On our final night in Prince Edward Island, we stop at a lovely restaurant in an old homestead. We've never taken all the kids to a nice restaurant and we are nervous that they will turn feral when confronted by our need for them not to be.

We run around with the kids outside to try to burn off some of their energy before disrupting the restaurant. A field next to the house is dotted with hay bales. I say, "Look at the hay bales. I love hay bales." Aila says, "No, they are cows." We go back and forth a few times on this point, but it is clear that she will not bend to reason. There can be an obstinacy about her nonsense and it's best not to challenge it. "They are hay bales," I say one last time, fruitlessly. "No," she says, with a sharp warning in her eyes. "They are cows." I back down. This is tantrum territory, even though she knows the truth.

Inside, the kids, bewilderingly, rise to the occasion and behave like perfect angels, pleased, I think, with our faith in them. The elderly couple at the table next to us keeps looking at us with warm glances. The woman finally says, "We had three kids close together. This period of life is hard. And then you miss it for the rest of your life. You're a beautiful family."

When the baby gets tired and cranky, David and I take turns walking her outside in the carrier to try to get her to sleep. When it is my turn, I walk back and forth along the fence beside the field. The hill skips upward so that the hay bales have a background of twilit sky and look as though they are perched and ready to fall off a ledge into nothingness.

I think about what the woman said, about this period of life being hard. I laugh to myself and wonder how I lived to be this lucky.

I sing Loreena McKennitt's song of the Yeats poem "The Stolen Child" as I walk, feeling Amy's head becoming heavy as she slowly falls asleep, her sweaty little head heavy in the crook of my neck. "Come away, O human child, to the waters and the wild, with a faery, hand in hand, for the world's more full of weeping than you can understand."

I loved this song when I was a child. The sky is almost dark; the hay bales are dimming into silhouette. The moon is getting brighter; it is shining now. A perfect warm wind is blowing. I look up at the silhouette of the old house the restaurant is in, the glowing lights on the second floor where my older children and my husband now sit. I look towards the barn. With its white paint and red trim it looks so much like the hollow exteriors of sets that I worked on as a child.

I feel a rush of breathlessness, my heart beating fast. The world looks large from here, and I have a thousand thoughts at once: where I would like to go, who I miss, what delights, who I might be, what words I might use to describe this moment one day. It's the kind of trance I used to go into often, before life went on tilt during those child-actor days. It's the feeling Lucy Maud Montgomery described as "the Flash," which she experienced herself and endowed so many of her young female characters with versions of. In *Emily of New Moon*, Montgomery writes: "It had always seemed . . . ever since she could remember, that she was very, very near to a world of wonderful beauty. Between it and herself hung only a thin curtain; she could never draw the curtain aside—but sometimes, just for a moment, a wind fluttered it and then it was as if she caught a glimpse of the enchanting realm beyond—only a glimpse—and heard a note of unearthly music. This moment came rarely—went swiftly, leaving her breathless with the inexpressible delight of it. She could never recall it—never summon it—never pretend it; but the wonder of it stayed with her for days . . . And always when the flash came to her Emily felt that life was a wonderful, mysterious thing of persistent beauty."

I was a romantic child, once, with romantic longings. When I first got the part in *Road to Avonlea*, and after I had recovered from the loss of the part in the school play, I lay on my stomach on our front lawn, reading an old, musty copy of *The Story Girl*, smelling its pages, biting into an apple and pretending I was in PEI, in another time. I had forgotten this. I had forgotten that I was once the kind of child who loved those Lucy Maud Montgomery stories. I read all of them, devoured them. I was one of those wholesome girls, before childhood got interrupted. In this moment, walking sleeping Amy along the fences, I have a feeling I haven't known since adolescence: that anything might happen and that it is thrilling to not know what that anything might be.

On the way home, I read "The Island" by the great Island poet Milton Acorn to the kids, using the light on my phone to illuminate the page as we wind through the darkened villages on our way back across the north shore, the dim outlines of hills and cliffs just visible beyond the road. When I look back, I see that they have fallen asleep.

Many times on this trip I will remember the vagueness of the boundaries between the beaches and the cliffs of my dream. PEI itself "dissolves the boundaries" in my own life, just like the dream that led me here. Things have become murky for me on this island in a way they couldn't have when I was younger—murky in the best possible sense, where whatever sharp narrative I've been spinning for years about parents and childhood and lost things has dissipated into foggier outlines. I wonder, now, if I escaped my childhood to arrive in this beautiful life, as I used to believe, or if I should be grateful to that childhood for leading me, so precisely, here.

The following summer, Eve attends a two-week session of a musical theatre camp and is enchanted by it, eagerly asking the counsellors for extra lines, a bigger part. I can't describe the feeling of seeing my child up there onstage, playing Baby Bear in *Shrek*, so nervous, so thrilled. When someone else is about to say a funny line, Eve hides giggles behind fluttering hands, laughing in anticipation. It's so gloriously for the sake of itself, for the sake of the kids involved. It's about the experience of the performance, not the performance itself. Eve asks me if we can sign up for a month or two next year, instead of just a two-week session. When I say, without hesitation, "Yes," Eve looks shocked and says, "I thought you would say no."

I tell Eve, "As long as it brings joy, as long as there is no one making money from it, as long as the experience is designed around the enjoyment of the children involved, and no one in charge has interests that are more important to them than that, you can act as much as you want to."

"But I'd like to do it professionally." Eve watches me closely, and gets very still, as though conscious that I might be easily scared out of this conversation. "You know, just because it was bad for you doesn't mean it would be bad for me."

I admit that may be right. But we won't take that chance. "Not with something you love so much."

I turn to Aila and ask her if she would also like to do the acting camp next summer. She looks up at me, her face a bemused emoji. "No way," she says.

Despite myself, I say, "But you're so good at it."

Aila looks straight into my eyes and says, "That doesn't have to matter, does it?"

Run
Towards
the
Danger

THE ACCIDENT

It is October 19, 2015. I am sitting on the living room floor, a full carton of Häagen-Dazs pralines and cream ice cream on the coffee table in front of me while my three-year-old, Eve, draws with crayons on the couch and my fourteen-month-old, Aila, sleeps with her head on my shoulder. It is election night, and I am watching television coverage of the federal Conservative government getting demolished for the first time in eight long years. As I spoon ice cream into my mouth, I watch the ocean of Tory blue that covered much of the virtual map of my country shrink into a blue puddle. I hug my neighbours on the porch. All is well. As I spoon a little more ice cream into my mouth, I acknowledge how good life is.

I pause. As with all the great moments of my life, I am momentarily distracted by the concern that I may be on the precipice of inevitable, impending disaster.

The next day I take Eve to preschool, clean the kitchen, play with Aila on the floor for a while, and then go upstairs to my desk to write. I have been hired to write the screenplay for a remake of *Little Women*. It's a perfect job. Every night at bedtime I tell Eve the stories of Amy, Beth, Meg, and especially Jo. Eve asks me to tell new stories of the March sisters every night, and I do, until I have told every story in the book and have to start making up my own. Eve asks if it's possible to visit the set when the film is made and I say yes, though I likely won't be directing the film. I want to have another baby, and I also don't want to return to directing when my kids are still so small, and risk missing any of these early years of theirs to fifteen-hour days on a film set, as that is the particular method by which I lost my own childhood.

Before I go to pick up Eve from preschool, I go for a swim at the local community centre. I've never been athletic but I've been taking swimming lessons lately, and, for the first time, I've felt myself substantially improve at something physical. I have felt my body change, from one of a basically inactive person to that of a person who moves. My arms have muscles. My legs feel strong.

I come from a family of athletic people, mostly tall, strapping WASPy people who easily take up any given sport and ace it. I've always been made fun of in my family for my lack of energy, stamina, and strength. My brother Mark still mocks me for helplessly throwing down my racquet and yelping, plaintively, "But I'm *sweating*!" when he tried to teach me how to play tennis when I was ten. He tosses "But I'm *sweating*!" at me often, and it has become a kind of code for my lack of perseverance and grit. It has become a shameful echo in the back of my head every time I falter in the face of a challenge. So, swimming means a lot to me. I'm working hard at it. I'm getting better. Maybe I'm not such an awful person after all. That may sound like an overstatement of the gravity for me of my lack of athleticism and my desperate need to overcome it, but sadly, it isn't. Almost everyone's family manages to make them feel like a failure, and it is in this context that I imagine the sweet glory of them being proven wrong and acknowledging it, which is, of course, a pipe dream.

After my swim, I shower and get dressed, then realize that my blow-dryer is not in my bag. I must have left it behind the last time I was here. I have wet hair and it is a chilly October day. I ask the woman behind the front desk whether she has seen the blow-dryer, and she suggests I check the lost-and-found bin.

I don't feel immediately compelled to ask her where the lost-and-found bin is. This blow-dryer holds no sentimental value for me. I can be a wasteful person. A lazy person. The kind of person who thinks to themselves, "Why rummage through a lost-and-found bin when you're sweltering in a winter coat?" The point is, I don't need that blow-dryer, it's not that important to me, and it would be characteristic of me to leave it behind. All of this is relevant only because, years later, I'm still resentful of the sudden burst of normal responsibility that led me to go looking for that blow-dryer.

The woman at the front desk points to a lost-and-found box in a corner. Obstructing half the bin is a large, free-standing poster advertising wellness or programming to achieve said wellness. To get to the bin I must squeeze between one side of the large poster and the bin itself. Above the box is a very large industrial fire extinguisher. I crouch down, squeezing by the poster, and rummage around in the bin, looking for my hair dryer. I become overheated, and curse myself both for my recklessness with belongings generally and for caring too much about this particular stupid blow-dryer. In frustration, I stand up quickly to fling off my coat.

I'm unclear on what exactly happens next. I hear a kind of metallic, dissonant musical crash. Something large has slammed into the floor beside me. I turn and look down to see the large fire extinguisher on the floor. It is rolling a little. My teeth ache as though they have moved around in my head. I've had nightmares about losing my teeth. I stand there, not moving, not speaking, and scan through what the possible remedies may be to losing all of one's teeth that don't involve dentures or surgery. I don't know enough about dentistry. I have this exact thought, "I don't know enough about dentistry." I clutch my jaw. Maybe it's broken. Or maybe I'm going to pass out. I suddenly realize that I should make sure that someone knows what has happened to me in case I lose consciousness. I hear myself say, over and over, to no one, in a voice that sounds like a disembodied robot, monotone and repetitive, "A fire extinguisher just fell on my head. A fire extinguisher just fell on my head. A fire extinguisher just fell on my head." My voice sounds like it is coming from beside me instead of from within me. The woman behind the desk seems to be gone. The only people here in the entranceway of the community centre to witness this moment are a couple speaking sign language to each other, who haven't heard or can't hear me. I am vaguely aware that this might be funny. After a few moments of contemplating the various ways I can tell this story to make people laugh, I become aware that the woman from the front desk is now standing beside me and is asking me if I am okay. I repeat to her the only words I seem to know now: "A fire extinguisher just fell on my head." She tells me to stay put so that she can go get her supervisor. I stand there for a few minutes, and then decide that I don't have time to wait for help for whatever injury has just occurred. I actually don't have time to have an injury at all. I need to get Eve and a friend from preschool and cook dinner for them as planned.

I walk out into the world as it will remain for me for much of the next three years. Cars are moving too fast. The sun is too bright. The noise of even the wind is unbearable. I feel as though I am underwater, but I am completely calm. When I set the intention to move my limbs, they don't move at the speed I think they will and I keep veering right. I try to walk a straight line down the middle of the sidewalk, but I keep walking onto people's lawns. I have to consciously move myself to the left side of the sidewalk in order to complete a new diagonal that sets me in a forward direction but loses ground again with the sideways movement. I reach a very busy street, which I usually jaywalk across, and pause. I am briefly aware that it is hard for me to judge when it is safe to go; the speed of cars is bewildering to me. I cross the street anyway, deciding once again that it is impossible that anything is really the matter with me. This is just not something life can make room for right now, with kids this age, with the job I have been hired to do. Everything must be fine because it has to be. There simply isn't another option.

I pause for a moment to send David an email from my phone: "A fire extinguisher just fell on my left jaw. No joke. Feel very weird."

That night I make dinner for Eve, Aila, and a friend from Eve's preschool. David has not been able to talk me out of going through with the evening's plans. My hands seem to move very slowly as I chop vegetables, and I have a dull awareness that perhaps I should be sitting down, but I continue to go through the physical movements of making dinner, which suddenly seem to be very plentiful. Each of these movements requires its own conscious thought. (Put the fish in a baking dish. Add water to the rice. Plug in the rice cooker. Open the oven door.) I try to separate my movements from the booming of the children's voices beside me, which is strangely difficult to do. They seem to be tangled together. How am I supposed to turn the stove on when there is noise in the room? I am aware that this is a new problem for me, and an odd one.

As the kids are eating the dinner I have somehow put on the table in front of them, Eve isn't listening or is throwing food or is doing something that is annoying me. I snap at Eve. I hold Eve by the arms to stop whatever activity is bothering me. Eve looks startled. So does the little friend sitting at the table. I let go. I back up all the way to the couch in the living room. I am confused about a lot of things right now, but I am certain that I don't ever talk to my kids that way, or touch them roughly. I sit down on the couch, away from the kids. I turn off the lamp and sit by myself in the darkness of the living room, my children and their friend, an alarmed little portrait, still visible to me in the kitchen at the other end of the house. David moves in to tend to them. I wave my hand in front of my face. I make a slow karate chop through the air.

I think to myself, "Did reality always feel this way? Did it always feel like watching TV? Did the air always feel thick, as though I could cut through it with my hand like butter?"

I share these questions with David. He watches me, closely. I answer myself.

"I suppose if I have to ask these questions the answer is no. Reality must not have always felt this way."

When the father of Eve's friend comes to pick her up, I tell him what has happened to me. He tells me that I am speaking very slowly. According to the notes that David was advised to make in the days following the accident, when my child's friend and her father leave I say, "I love you guys." David writes a comment: "An uncharacteristic salutation given that they are not that close."

It still makes me laugh to read this clinical documentation of my embarrassing farewell.

I call my sister Susy in BC who is a family doctor, and she tells me that it sounds as though I have a concussion.

THE AFTERMATH

Over the next few days I get a lot of advice from well-meaning people, including doctors. The advice, combined, is: lie in a dark room; don't lie in a dark room. Less screen time; no screen time. Get outside; take it easy. Do nothing for three weeks; don't do nothing for three weeks. Go for a walk; stay in bed and nap as much as you can. Take a break from anything and everything whenever you get symptoms. Slow. Down. My own family doctor kind of shrugs when I ask her what she thinks has happened to me, and says, with a bewildered look in her eyes, "*Something* happened."

I've had plenty of health issues, but I've never heard so many people, including doctors, so blatantly disagree with each other. I feel as though

I am in a country of roads that go nowhere, no maps, total confusion. When you are not functioning, and no one seems to know what to do, and professionals are contradicting each other or shrugging their shoulders and saying "*Something* happened," a kind of panic should set in. But I am not able to conjure a normal response. I just feel numb. Whatever part of my brain that used to hold my anxiety seems to have been knocked out of commission by the fire extinguisher.

I hear from a few friends who have had concussions that have dragged on for years that they wish they had rested more in those first weeks. They wonder if maybe things would have turned out differently for them. I know a screenwriter named Meredith who has had a concussion for two years. She wears wraparound shades and a wide-brimmed baseball cap at all times, even indoors. For the first year she wore a ski helmet at home when her kids got wound up to prevent them from accidentally bonking her head. She hasn't worked since her concussion. She sends me a long, compassionate email advising me to take it easy. "Sleep is your friend," she writes. "Rest is your friend."

Unable to make much sense of anything, I opt for lying in bed and try to keep working on my second draft of *Little Women*. But the words are getting mixed up now; I don't understand what I'm writing or why I'm writing it. I don't understand how to fix a structural problem I've made for myself. I want the film to live in the present tense, beginning with the sisters as adults and flashing back to their early life. I want to make sure we don't just marry Jo off at the end, which would be an affront to Louisa May Alcott, who never wanted to write that ending in the first place. I've had conversations about all of these ideas with the producers, and I am halfway through my second draft, but now I have no idea how to finish it. The words all blur together.

I let the producers know that I've had an accident and I need to take a pause and it isn't just because I've recently lost a fight with them to have Jo March fall in love and end up with a woman (Frieda Bhaer!).

They are compassionate and understanding about my injury. During a phone conversation I ask Amy Pascal, one of the producers, if I sound weird to her. She says, "Honestly, you sound a little weird."

I don't know what I sound like, or what I used to sound like. I don't understand much of what is being said to me. I just know that I can't get this job, or any other job, done in my current state.

About two weeks later, David sits at the end of our bed as I drift off to sleep and begins to sob uncontrollably. It's only then that it occurs to me that it is possible that something very, very bad has happened.

He says, "I'm so sorry this happened to you."

I wonder, as though from across a great distance, if I will get better.

After about three weeks of lying in bed most of the time, I get my first headache. Up until now I've felt dizzy, underwater, confused, nauseous. Now my head begins to pound in a way that makes me feel as though I am having an aneurysm. I'm not. It's a migraine and it is incapacitating. The migraines, once they start, don't ever stop for long. Now every small noise coming from downstairs relentlessly booms in my head. Even from my bedroom, the sounds of my family in the kitchen sound as loud as if I'm on the side of a highway. As the headaches become worse, I try to nap more frequently, taking to heart the advice to rest more.

David takes over most of the daily tasks of getting the kids dressed, fed, and to their activities. I often watch out the bedroom window as he pushes our children down the sidewalk in the double stroller towards a swimming lesson or a playdate or to the park. I'm grateful to have such a competent, loving partner. I'm even more grateful that I can't feel much. I know that what I would be feeling, if I were capable, would be unbearable as I watch my life walk away from me every day.

When I sit in the kitchen with Eve and Aila in the mornings, we have to constantly remind Eve to speak more quietly so as not to exacerbate my headaches. Eve doesn't understand this, or why I'm not doing the walk to preschool in the mornings anymore. I try to be with Aila as much as possible, even while lying in bed, but sometimes her babbling shrieks or cries become too loud for me to take. I miss seeing her daily life, getting to know what words her new little sounds are referring to. I miss taking her to song circles and drop-in centres. I am aware that there is devastation in all this and I feel a dull ache, but I know that when I am better, if I get better, that ache will be much sharper than it is now. If things persist the way they are now, my heart will fight its way through the brain fog and scream its grief for the moments it has missed.

I try to think of ways I can be involved in my children's lives from this static place I am living in. I order a book of Greek myths for children. Every day I give myself the task of reading, slowly, in pieces, one of the condensed versions of these myths and trying to remember the general outline of the story so that I can tell it to Eve at bedtime. It is hard to read the stories. It is even harder to remember them. Sometimes it takes me a few days to read and remember one. In this way, I tell myself, I am making my brain work at least a little bit, and bringing something beautiful from the outside world to Eve, to whom I am, for the most part, bringing very little from beyond the walls of my bedroom.

Friends drop off meals, realizing that this concussion isn't passing as quickly as everyone had hoped. My brother Johnny drops off food and activities for my kids regularly, my sister Susy and several friends call me every few days to check in or drop off groceries, and two of my friends pick a day of the week and always, without fail, drop off dinner for us, though they each have three kids of their own. I am conscious, through the haze, of how lucky I am, and of how much worse this could be.

I have to tell the producers of *Little Women* that I still can't write, or even look at a screen for more than five minutes, and that I don't know when I will be able to. Understandably, they begin to look for a new writer.

My memory of this period is dim, and the timelines jumbled, but at some point during these foggy months I go to a couple of family gatherings of around seventeen people, where I find myself off-kilter, and completely slaughtered by the noise, chaos, and light. When I am exposed to this level of activity and noise, a pain shoots like a diagonal lightning bolt from the top left side of my head down across my body and into my stomach, where it turns into nausea. Even though I know I will feel sick for days as a result of the barrage of stimulus, I go, and as best I can, I pretend to be well.

Some family members have asked David, as he struggles alone to corral our toddler and baby at a Christmas party I did not feel well enough to attend, whether I might be "malingering." It's a word I have to look up. *Malinger* means "to exaggerate or feign illness to escape duty or work." When I see these people, they say things like: "You seem really quiet, Sarah. Is there something wrong?"

It is clear that this is not an invitation to reiterate that I have a brain injury. I try my best to pretend that I'm fine and sneak out for fresh air when I think no one will notice, so that my seeming unwell will not provoke fresh anger or doubt, which I find painful to encounter in the middle of the confusion over what has happened to my mind.

I've had a lot of illnesses and physical problems, many of them invisible: endometriosis, scoliosis, placenta previa, and now a concussion. I think it's starting to get on people's nerves and make them suspicious.

I go to a physiatrist at a head injury clinic. This doctor is hopeful. Her advice is to push myself just up to my threshold of activity, where I get symptoms, and then come back down when I've touched it. "If you go beyond your threshold," she says, "you will set yourself back."

She tells me to listen to my body, to be aware of when symptoms are arising. This is a familiar phrase to me. "Listen to your body" is something I've learned in yoga, in meditation. It feels like a gift to be told to develop this skill further, to become a good listener to the subtle, nuanced messages my body is giving me.

The physiatrist tells me that I need to walk outside every day until I feel my symptoms coming on. When the symptoms become too much, I need to turn around and return home. I walk only three houses past my own the next day and suddenly I get dizzy and feel like I'm going to vomit. The light seems to be strobing even on an overcast day. Every car passing me sounds like a tractor trailer, and I'm in excruciating pain. I take the doctor's advice to listen to my body and turn around and go home again.

I start looking for alternatives. I'm not the kind of person who is generally prone to buying snake oil and I generally have a strong suspicion of anything that isn't backed up by random sampling trials or credible studies or isn't prescribed by a doctor. But my life is gone from me now, doctors are offering me conflicting advice or none at all, and if someone is selling bottles of snake oil with the words "Concussion Cure" on them, I will buy in bulk.

I spend thousands of dollars and enormous amounts of time over the next several months going to appointments in strange places in the suburbs. I go to a neuro-feedback specialist who tells me, after I spend an exhausting day watching balls bounce around a computer screen, that I am in the "one percentile" for attention span for my age and gender (this will haunt me for years), a nutritionist who tells me to stop eating gluten and dairy, and a chiropractor who apparently helped cure hockey player Sidney Crosby. (I will later realize that almost everyone out there specializing in concussions has a rumour swirling around them that they cured Sidney Crosby. After a while, whenever anyone starts to rave about a concussion miracle worker they know, I say, "Let me guess, he treated Sidney Crosby." The answer is invariably yes.)

Craniosacral massage and a nine-week mindfulness-based stress reduction program do offer some temporary relief from the headaches. I meet five other people in the meditation program who are suffering with long-term concussions. We get together once in a while to share notes and resources on the various fixes we have been exploring. One woman is really into cold laser therapy, even though she admits it makes her headaches substantially worse. It's a motley crew, and, for the most part, fully half of us don't show up to the get-togethers. We are either in too much pain or we've forgotten. (Note to self: the presence of a brain injury is not a good organizing principle for a social group.)

I go for my three-month follow-up with the physiatrist. She had expected me to be better by now. I tell her that I still have brain fog most of the time, I have occasional headaches, and I still can't multitask or think clearly. She tells me to start using an exercise bike every day. She wants me to take gabapentin for my headaches and anxiety. I tell her that I don't have much anxiety right now and the headaches have become infrequent. She sends me away with a prescription anyway, and, towards the end of the appointment, she tells me that she suspects that the source of my headaches may be the whiplash I suffered when the fire extinguisher hit me, and that the soft tissue in the neck and shoulder may need to be worked on. She recommends that I go to see a physiotherapist with additional training in manual osteopathy named Kanchan Masand. She says she can't show me a study that will prove that Kanchan's treatment bears results, only that every patient she has ever sent to her gets better.

I never fill the prescription for the gabapentin, but I go to see Kanchan, and after just a few treatments, the manual osteopathy gives me relief from the more severe symptoms for days at a time. But Kanchan is also incredibly wise and has a shaman-like quality. She has the rational, scientific mind of a doctor and the nurturing demeanour of a healer or therapist. She has seen quite a few people with concussions and has figured out a way of encouraging them to begin "playing" with limits. She walks me through my day, how I can try to manage more and challenge myself without being destructive. She is compassionate, kind, a great listener, and also a cheerleader.

When, after a few sessions and more exercise that she has encouraged, I see a little bit of improvement, she says, "All right, now I want you to bug your brain a bit more, so I can see how it responds." She tells me I have to go into a social situation with several people, an environment that she knows will trigger my symptoms. She tells me to start paying attention to how the situation is affecting me. This is the first time someone introduces the concept of pushing *past* my threshold instead of just touching it and then fleeing.

After several weeks of walking more, seeing Kanchan every week, meditating every day, riding an exercise bike, and following Kanchan's instructions to let myself get "bugged a little more," the crushing migraine headaches are now rare and I am able to walk to my kids' school every day. I still can't write, and don't understand much of what is said if there are many people in a room. I still can't be in crowded environments for long without a bad headache coming on, and I still can't bear overhead light and noise. I still have a diminished capacity to think or focus or handle any sort of multi-tasking, but slowly, under Kanchan's guidance and care, I see some real improvement.

Five months after the concussion, I have to return to work. My option on a miniseries I have written based on the Margaret Atwood novel *Alias Grace* is about to expire, and we are running out of money. I've wanted to adapt this book since I was seventeen, and I have worked on the scripts for this limited series for years. Now I don't understand the six scripts that I wrote before the concussion, but I don't have to direct them myself and it must go forward, whatever state I am in. I go to LA with the director and producer to meet with several companies that are interested in making the show.

In the airport, I put my bag, the diaper bag, and the stroller on the conveyor belt of the security machine. The rush of people around me, the noise of the moving belt, and the stream of objects in front of my face, coupled with the dozens of tiny decisions that must be made in this situation, make me feel nauseous, dizzy, my vision blurry and my head hurt. Look at shoes. Untie shoes. Take off shoes. Put shoes on belt. Give passport before or after I put my shoes on the belt? After. Bop baby in carrier to stop her crying. Take carrier off before going through the screener? When you have a brain injury, you have a unique opportunity to witness how much processing your brain is normally able to do with unnoticed effort. So many small decisions, observations, and conclusions are reached in a twenty-second period. It is a marvellous thing, the brain, when it works. Having it not work well anymore gives you a sense of awe at what it does normally, and causes you to wonder why everyone isn't very tired all the time after the mountain of cognitive work that every interaction and activity requires.

I begin to doubt my ability to get through this series of tasks. How many things did I put on the conveyor belt? Will I remember that number once I'm through the scanner? I should tell someone else. "David," I say, "I just put seven things on the conveyor belt."

He laughs. "Medal's on the way."

The executive producer, Noreen, has scheduled just two meetings a day in LA, with space in between them so that I can get through them without getting a crushing headache. When my concussion headaches come, my left eyelid droops noticeably and I'm unable to hide, for the most part, that something is wrong with me. At best I look like I'm not very smart; at worst, I look like I'm a zombie having a stroke. It's not a great look for someone trying to sell a TV show.

The most enthusiastic of the companies we meet with have read the first few episodes and they'd like me to walk them through what happens in the rest of the series. I stare, silently, into the space in front of me. I have no idea what happens in those episodes. I've reread the scripts in preparation for this meeting, but I don't remember a word of them now. Something to do with who really committed the central murder in the story, I think. But at this particular moment, I don't even remember who gets murdered. They ask me a softer question. Maybe I can just describe the arc of each of the characters? After a lot of thought, I realize that I can't do that either. I look helplessly at my collaborators, who try to fill in the blanks. After this shitshow of a meeting, the company decides to pass on the project. Thankfully, Netflix is just as enthusiastic; they have insightful comments and, even better, they don't ask any questions that require me to remember anything.

I make it through production, with limited hours on set. I try not to "cross my threshold," as I've repeatedly been told not to do, but I often must to get the required work done. This is nowhere near the hours and energy it would require for me to direct again one day, and I'm barely making it through. I try to look at the bright side. I've never been particularly ambitious in the sense of having an overall career; I'm reasonably happy with a couple of the films I've made and I don't feel like I have to make more to be a whole person. Now I can concentrate on my kids in a way I wouldn't have been able to do before.

Eve confirms this many times. One day, shortly after the injury, I sit in the darkened living room on the floor, playing "toys in my backpack," a game that involves passing plastic items of food for Eve to pack in a small backpack. We play this every morning since I got injured, and as long as I don't look directly down at the objects I am passing (too many things passing in front of my field of vision makes me hurt), I can play this for an hour at a time.

Eve turns from the plastic banana I have just passed and says to me, "Usually it's not good if people hit their heads. Except you. It's really good when you hurt your head really badly."

"Why?" I ask.

"Now you sit on the floor with me all the time. You used to move around a lot more."

It's true. I am able to give myself to my children in a way I couldn't before. I am here. Not anywhere else, either in mind or body. (It reminds me of when my mother, after one of her chemo treatments, when I was around ten, sat in the window of our living room, knitting me a sweater for the first time. She was someone who had to rush around madly in this world, to care for five children, to pay the bills, to build a career in an industry where women were a rarity, to escape a stillness that would invite the barely contained pain of a difficult childhood to make itself known. I remember standing in the backyard on a cold autumn day, seeing her in that window knitting, and being grateful for the static comfort of her illness, grateful that she was all mine for what I wrongly assumed would be a brief interlude in her well-being.)

And so life goes on, at a different pace than before. Over the next few years I modify my life to accommodate my limitations and, as a result, I generally feel okay. I am slow, unable to multi-task too much, but not in pain. It's not obvious to most people now that I have any lingering symptoms. But if I have an occasional "ambitious day" (take the kids to school, see a friend, grocery shop, make dinner, *and* write a bit), I end up with a crushing headache that takes at least a day of lying in a dark room to resolve. I tell myself that it's good for me to learn to slow down, to talk less, to socialize less, that I've always moved too quickly, talked too much, and packed too much in anyway. I accept that I'll never be my former self again. I accept my new baseline and make peace with it.

Then, in an irrational fit of optimism, we decide to have a third child.

THE REGRESSION

We have a third baby. A beautiful baby. We have a golden summer. Little Amy nurses all night, but we are outside all day so I hardly feel the sleep deprivation. We go to PEI and walk beach after unbroken beach. Aila collects shells with me for hours and hours, Eve runs far ahead into the distance, the baby sleeps on me in her carrier, lulled by the waves.

We return home, David starts his new job in another city, and life gets harder. After four months of nursing the baby through the night, David commuting to work—which leaves me alone with the three kids in the early mornings and evenings on some days—and multiple sicknesses and injuries among my children (some of which have me rushing to the hospital with a newborn under my arm and a bleeding four-year-old), I feel myself start to go off the rails. I wake up on the morning of Halloween, surprise Aila awake, the baby attached to my breast through a gap in the thick felt Mummy Pig costume I am wearing to match her Peppa Pig, and suddenly feel myself drenched in sweat. In the last month and a half we've had, between us, strep twice, allergic reactions to antibiotics, impetigo (which keeps Eve up for many nights, screaming while trying to scratch boils off facial skin), a major tongue laceration, and a sprained ankle. I go to the school Halloween parade with the baby in the carrier, a "happy mom" smile plastered on my face, and feel the world start to go off-kilter again. That night, I walk towards David, who is greeting us on the street in a mob of trick-or-treaters in his own giant Daddy Pig costume, and I yell at him in an English accent, my Mummy Pig head bobbling on top of my head: "Daddy Pig! Glad you're here! Mummy Pig isn't well!"

Over the next few days I slide quickly backwards. The headaches that
I was able to sleep off after a day are now not going away. I don't
understand anything. I feel as though it was only yesterday that fire
extinguisher fell off that wall and slammed me in the head. This can't
be happening. I've worked hard, for years, to get myself back. I've
been doing so much better.

I don't retain much of what happens over the next two months to my
memory. I know that my kids get sick over and over again, and that
my concussion symptoms continue to worsen. I go for walks only at
night, when the light won't bother me. Thankfully, two days a week
we have a part-time caregiver for our kids, Mai, a brilliant, empathetic,
and wise early childhood educator who alleviates enormous amounts
of stress for all of us. I'm not just grateful that she is there; I'm acutely
aware that without her, we would be sunk.

I'm anxious to keep the news of the recurrence of my concussion symptoms from the members of my family who don't believe I had a serious
long-term brain injury in the first place. I'm concerned about their
anger and disbelief reaching me somehow and destabilizing me in my
weakened state, though we don't have a lot of contact anymore beyond
big family gatherings.

I see another specialist, one of the best in the country. He takes an
enormous amount of time with me and has a compassionate bedside
manner. He asks me how many concussions I have had. He asks me to
think hard about this. I tell him that I don't think I have had other
concussions, but I remember one incident that might be of significance.
When I was eleven years old I was in a scene in a TV show in which
my character was kidnapped and tied up in a covered wagon. While
technicians rocked the wagon, much of the set decoration came loose,
and a heavy, full mason jar of preserves perched precariously on a shelf

above me toppled and cracked over my head. I tell this doctor that I remember being dizzy, tired, and out of it for a day or two. "That's a concussion," he says. He writes it down in his notes.

The more head injuries you sustain, he says, the more likely you are to have a concussion that doesn't resolve easily. Remembering this other concussion gives me a strange comfort, a kind of explanation for the wild interruption to my life, that I haven't had before now.

He tells me to walk more. To sleep-train my baby so I can get more regular sleep. To ride a stationary bicycle. To be positive. I ask him if I'll ever make a film again. He pauses. He sighs softly. He says, "I think it's a good goal to have." His tone is gentle. He looks slightly guilty, as though he's just humoured a toddler by telling them they might be able to read the complete works of Shakespeare if they try hard enough. As if he knows this will only lead to a later tantrum, but perhaps it's worth it for the solace it might offer me in this particular moment.

Around Christmas, Eve's head gets slammed by a heavy school door. Thankfully, the concussion symptoms last only a week, but when David plugs in the lights for the Christmas tree, Eve and I both immediately yelp and turn away, nauseated by their brightness. We hold each other and laugh. Eve says, "I'm glad to know how you feel."

THE CURE

One day I see my friend Meredith, she of the wraparound shades, wide-brimmed baseball hat, and ski helmet to protect her from her children, whipping down the street, hat off, no shades, smiling. She doesn't see me and I don't stop her. It is too arresting a sight. I'm afraid that if I get her attention this image will somehow dissolve or reveal itself to be some kind of taunting hologram. What happened to her?

Later that day I email her to ask how she is doing. Without asking directly, I want to either confirm what I have seen or be told that it was an illusion. I need to know if I should have hope, if I *could* have hope, but I'm too afraid to put this question into words because then I might feel the sting of having been wrong. Perhaps I saw someone else who looked like her and she is not better. Perhaps she is still in her house with her ski helmet securely on, her hands in front of her face for extra insurance against the potential of a catapulting child.

Meredith writes back: "I went to this clinic in Pittsburgh, and I am doing really well. No dark glasses, no hat, no naps. Functioning almost normally, and looking to be 100% over the next while. I am so thrilled and over the moon. It has been four years."

She sends me a long chain of emails between her and people I know of who have had concussions, describing this clinic in Pittsburgh. The emails on the thread all have a whiff of the ecstatic at being suddenly, unexpectedly, miraculously better. That elation is what I read in her email too. It is what I had read in her body as she flew down the street. She attaches a video for me to watch and advises that I listen to it instead of watching the screen, since that will likely provoke a headache.

I click on the video, turn my head away, and listen to Dr. Michael ("Micky") Collins, of the University of Pittsburgh Medical Center's Sports Medicine Concussion Program, describe concussions. He describes concussions as an "energy problem" inside the neurons. "And that energy problem is what causes the behavioural problems that occur with concussion."

He describes the various types of concussions. (I have never heard of "types" of concussion.) "It's complicated," he says, "but it's also kind of fun. Because we get patients better when we know how to break it down and treat it the right way."

As he points to a diagram of the brain, he explains the process by which neurons develop this "energy problem," and I realize that in the years of suffering with a concussion, no one has ever explained to me what a concussion *is*. I have not, until watching Dr. Collins describe it in detail, understood the mechanics of what for much of the last three and a half years has robbed me of time with my children and work and joy and music and dancing and parties and my relationships with two of my siblings. But the thing that makes me turn my eyes towards the screen that hurts them is when he says that concussions are manageable. Concussions are treatable.

I ask a respected concussion specialist in Toronto his opinion of this clinic. He tells me that Dr. Collins is very charismatic, he makes a lot of promises, it costs *a lot* of money to go to his clinic, and that I am not missing *anything* by not going to Pittsburgh. He thinks this is snake oil, I can tell. I recognize on his face a weary look I myself display when anyone suggests that there is something in the private US healthcare system that cannot be done here.

My friend Virginia intervenes. She knows someone who has just received treatment from this clinic and is completely better. She tells me I am in crisis and not thinking straight and I *must* go. She speaks to David with the same authority. We listen. This is not the first time in my life that I've needed someone to be bossy, to not ask what I need but instead to know what must be done, to bulldoze my doubts and inaction.

Perhaps it is snake oil, but I'm in the market for snake oil. I've also seen, first-hand, the results of this particular snake oil, and I like what I've seen. I do another google, for insurance, on Dr. Collins and I find the photo that every medical professional working in the area of concussion would die, or likely kill, for: a photo of him sitting next to Sidney Crosby.

It costs $2,500 American for two visits to the UPMC concussion clinic. With the cost of flights and hotels, it is expensive, and as a Canadian I have an allergy to for-profit healthcare as well as the notion of having to pay for it, but based on the warnings, I'd thought this clinic was going to cost me my firstborn. I fill out forms, many of them, and include David's incredibly detailed notes on my condition from those first terrifying months.

My friend Kate, who works as a family support specialist in a neonatal intensive care unit, agrees to come with me to the appointment, to help me navigate, and to take notes, as I will inevitably forget a lot of what is said. Mai comes as well, to take care of the baby while we are at the appointment. She agreed without hesitation to come for this two-day trip to Pittsburgh so I wouldn't have to leave Amy, who is still breast-feeding. I silently thank Mai, over and over, like a kind of incantation when I'm not thanking her out loud, which makes her generally uncomfortable, I think.

On the plane the baby falls asleep while nursing. Her face is cherubic as her lips lose their hold of my breast and her head falls back into the crook of my arm, her cheeks flushed. I listen to my body. My body tells me that this trip is too much for my brain to handle right now. I try to quiet the banging drum in my head, but I'm so concerned that I've over-stretched myself that I can't.

The next morning, Kate and I wait in a brightly lit waiting room with a TV blaring. "This room was clearly not designed as a concussion clinic," I mutter to Kate. A young, affable resident ushers us into a clinic room.

After a twenty-minute neurocognitive computer test that makes me break into a sweat ("one percentile for attention span for my age and gender" echoes in my head) and a short examination by a resident, Dr. Collins comes in, in what I like to call a burst of AMERICA! He is confident, direct, to the point; he owns the space. If personalities had weather systems attached to them, our hair would be blown back. He examines me, looking intensely into my eyes as he quickly moves me through a battery of tests involving dots on popsicle sticks and asking me to stare at my thumb while rotating my head to the right and left. He speaks quickly and loudly. Kate diligently takes notes. I tell him about my symptoms, both minute and large.

"Stop tracking your symptoms! Stop processing your symptoms! Don't waste your time!"

He is yelling at me. Then he turns and yells at Kate. He points at her notebook. "You stop tracking her symptoms too! You're not helping her!"

He tells me that from now on I am to start paying attention to my recovery times instead of listening to my body's symptoms.

He explains that the clinical trajectories of my concussion have been diagnosed as primarily vestibular with post-traumatic migraine and anxiety. He shows me a diagram of intersecting circles of six types of concussion. He points to the vestibular circle, the anxiety circle, and the migraine circle. He draws a line between the vestibular circle and the anxiety circle and then down to the migraine circle.

When the fire extinguisher fell on my head, he explains, it led to vestibular problems. This in turn switched on my anxiety, which, along with bad advice, led me to stay in a dark room for a long time, which led to my migraines beginning. This fed deeper into the anxiety, which fed more into the vestibular system acting up. He sees this a lot, he says. When patients have vestibular dysfunction, the same parts of the brain that control emotional functioning get affected, so patients who have vestibular dysfunction have an autonomic reaction where their heart rate increases and they develop anxiety. He again points to the vestibular circle and then the anxiety circle.

But—"and here's where it gets complicated," he says—because this pathway is now there, the anxiety can now talk back. He explains that the vestibular symptoms aren't psychological, but because these two systems have become so good at talking to each other, now my anxiety can switch on my vestibular problems. "You have to break the communication," he says. "You need to stop *this*"—he points to the anxiety circle—"from talking to *this*"—he points to the vestibular circle— "which talks to this"—and back down to the migraine circle.

I tell him that I'm not sure about the anxiety piece. I'm generally a fairly anxious person, but the one thing I haven't felt a lot of since the concussion is anxiety. "I've felt kind of numb," I say.

"What does a frog do when it's scared?" he asks. He freezes, his eyes popping out of his head. There is an awkward silence before I realize he is imitating a frog.

"Oh. Right," I say.

"What does a goat do? You can just push it over." He freezes again, his limbs rigid, and begins to tilt to one side. He chuckles a little as he recovers from his frozen goat impression and steadies himself.

I look at him, confused. This guy is weird.

"You froze when this happened. It's a way of manifesting anxiety." He looks me right in the eye and leans in close, as though he doesn't already have every molecule of my attention. He says, "If you remember only one thing from this meeting, remember this: run towards the danger."

I should now view my symptoms, he says, not as something to be avoided but as "opportunities" to increase my threshold of tolerance. I must learn how to run into the discomfort instead of away from it.

In order to fully recover, I require daily exposure to anything that has traditionally triggered symptoms or caused me pain. Grocery shopping, parties, screen time, driving, film sets, all of it. My avoidance of the things that have bothered me has made it more and more difficult for my brain to cope with them.

I will also be given a rigorous routine of vestibular and physical exercise. I am to do these every single day, without fail. I must eat three regular meals a day, stay hydrated, and be on a strict sleep schedule.

When I feel a headache coming on after being in an environment or participating in an activity that triggers my symptoms I must not lie down or rest but do the dynamic exercises they are going to show me, or go for a fast walk. Then I must go back into the environment I was exposing myself to. In other words, instead of "touching my threshold and then coming back down" as I have been advised so often—*Keep. Going.*

"You're going to do everything you now think you can't do. You're going to be social, you're going to do a dynamic workout every day, you're going to be in the environments that bother you the most. You need to retrain the system.

"If I find out you've been lying down in the day, or napping, I will scream at you. I will. I will scream at you!" He spins towards Kate and jabs a finger at her. "I will! I will scream at her!"

Kate almost drops her pen in alarm.

"And stop taking notes! You make me nervous and you're not helping!"

I don't want to ask him if I will ever get back to one hundred percent, I don't want to hear the same soft sigh and hedged answer I heard from the specialist in Toronto, but I can't help myself and I ask him anyway.

He says, without hesitating, and still kind of yelling: "YES! I guarantee you will get back to one hundred percent! And sooner than you think."

"How long do you think?" I ask.

He considers me thoughtfully, then says, "Four to six weeks. This is a fairly straightforward case."

I wonder now, truly, if he is a charlatan. I've been suffering with concussion symptoms for three and a half years and, at my best, I've been operating at around sixty percent. I'm also well versed enough in the language of doctors to know to be suspicious when someone offers this kind of guarantee of a cure with a timeline, especially when it comes to an injury that no one seems to understand much about.

"But you're going to have to work really hard," he adds. He leans in like a football coach. "WE'RE GOING TO HAVE TO PIN OUR EARS BACK AND GO AFTER THIS THING!"

I wonder if he's going to head-butt me to emphasize his point and I jerk my head back slightly, wary of being re-concussed.

I glance at Kate, who immediately looks away from me. We are both on the verge of giggles, and hysteria will break loose if one of us even smiles. We are polite Canadians, unused to being yelled at. Even the positive things we say are said with a note of apology.

He tells me that I, and the people around me, have been accommodating this concussion in hundreds of ways, some conscious and some invisible to me. My job is to find out what those accommodations are and to strip them away so that my brain can reacclimatize and be in the world as it used to be. If a room doesn't feel too bright to me, I am to ask the other people in the room if it is bright enough for them and adjust the lights accordingly. If I am watching TV with someone else and the volume isn't hurting my head, I am to ask them if it is loud enough for them.

Suddenly his tone softens and he tilts his head as he says, compassionately, "You're a screenwriter. How do you spend so much time in front of the computer? It must really hurt."

My guard down, I enthusiastically share with him my discovery of an amazing light filter app called f.lux, which cuts the blue light of the screen and has allowed me to look, without aggravation, at my computer for short periods of the day. But it's a trap. His eyes narrow and he swipes his hand across his throat like a knife.

I am alarmed. "I have to get rid of it?"

"Yup. Gone. And you need to work your way up to more and more time in front of the computer."

Though he has already (insanely) guaranteed me a one hundred percent recovery, I want to confirm the details. I ask him if I will ever make a film again.

He says, "Absolutely you will make a film again. I'll put it this way. You're not going to be totally better *until* you make a film again. Because that is part of what makes you, you. Right now, you are bartering between different areas of your life, and that must stop now. All areas are equal."

I tell him that a doctor in Canada told me, with skepticism, that making a film one day seemed like a "good goal for me to have."

Dr. Collins shakes his head, and I can see that he is trying to contain his frustration. "That's an awful thing to say to someone."

I ask him, tentatively, what will happen if one day I push myself the way he is suggesting only to reap the terrible rewards the next day, when I am alone with my kids, trying to get them fed and to school while breastfeeding the baby at the same time. What if I have a terrible migraine as a result of pushing myself too hard and can't do what is required of me?

"ATTACK, ATTACK, ATTACK!" is his immediate response. "PUSH THROUGH IT. ATTACK ATTACK ATTACK!"

I feel Kate look down at the notes in her lap. We cannot look at each other. There will be no method by which we can explain a sudden outburst of laughter to someone this intense.

"JUST KEEP GOING."

I nod. I feel nauseous and terrified, but I try to put aside my doubts about his huge claims of recovery, I try to put aside my characteristic awkwardness in the face of such confidence and my feeling of being overwhelmed by what is being asked of me. I try to focus on my mental picture of Meredith flying down the street that day, liberated. I tell him he treated a friend of mine, another screenwriter in Toronto, and she is doing really well.

"What's with all the female filmmakers from Canada?" he asks. "What is going on up there?" He's had a weird number of Canadian female filmmakers and screenwriters come down to his clinic with concussions. (Indeed, I myself now know at least four Canadian female filmmakers who have been to this clinic.) "The front desk keeps asking me what is going on in Toronto."

I tell him that we're a competitive bunch. The pool of female film-makers is small, but even smaller is the pool of money to make films. We've taken to bashing each other over the head to put each other out of the running for the public money. Hence, more business for him, and an added bonus of appearing as the doctor character in lots of overly serious, low-budget movies that people will never see.

He stares at me.

"I'm joking," I say. I let out a bad laugh, an embarrassing laugh, to make sure he knows I'm joking.

He gives me a small smile with about a quarter of one side of his mouth. It's the slightly resentful smile you give when someone thinks the boring joke they just told is really funny and it's too awkward to not smile, but it pains you to do so for the dignity it costs you. I hate this moment. I'd like it to end.

He leaves the room and Kate and I erupt into wild, bewildered laughter.

THE PROGRAM

The physiotherapist takes me into a busy three-storey gym. She tells me to stand with my back against the wall and to look out at the room while she takes me through a series of exercises. The constant motion in the room, the noise, the overhead light make me feel dizzy and nauseous. She smiles. "This room wasn't designed for concussion patients but we couldn't have designed it better ourselves."

I look out at the noisy, busy, bright room and say, "Right. Run towards the danger."

As she takes me through a sequence of (for me) challenging exercises, I ask her if Dr. Collins is always so yelly.

She says, "Oh, did he yell at you?"

"Kind of," I say.

"Well, he's been doing this for a long time, and he's seen a lot of patients, and he's also a clinical psychologist, so he can tell within about a minute of meeting you if you need to be listened to compassionately or if you need—"

"I needed to get screamed at," I say.

Back in her office, the physiotherapist asks me what I used to do for exercise. I tell her that I used to do yoga regularly but I haven't done it in ages. Downward dogs and being upside down in general now make me feel as though my head will explode. She nods and types. Before I leave she hands me a sheet of paper with my exercise regimen for the next six weeks. Every day I am to walk fast for twenty minutes and go through three repetitions of physical exercises— squats, weights, planks, and so on. At the bottom of the sheet is a picture of someone doing a downward dog with "x 30" written beside it. I look up at her questioningly. She says, "Yup. You're going to do them."

Next I meet with Anne, the vestibular therapist, who gives me a series of exercises to do. I keep my eyes on my thumb as I move my head rapidly side to side, then quickly up and down. I throw a ball to her behind my back and as I move my head to look over the other shoulder she throws it back to me. We do this ten times. I feel dizzy, nauseous, and unable to believe that I am to do all of this every day for a month and a half. Anne reiterates what Dr. Collins has told me, that my main job now is to stop making environments accommodate me and to instead increase my tolerance of different environments. When I hit a moderate level of discomfort, it is a cue not to lie down and rest but to switch activities or exercise. Anne is kind, patient, compassionate. She watches me incredibly carefully as she assesses me and develops my program.

At the end of the day, I meet Dr. Collins again. He is softer now, calmer. "I'm sorry you didn't come here sooner," he says. "I'm sorry you've suffered for so long. This must have had a big impact on your life. On your kids."

I am quiet. I nod.

He asks me how confident I am that this will work. He asks me this question in a way that implies that the entire outcome of my care may depend on my confidence in it. I tell him that it's hard for me to believe that I will get better as quickly as he says I will, but I've seen the results with one of his patients, so I feel I should probably just have some faith. This is the Canadian equivalent of "FUCK YEAH" but he hears it the way Americans tend to hear these types of equivocations from me, with a mixture of pity and frustration. In response, he says what I now say to everyone I meet with a concussion who I advise to go to the Pittsburgh clinic:

"Well, what you've been doing so far hasn't been working very well, so it's worth committing to it."

THE RECOVERY

After our football-coach impressions of Dr. Collins ("ATTACK! ATTACK! ATTACK!"), Mai says, "I can't tell—did you like him or not?"

Kate and I both shrug and try to explain. We don't know, but we've been stunned into a new way of perceiving things, our world view cracked open a little. Our expectations, our relationships with ourselves, with our children, and our sense of what is actually compassionate have all shifted somehow based on what we learned today about how the brain works, about how one gets better. We are questioning some of the basic tenets of "wellness" wisdom we have previously taken to heart, which implores us to take it easy and be gentle and accept our limits without specifying what limits are acceptable.

While I'm not a fan of men shouting at me or telling me to push harder—I've had enough of that in my life—I've also never been on a sports team or had a coach whose ultimate goal is for me to succeed, not only by pushing me but also by being there to help me get there. I've had plenty of critical exhortations from my family to just "push harder" and not be so weak, all of which have served to drive me deeper into the cave of myself, yet there is an exhilaration in feeling that someone is pushing me forward while rooted firmly on my side, offering support and expressing their unshakable belief in me.

When I get home, I follow the treatment plan to the letter. I start every day by throwing a ball behind my back and having Aila catch it and throw it back to me as I whip around to the other side. We do this dozens of times. She tells me she likes the feeling that she is helping me to get better, but one day, without looking up at me, she says, "We keep talking about you getting better. But I like you now. Will you be different when you're better? I don't want you to be different." I try to assure her I will be the same, with more energy. But inwardly I wonder if I'm telling her the truth. I've never lived this way before, or pushed myself this hard. I have no idea what will come of it.

I never miss a day of the exercises. I take the kids to school. I make dinner. I clean the kitchen. I try to do many of the errands David has done for the last few years, running to grocery stores, getting things fixed. I write. I socialize. When my children ask me to play, I say yes, no matter what, no matter how raucous the game. I write a screenplay. I sign on to direct a few episodes of a web series, keeping in mind the advice that I won't get better until I do my job again, but mindful that I have a baby who I am not yet ready to leave for a longer project. I go everywhere I am invited, usually with the baby in tow. I'm in a kind of manic haze. It hurts like hell, I feel nauseous, and especially in those first weeks, I get the beginnings of what used to turn into crushing migraines. But when I feel those beginnings, instead of going to bed, I go for a fast walk on busy sidewalks or do an intense dynamic workout. By the time I am done, the headache has usually faded substantially. I learn to push through, and to have faith that I will feel better when I do so. In short, I learn to stop listening so attentively to my body. A friend who is cheerleading my recovery says to me, almost every day, over text or the phone, "This is hard, but you can do hard things."

Every now and then the noise of my children hurts my head at the breakfast table and I ask them to stop screaming.

Eve, who is seven now, does an impression of my impression of Dr. Collins and screams back at me: "RUN TOWARDS THE DANGER, MOM!"

"ATTACK ATTACK ATTACK!" screams Aila at the top of her lungs, in her best American accent. "MOM! PIN YOUR EARS BACK!"

And then they get louder. They will be quiet no more on account of my concussion. They know it won't help me.

It is perhaps two weeks after my return from Pittsburgh that I get a glimpse of the reward that is to come. David has made a plan for us to go out for dinner with his colleague and his partner, who I have never met before. As Amy is still exclusively breastfeeding, she will come with us. Since the concussion, this has been my idea of hell. The energy it takes just to focus on what someone is saying in a loud restaurant, let alone to deliver the social niceties necessary with people I don't know while juggling a baby, is the kind of thing that sinks me. Sometimes, after a scenario like this one, my left eyelid sinks and covers half my eye as my head throbs in pain. But I go. It's part of my treatment.

David's colleague and his partner are kind, thoughtful, and curious, the kind of people you meet once and know you don't want to let go of. I nurse the baby, put her back in her stroller to sleep, and then, halfway through dinner, I realize with a jolt that I have understood absolutely everything that has been said in the conversation thus far. I understand, I contribute, I don't hurt. A light has turned on and illuminated all that has been hidden from me these last three and a half years.

As we are walking home, I am suddenly deeply aware of how far I have been from feeling like myself for the last few years. Even on my good days, during my "okay" months, I was light years away from feeling this clarity, this aliveness, this presence in the world. I tell this to David and I start to cry, knowing now that I will get better. Until this moment of total faith that this will work, that I will be back to myself, and of knowing what it is to be alive in my brain again, I have not registered the weight of the loss of the last few years. Three of the four years of my second child's life. Three of my oldest child's seven years. I have been there with my whole heart but only half my brain. I weep for how little I knew about how altered I have been.

This moment of clarity passes. But there is another one two days later, and another the day after that. Then they start to come on top of each other. Several a day, lasting longer and longer. After four weeks, I feel this intense vibrance and presence all the time. After six weeks, I never have headaches, brain fog, confusion, dizziness, or fatigue anymore. I am myself. I am back. I can do anything I did before and more. Because now that "run towards the danger" organizes my life, I find that I jump into the tasks that scare me, the ones I have always avoided.

It's strange, this paradigm shift. It's hard for me to get used to the idea that this culture I've been steeped in of "listening to your body" and "self-care" has its limits. That's not to say that it's unimportant to learn how to do these things if you're someone who doesn't do them at all. But over the years I've been told, by pretty much every medical professional, every yoga instructor, every meditation teacher, to listen to my body *more* without anyone ever asking me how much I was listening *already*. When I listened to my body through my malfunctioning, concussed brain and it told me it couldn't do things, I confirmed its limits. It heard, "You're right. You can't do those things." I listened to my body. But my body listened to me, too.

When I first met him, Dr. Collins had said: "When you have a concussion, you don't have good instincts about what will make you better. You want to lie in a dark room. You don't want to be social. You want to drop out of your life. That bad instinct, coupled with bad advice, makes you much, much sicker than you need to be."

At my follow-up appointment in Pittsburgh six weeks later, I can feel the team's elation at my results. Dr. Collins, no longer in football-coach mode, says, "I can't tell you how gratifying it is when we see someone improve the way you have. You worked so hard for this. We are all so proud of you."

He asks me if other people have noticed the change in me. I tell him that my next-door neighbour, who never knew me before the accident, saw me walking down the street the other day and didn't recognize me until I was very close. "What happened to you?" he had said. "You look like a different person, like someone turned on the lights."

Dr. Collins says, "I'll bet your kids are happy to have you back."

I tell him that my middle child, Aila, never really knew me before the concussion. She was one year old when the accident occurred. So now she is getting to know me, really know me, for the first time.

He takes a small inhale of breath. His eyes well up.

I tell him that Aila is often bewildered at how much I can play boisterously now. "You are such a *fun* Mom! You really know how to play!" she often exclaims, delighted.

I give him a drawing Eve has made, a cartoon of an animal-like creature soaring through the air, long ears flying in the wind behind it. In
a bubble above the airborne creature are the words, "Let's pin our
ears back and go after this thing!" I take a picture of Dr. Collins holding up this drawing to give to my kids. For them, Dr. Collins is a kind
of folk hero, a wizard who gave them a mother who can play and
dance and be unafraid of things.[5]

When I say goodbye to Anne, the vestibular therapist, I thank her. "You
must have people thanking you for getting their lives back every single
day," I say to her.

She says, "It never gets old."

The physiotherapist takes me to the gym to go through my new workout
regimen. I see a young man in the gym, maybe in his early twenties, long
unkempt hair, pale, riding an exercise bike and crying. I imagine that he
has been in a dark room for months, maybe years. I imagine that he is in
agony in this physical therapy room, with the noise of the exercise
machines, the glare of the lights above him, a sense of the uselessness of
hurting himself in this way, in a body he doesn't know anymore. I imagine that he is, right now, taking one step off the edge of a cliff and that he
will, eventually, sooner than he thinks, land in a life he recognizes, a life
that, upon his return to it, will be better than he remembered it.

There isn't a day that goes by when I'm not grateful to be able to think
clearly, to not have to modify my life to accommodate an injury that no
one can see and so few understand. I feel elation at being able to manage
the simple things in life as well as having the ability to work and dance
and play.

Despite all this, the concussion has left marks on my life. Though they
believed I suffered a concussion, and were quite supportive when I
was first injured, the disbelief in the longevity and severity of my

concussion that some of my family still carry bewilders and hurts me somewhat. Months after my recovery, when an ophthalmologist tells me that a damaged optic nerve is responsible for the poor sight in my left eye and is likely a result of the injury from the fire extinguisher, I let out a kind of involuntary sigh of relief, so gratified am I to have some physical evidence that this really happened to me.

"But I'm sweating!" is what I think some of my family heard during the years when I couldn't attend many noisy family events, or needed to take a walk when a headache came on. As with all cracks and fissures in families, this one has many layers, ancient and calcified, but knowing of their doubt was sad and stressful and caused me to continually doubt myself and perceive myself as weak when (as Dr. Collins showed me) I needed to feel strong. At times I found that I heard some of my family's skepticism more loudly than my body's own pleas, and judged myself harshly for how ill I felt.

Being able to measure what one used to be capable of and finding it significantly altered, and having a felt sense of what it was to be inside that previous self, are two very different things. So many people I have spoken with who have experienced a concussion speak of this pain of not being believed, of not being able to fully believe themselves.

NOW

As I write this, Canada has just had another federal election. *Little Women* is in theatres. I watch it with my kids. Eve, who remembers me telling the story, years ago at bedtime, of Amy March falling through the ice, is inspired by the film (which has been beautifully realized by Greta Gerwig) to scamper upstairs before bed to write tales of childhood.

It has been four years since I lost my brain the way I knew it. It has been only eight months since I've lived the elated life of having regained it.

I'm back in the world now so fully, and there is a strange symmetry to a federal election and the project I was working on when I got smashed over the head both coming back into view again.

These days I try, in the chaos of everyday life, to be mindful of the contradictory lessons I learned from needing to slow down and then to speed up again. I learned to breathe, fully, and to be in the moment. I learned to sit on the floor and play with my kids and let the tasks and obligations of everyday life fade far behind us as we played with small objects or read books or talked. And I learned to have faith that I could do more than I thought I could, to not be afraid, or to proceed despite my fear. I wonder, sometimes, if I can find a way to live in the middle of all the conflicting things I have learned. Can one run towards the danger at the same time as being present in the moment? I don't know. But at least I have my brain back, to help me sort it out.

These days I take my kids to school, I take my baby to busy drop-in centres, I write scripts. There is no physical limit to the screen time or social time I can manage. I can play tickle monster with my kids endlessly, and delight in their screams of excitement. I can understand what people are saying in crowded rooms. I can understand what I am writing and what I have written.

Now in my forties, I have changed in ways that reach far beyond the limits of my concussion recovery. I know now that I will become weaker at what I avoid, that what I run towards will strengthen in me. I know to listen to my body, but not so much that I convince myself I can't do things or that I can't push myself; not so much that I can use the concept of listening to my body as a weapon against my vitality. I do the highway drive I'm nervous about doing. I prepare to make a film. I write the book I've always wanted to write. "Run towards the danger" is a way of being that I have taken into my life with me; a treasure, a spell, a sword.

ENDNOTES

1   In Andrew Yule's book about the production, *Losing the Light*, he refers to my having arterial hypertension and respiratory arrhythmia as a result of the shoot. I have no memory of this, but it causes me to wonder if I was in fact given the clean bill of health that I was led to believe.

2   These incidents are detailed in *Losing the Light*.

3   Excerpt from "There's No Business Like Show Business", music and lyrics by Irving Berlin, Copyright 1946 by Irving Berlin Music Co.

4   A subsequent adaptation of the *Anne* books by CBC and Netflix—*Anne with an E*—painstakingly tried to inject more reality and inclusion.

5   I've wanted to write this essay for a very long time, but I've been paralyzed by the idea that I am writing about a failure of healthcare in Canada at a time when the fight for public healthcare is at a critical point south of the border. I've had, over the course of my life, major spinal surgery, a high-risk pregnancy on bedrest in the hospital, a baby in a neonatal intensive care unit, three C-sections, and a surgery for severe endometriosis. It has all been covered by universal healthcare. I have had, with few exceptions, wonderful care. And still I see such nightmarish portraits of our healthcare system painted in the US media. I'd be horrified to think that this

story might play into harmful propaganda about our public health-care system being unable to deliver what private healthcare in the United States can. A premier of Newfoundland, Danny Williams, famously went to the United States to have a heart valve replace-ment that was pioneered in Toronto. Though the best outcomes in the world for the particular surgery he needed were in his own coun-try, he went south of the border. Dr. Danielle Martin, a Canadian doctor and prominent advocate for universal healthcare, told this story to a US senate committee, adding, "Sometimes people have a perception, and I believe this is fuelled in part by media discourse, that going to where you pay more for something necessarily makes it better, but it's not actually borne out by the evidence."

When I was in Pittsburgh on my last visit, the clinic referred me to an optometrist who helped me put my own experience in perspec-tive. His wife is Canadian, and he spends a lot of time up here. He said, "When it comes to eye surgeries, you guys are always five to ten years ahead of us. With concussion, it's one of the few areas I've seen where you are consistently behind. It has nothing to do with private versus public. In many cases, the public system in Canada is way ahead of where we are here in terms of innovation."

ACKNOWLEDGMENTS

My husband David embraces life, undaunted, no matter what it throws at him. Being in his presence has made everything feel possible, including the writing of this book. I am grateful every day that I get to walk through the world with someone so alive.

I have had the absurd luck of having the brilliant Nicole Winstanley at Hamish Hamilton and Virginia Smith at Penguin Press as my editors. Their wisdom, insight, and ability to give clear direction wrapped in enormous compassion is breathtaking. One day, I hope to be a skilled enough writer to actually deserve editorial notes as beautifully written as the ones I received on this book. They gently guided me with the questions I was afraid to ask myself, and so I found myself, often, running towards dangers I hadn't even identified were there. Nicole was also the first person, over a decade ago, who ever asked me if I'd considered writing a book. It unearthed a lifelong desire in me that I had almost buried.

The legendary Sarah Chalfant guided me thoughtfully through the process of getting this book published with unrivalled class, patience, and openness.

Shaun Oakey was the skilled, watchful eye who presided over the copy edit; if I had dared to sneak a semicolon into this sentence, he surely would have challenged it.

Ben Phelan helped me with fact-checking and kept me very entertained while doing so.

Thanks so much to Lauren Tamaki for the tender, thoughtful illustrations on the title pages, and to Kelly Hill for giving the book its stunning design.

Yvette Lang provided helpful research and support.

Rick Salutin has been a constant in my life, and he was with this book too, spending many hours helping me navigate my own feelings around it, as well as the book itself, and never acting like he wanted to be anywhere else.

Gaby Morgerman, Frank Frattaroli, and Pam Winter read the first draft of every essay and spent hours on the phone with me as I tried to shape and understand them. They, as well as Celia Chassels, have been my guides through my years as an actor and director, and have helped me navigate the film industry with wisdom and huge amounts of patience.

At a time when I didn't have much confidence, Miriam Toews pushed me solidly forward. Her awe-inspiring warmth and belief that this book was ready to go out into the world made me move forwards just when I was preparing to take a giant leap backwards.

My cousin Sarah Rigler provided insight and unconditional support as I was completing these essays.

Kate Robson supported me in countless ways throughout the process of writing this book, and I am so grateful for her willingness to constantly be there, especially during my difficult concussion days.

My brother Johnny makes me laugh harder than anyone in the world and is kind in ways that require courage. I was terrified to show him this book, and received nothing but support when I did. Through all of it, he's my person. He doesn't get nearly enough airtime in this book, given how large a character he is in my life.

My sister Susy has always encouraged me to write. It has meant the world to me that she has seen me this way. And I aspire to have her warmth, tolerance, and resilience.

I was lucky to grow up in the same house as the best big brother in the world, Mark. He introduced me to poetry, politics, adventures, inappropriate jokes, and the idea of being loved unconditionally.

My sister Jo is the real writer in our family. She has held some of my secrets, and encouraged me to share some of them so I wouldn't have to continue to carry the weight of them alone.

My Auntie Ann nurtured me in ways that were formative and I am grateful to have had her as a model every day that I am a parent myself.

The following people provided essential support and insight: Justin Safayeni, Andrea Gonsalves, Alison Pick, Kevin Morris, Scott Thornley, Shirley Blumberg, and Emily Jade Foley. I was very lucky to benefit from the wisdom, support, and careful legal oversight of Linda Friedner and Iain MacKinnon. Nicole Stamp provided incredibly clear, practical, wise feedback.

I am grateful for both the rock-solid friendship and the helpful feedback of the following people during the process of writing this book:

Jack Hourigan, Iris Ng, Chris Curreri, Sarah Mitchell, Day Deans-Buchan, Margaret Atwood, Patrice Goodman, Ava Roth, Virginia Johnson, Louis Trochatos, Atom Egoyan, Andrea Addario, Cathy Gulkin, Anton Piatigorsky, Luc Montpellier, Jessica Reid, Susan Magotiaux, Harriet Sachs, Clayton Ruby, Emma Ruby-Sachs, Jane

Saks, Joe Carens, Jennifer Nedelsky, Hannah Sung, Chi Nguyen, and the whole Azevedo family (Bev, Frank, Jessica, Chrissy, and Frankie).

Jaimie Donovan convinced me to switch gears and prioritize finishing this book on a walk in November 2019. Sometimes a walk with a good friend can be life-changing.

Megan Sandomierski, my sister-in-law, has been there for us time and time again these last nine years since having children. I am grateful for her presence and love.

I mention Maiko Takagi only briefly in this book, but our lives would not be possible without her. She is wise, empathetic, a role model to me, and I am astonished by our good fortune to have her in our lives.

My friend Gisele Gordon spent many hours guiding me through the practical intricacies of how to live with a concussion. Were it not for her understanding, help, and practical care in that first year after the injury, and her friendship in general, I would be lost.

Ava Roth and Kristen Thomson dropped off weekly meals for us during the hardest days of my concussion and have showed up in so many ways throughout the past several years.

Corey Mintz got me through my recovery from my surgery and the most awkward years of my teens. He remains a trusted, beloved friend and is a great food reporter.

Thank you to the women who had the incredible courage to come forward in the Jian Ghomeshi case. Lucy DeCoutere, Linda Redgrave, the unnamed complainant, as well as the other women who wrote articles or came forward to the police and whose charges did not make it to court. You started a movement. It won't be forgotten. The world is changing because of you.

Melanie Randall and Lori Haskell were invaluable guides and supports when writing "The Woman Who Stayed Silent." Both of them do groundbreaking work around the issue of sexual assault. They are also amazing friends.

Elaine Craig's book, *Putting Trials on Trial*, was a huge help to me in understanding the challenges for women who come forward in sexual assault cases.

Chris Murphy made me keep thinking about telling the story in "The Woman Who Stayed Silent," and his words stayed with me throughout the years. He has been there in a real way to advise and support throughout the process of making the decision to tell this story.

Thank you to every medical professional who was involved in my care at the Hospital for Sick Children (SickKids) and Mount Sinai Hospital in Toronto. There are many people at both these places who had an impact on me whom I haven't mentioned in this book.

Judith Neilly is not mentioned in the essay "Run Towards the Danger" but her osteopathy and cranial-sacral treatments provided me relief during the early days of my concussion.

Kanchan Masand made recovery seem possible and probable and has helped so many people with concussions and other injuries and illnesses. I am lucky to have been in her care.

Dr. Michael (Micky) Collins and Anne Mucha and the team at the UPMC concussion clinic gave me my brain and my life back.

I have a wee "concussion club" of women writers who had concussions and who all went to UPMC to be treated. I am so grateful to have Semi Chellas, Tassie Cameron, and Meredith Vucinich to share and listen with.

Dr. Douglas Hedden, when I was fifteen, saved my mental health in ways that are hard to calculate, with his compassionate ability to see and treat me as a whole child instead of solely a scoliosis patient. He also read the entire manuscript carefully and provided thoughtful insight on every essay. I can't believe my luck that I had him as a doctor at that crucial time in my life.

Dr. Marvin Waxman was thorough enough to find my scoliosis during a routine insurance medical exam for a TV show. Nice one!

Dr. Kate Hays was the performance psychologist who worked with me on my stage fright. Her work was life-changing for so many.

I am grateful for the mentorship of Michelle Fisk, my kind, wondrous dressing-room mate in Stratford.

Marti Maraden put a kid's well-being before her play. She is one of a kind.

Thank you to the cast and crew of *Alice Through the Looking-Glass* at the Stratford Festival in 1994. And sorry about that winter Elgin run!

Laurie Farrance, my tutor and guardian on the set of *Road to Avonlea*, was there for me in untold ways during the hardest years of my childhood. There aren't enough pages to describe the care she put into my well-being, and I'll always be grateful. She doesn't get nearly enough space in these pages.

Eric Idle was a safe haven for me when I was eight and nine, and validated my memories, more than once, as an adult. He was also a careful reader of this book as it progressed and filled in gaps that were essential to my understanding of that time.

Richard Conway read the essay "Mad Genius" and provided feedback, even as he was struggling with major health issues. I will forever be grateful to him for validating my experience and adding much-needed background on how and why certain things happened during the filming of *The Adventures of Baron Munchausen*. Kent Houston also provided support and valuable feedback on this essay.

Charles McKeown was very kind to me during *The Adventures of Baron Munchausen* and was a valuable resource in recalling details from that production.

Zachary Bennett has talked through and explored the experience of being a child actor at length with me and has been an inspiration in embarking on the unpacking of these experiences. I knew he had my back when I was ten, and it's never changed.

Mag Ruffman remains an essential part of my life. Childhood was made lighter because of the magic she brought to it, and she continues to bring the same sense of wonder to my own children, as does her incredible husband Daniel Hunter. Their practical and emotional support made the completion of this book possible.

I have heard stories of many crew people on film sets (grips, electrics, drivers, wardrobe assistants, et cetera) who at various moments stood up for children and risked their own jobs in doing so. I have witnessed it myself more than once. Thank you for these courageous acts. Even if you didn't succeed, the fact that you tried is remembered.

Dr. Thomas Socknat was my professor in the academic bridging program at the University of Toronto. He lit us all on fire with his passion for Canadian history and his entrancing storytelling, and he graciously answered all my questions about the PEI Tenant League.

Dr. Paul Bernstein, the legendary ob-gyn who retired recently (but still assists at C-sections because it makes him happy), took the time to advise me on the medical details in "High Risk."

Dr. Jose Carvalho provided valuable feedback on "High Risk."

Mary Ellen Cooke, the anesthesiologist extraordinaire, was a uniquely detailed reader of these stories, and was very generous with the time she put into both reading and responding to them. She was helpful in understanding the medical details, validating my experience, and she is just a sheer delight to know. She also advised me to apologize to Soap-Opera-Hot Doctor who was actually very nice. See below.

To Soap-Opera-Hot Doctor: you are a lovely person and were a great neighbour and I hope my teasing portrait of you didn't offend! You wear just the right amount of face moisturizer.

Dr. Sarah Freke held many of these stories for years and helped me process them all. I don't know who or where I would be had I not been in psychoanalysis and psychotherapy with her since I was twenty-two.

My mother routinely sacrificed sleep in favour of reading books and read me a story every night before bed no matter how crazily busy she was. I am grateful for what this instilled in me and of course for the laughter, warmth, and fun she brought to the world. There won't be another like her.

My father, Michael Polley, was a miraculous person and we remained close until his death in 2018. My 2012 film, *Stories We Tell*, paints a fuller, kinder portrait of who he was than I have in these pages. Perhaps it is because I made that film while he was living that I felt licensed to explore some of his flaws in this book, after his death. Whatever those flaws were, he was enlightened in ways I have yet to encounter in another person, and he was capable of generous responses in situations where most wouldn't be. I'm lucky, in so many ways, that he was my dad. You always said you were uncomfortable with the way I portrayed you as a hero in that film, Dad. So—here you go! Consider it evened out.

A NOTE ABOUT THE TYPE

Pierre Simon Fournier le jeune, who designed the type used in this book, was both an originator and a collector of types. His services to the art of print communication were his design of individual characters, his creation of ornaments and initials, and his standardization of type sizes. Fournier types are old style in character and sharply cut. In 1764 and 1766 he published his Manuel Typographique, a treatise on the history of French types and printing, on typefounding in all its details, and on what many consider his most important contributuon to the printed word—the measurement of type by the point system.